ArtScroll Mesorah Series®

Rabbi Nosson Scherman / Rabbi Meir Zlotowitz

General Editors

הגדה של פסח
כי ישאלך בנך

WITH
ANSWERS

THE CLASSIC COMMENTATORS
RESPOND TO OVER 200 QUESTIONS

BY RABBI YAAKOV WEHL

THE
HAGGADAH

Published by

Mesorah Publications, ltd

FIRST EDITION
First Impression . . . March 1997
Second Impression . . . January 1999
Third Impression . . . December 2001

Published and Distributed by
MESORAH PUBLICATIONS, Ltd.
4401 Second Avenue
Brooklyn, New York 11232

Distributed in Europe by
LEHMANNS
Unit E, Viking Industrial Park
Rolling Mill Road
Jarrow, Tyne & Wear NE32 3DP
England

Distributed in Australia & New Zealand by
GOLDS WORLD OF JUDAICA
3-13 William Street
Balaclava, Melbourne 3183
Victoria Australia

Distributed in Israel by
SIFRIATI / A. GITLER — BOOKS
6 Hayarkon Street
Bnei Brak 51127

Distributed in South Africa by
KOLLEL BOOKSHOP
Shop 8A Norwood Hypermarket
Norwood 2196, Johannesburg, South Africa

THE ARTSCROLL MESORAH SERIES ®
THE HAGGADAH WITH ANSWERS
© *Copyright 1997, by* MESORAH PUBLICATIONS, Ltd. and Rabbi Yaakov Wehl
4401 Second Avenue / Brooklyn, N.Y. 11232 / (718) 921-9000 / www.artscroll.com
ALL RIGHTS RESERVED

ISBN:
0-89906-384-5 (hard cover)
0-89906-385-3 (paperback)

Typography by CompuScribe at ArtScroll Studios, Ltd.
4401 Second Avenue / Brooklyn, N.Y. 11232 / (718) 921-9000

Printed in the United States of America by Noble Book Press
Bound by Sefercraft, Quality Bookbinders, Ltd. Brooklyn, N.Y.

Dedicated

לז״נ ולע״נ

ר׳ אהרן בן ר׳ יעקב שמוא׳ ז״ל וועהל

(נפטר י״ד אייר תשד״ם)

וזוגתו מרת דר. פרומט שרה ע״ה וועהל
Dr. Selma Wehl המכונה

(נפטרה ג׳ ניסן תשמ״ז)

תורה ומצוות *for* מסירת נפש *Whose*
acted as a beacon of light for us
and for the thousands of friends and patients
whose lives were enriched
by their medical genius and ever giving kindness.

Their sacrifices for the mitzvos of
Tefillah, Shemiras Shabbos, Bris Milah and Pesach
were legendary and knew no limits.

Indeed, their way of life reflected the
true ideals of תורה *and* דרך ארץ.

Their lives personified the highest
and most noble meaning
of the concept
זמן חירותינו!

By their Children, Grandchildren
and Great-Grandchildren

In memory of
לז״נ

Opa Wehl

ר׳ יעקב שמוא׳ בן ר׳ מאיר ווהל ע״ה

Who despite being widowed at a young age
through the illness of his dear wife,
our beloved grandmother

האשה פרדכה רבקה בת ר׳ יהודה ע״ה

Brought up his family in the true way of
קהלות אה״ו – המבורג,
תורה עבודה וגמילות חסדים
and in whose house I and my brother

ר׳ קלונימוס פנחס בן ר׳ קליינימסס פנחס ע״ה
grew up after my sainted father

ר׳ קלונימוס פנחס בן ר׳ זאב ענגלנדער ע״ה

passed away at a young age.

Under the guidance of our dear mother,
who despite a life of trials and tribulations,
kept faith with everything that represented
the תורה *and* ארץ דרך *way of life*

האשה דייכא בת ר׳ יעקב שמוא׳ ע״ה

Opa, your house was open to תורה *(shiurim),*
עבודה *(your kloiz)* וגמילות חסדים *(always with orchim).*

We hope that we have carried the torch forward.

With love and respect,

Eva

These approbations were issued for the Hebrew edition of this work.

הרב הגאון ר' חיים פינחס שיינברג שליט״א
ראש ישיבת תורה אור, ירושלים

יום ב' לפרשת את הברכה אשר תשמעו תשנ״ב

כבר איתמחא גברא בספרי' הראשונים עקבי אהרן ופשר דבר על מסכת שקלים ועל מסכת חגיגה ומאד שמחתי לשמוע שעכשו בא לזכות את הרבים עם חבורו החשוב על ההגדה של פסח. כבר ידוע לכל שבמצות סיפור יציאת מצרים הקפידה התורה ״שענין זכירת יצ״מ בלילה הזה תהי' ע״י שאלה ותשובה״ וכידוע מכל הפוסקים, ולכן דבר גדול עשה המחבר שלקט רובא דרובא מקושיות הראשונים והאחרונים ואסף כעמיר גרנה ועשאם לבית אחד כולם על מקומם הראוי.

החיבור הנ״ל בודאי יביא תועלת גדולה לכל ת״ח ולכל בן תורה הרוצה להתדבק באור תורתן של הראשונים והאחרונים על ההגדה ובפרט לכל אב ולכל רבי המלמד בישיבה להועיל לו לקיים מצות ״והגדת לבך״ ולהכין תלמידי' ל״ליל התקדש חג.״ ״הזמן קצר והמלאכה מרובה״ קודם החג שכל ישרא' טרודים בהכנות החג ואם כן בודאי יחזיקו טובה להספר הנ״ל ולמחברו. ובאתי בזה לעודדו ולחזקו ולברכו שכשם שזכה ספרי' הראשנים נתקבלו על שלחן מלכים מאן מלכי רבנן וביניהם גדולי תורה, מגידי שיעור וחובשי בית המדרש, כן יזכה שהההגדה הנ״ל תתקבל ברצון ויעלה על שלחן מלכים, תלמידי חכמים, מרביצי תורה וכלל ישרא'.

אני מכיר את המחבר הנ״ל כשלשים שנה ומלבד ספרי' החשובים כבר זכה להעמיד תלמידים גדולים וחשובים הלומדים אצלנו בישיבתנו הק' ובשאר ישיבות הק' הן בארץ ישרא' והן בארצות הברית ויודע אני שלא מש מאהלה כל ימי' הן כר״מ והן כמרביץ תורה כמגיד שיעור דף יומי קרוב לעשרים שנה.לכן הנני מברכו שיזכה להמשיך בעבודתו הק' להעמיד תלמידים הרבה ולהרביץ תורה מתוך הרחבת הדעת ויפוצו מעיינותי' חוצה וישקו עדרים מתורתו ומספרי' הן בע״פ והן בכתב.

הכותב וחותם לכבוד התורה ולומדי'

[signature]

חיים פינחס שיינברג

ראש ישיבת חורה אור ירושלים עיה״ק תו״ת

מורה הוראה קרית מטרסדורף.

הרב הגאון ר' טובי' גאלדשטיין שליט"א

ראש הישיבה, ישיבת עמק הלכה

ברוקלין, נ.י.

בס"ד

לכבוד הרה"ג מופלא ומופלג וכו' מרביץ תורה ברבים הרב ר' יעקב וועהל שליט"א

היות שכבר זכה בע"ה להוציא לאור שני ספרים בהלכה ונתקבלו דברי' בחוגי הלומדים וכולם משבחים מאד את דברי' היקרים **ועתה הראה לי חיבורו על ההגדה של פסח ליקוט מראשונים ואחרונים ז"ל והוסיף מדלי' כמה דברים יקרים מאד בשכל צח וישר**, לומד בתורה הק' בשקידה עצומה מאד, ואני מברך אותו כשם שזכה שהספרים שלו נתקבלו בחפץ לב בין רבנן ותלמידיהם כן יזכה שספרו השלישי תתקבל ברצון, ורבים יהנו מהבושם הזה, ויזכה עוד להגדיל תורה ולהאדירה,

הכותב מתוך שמחת הלב, ידידו עוז, החפץ ביקר תפארתו,

טובי' גאלדשטיין,

היום עש"ק שמות כ"ב טבת תשנ"ג

פה ברוקלין

אב"ד דעברעצין ונייהייזל יצ"ו

בעמ"ח שו"ת באר משה ז"ח

בלאאמו"ר הרא"ש, בעמ"ח ספרי נפי אש ומליצי אש וש"ס

ברוקלין יע"א

בעזהי"ת

מתוך לב שמח וחדות הנפש כתב שורות אלו להעיד על **מעשה אומן לקוט מן הראשונים והאחרונים בדרך שאילה ותשובה** של מע"כ ידידינו הרה"ג המופלא ומופלג בהפלגת חכמים ונבונים מתמיד רב ועצום חריף ובקי ירא וחרד לדבר ה' מו"ה יעקב וועהל שליט"א שהגיש לפני קונטרסים נאים מלאים **חידושים מפוארים** על ההגדה של פסח עיינתי בהם הרבה כאן וכאן **וישרו בעיני ונתמלא הבית אורה** אורה זו תורה ואשרי לו ואשרי חלקו שזכה לכך ונתקיים בי' דרשת חז"ל על ושננתם שיהא דברי תורה שינונים בפיך בלא גימגום ומדזכה לנפשי' רוצה לזכות גם את הרבים ולהעלותן על מכבש הדפוס שיהי' מצוים בבתי מדרשים ובבית **תלמידי חכמים** ונזכה כולנו ביחד לקבל פני משיח צדקנו במהרה אכי"ה"ר.

וע"ז בעה"ח עש"ק לס' הדברים שנת שנ"ב לפ"ק

פה ברוקלין יצ"ו

משה שטערן

אב"ד דעברעצין יצ"ו .

הרב הגאון ר' משה שטרנבוך שליט"א
סגן נשיא העדה החרדית בעיה"ק
מח"ס מועדים וזמנים ועוד
ראב"ד דק"ק חרדים ביוהנסבורג

הכתובת בירושלים:
מישקלוב 13 הר—נוף, ירושלים
טל: 435780 פקס: 529610

בעזהי"ת, יום ג' אלול תשנ"ב

לכבוד הרה"ג המופלא ומופלג וכו' ה"ה הרב יעקב וועהל שליט"א

אחדשה"ט וש"ת כראוי

קבלתי עלים מספרו על הגדה של פסח דבר נאה ומתקבל, ליקוטים וביאורים, וכבר אתמח' בספריו הקודמין, והסכימו לספריו גאוני ישראל שליט"א, ופה מו"ל דברי הלכה ואגדה יחד, וישמחו בזה המעיינים שהכל מוכן כשלחן ערוך, ואינו צריך לזה הסכמה, שהמעיינים ימצאו כאן כשלחן ערוך הגדה מסודר ומתוקן יפה וניכר שעמל וטרח הרבה, ויהי רצון שהספר יתקבל ויביא לכבוד שמים בספור נפלאות הבורא ית"ש במצרים, ולאמונה בהשגחת הבורא ית"ש, ויזכה עוד להגדיל תורה ולהאדירה, ובקרוב נזכה לגאולה שלימה אמן.

בידידות

משה שטרנבוך

הרב הגאון ר' שמעון שוואב
רב דק״ק
קהל עדת ישרון
נוא—יארק, נ.י.

ב' אלול תשנ״ב

כ״ת ידידי הרה״ג המפואר חו״ב מוהר״ר יעקב ווהל שליט״א:

אם אמור יאמר לכ' המחבר הספר הזה מה לך אצל ה״הגדה״ כלך לך אצל שקלים
וחגיגה ושאר מס' הש״ס להוסיף ולחדש חידושי הלכה כאשר ראינו כבר חכמת תורתו
ועומק הבנתו בעבר— אז יש לו תשובה ניצחת שהספר הזה היא קנקן חדש מלא
ישן, מלא וגדוש מפירושי הראשונים וגדולי האחרונים על עניני הגדה של
פסח ויש בו תועלת לאבות ולבנים להכין א״ע לכה״פ שלשים יום לפני החג
לסידור פסח כהלכתו וגם להבין את כל דברי ה״מגיד״ על בורין. אמנם צריכים
להזהיר את הכל שעיקר מצות הלילה הזה הוא סיפור הנסים והנפלאות של יציאת
מצרים ולהבינם גם לנשים בדברים פשוטים של דברי ההגדה שיסדו עמודי העולם
אבותינו ורבותינו הקדושים, ובאופן שלא לדחות את הקץ של חצות הלילה לגמור את
אכילת אפקומן]ולכמה פוסקים אף אמירת ההלל[— ואני מובטח שזאת כונת כ״ת של
המחבר היקר והנעלה מאד שהשקיע רוב עמל ויגיעה וכשרון להכין את הדרך
של לימוד ״ההגדה״ באופן של שאילה ותשובה, ממש קילורין לעינים— ואי
לזאת יחולו כל ברכות התורה על ראש כ' המחבר שליט״א ויה״ר שיפוצו מעיינותיו
חוצה ורבים ירבו מאורו ועתידו לגאון ולתפארת וחפץ ד' בידו יצליח—כעתירת מוקירו
ומעריצו בכל לב

שמעון שוואב

❧ Preface

The first mitzvah in the Torah is the positive mitzvah to believe that the One Who gave us the Torah on Mount Sinai through our teacher Moses is the God Who took us out of Egypt, as it says at the giving of the Torah: "I am HASHEM, your God, Who took you out of the land of Egypt" (*Semag, Sefer HaMitzvos*, mitzvah 1).

[It is an obligation] "to know that He Who created heaven and earth is the sole Ruler of the higher and lower spheres and of all four directions of the universe, as is stated: "I am HASHEM, your God. [Who took you out of the land of Egypt] . . . Just as we are commanded to believe that He took us out from Egypt, . . . so too believe that I am HASHEM, your God, and in the future I will gather you and save you (*Semak, Sefer HaMitzvos*, mitzvah 1).

T he Exodus of the Jewish people from Egypt was not an isolated event. It is the cornerstone of our accepting the Torah and the foundation of our nation's experience until the ultimate salvation, which will take place with the advent of the Messiah. Thus, the understanding and retelling of the story of our redemption, while primarily performed to fulfill the commandment to retell the story of the Exodus on the night of Pesach, actually fills a much broader purpose. *Hagaon Rabbi Moshe Sternbuch, shlita,* in his approbation to the Hebrew edition of this Haggadah, writes: "May it be the will of the Almighty that this *sefer* be accepted, and may it bring glory to Heaven through the retelling of the wonders of the Creator, may His Name be blessed, which He performed in Egypt, and to a full trust in the Divine providence of the Creator, may His Name be blessed." This is an awesome task, and we pray that, with the help of *Hashem Yisbarach* and in the merit of preceding generations, we have achieved this goal to some extent.

The basis for all of our people's trials and tribulations and our ultimate rescue from them can be found in the covenant between God and our forefather Abraham — The Covenant Between the Parts (*Genesis* Chap. 15). The *Malbim* points out that God's guarantee to protect Abraham's descendants for all time has stood by us in all our troubles and misfortunes.

In this connection, I must express my gratitude to *Hashem Yisbarach* for saving my parents and myself and bringing us here to America, sparing us from the horrible fate that befell European Jewry during the Holocaust. He granted me the merit to be counted among "those who attend the Beis Hamidrash" and He enabled me to disseminate Torah knowledge, by being a Rebbi for over twenty-five years in a Yeshiva High School, being a member of the *hanhalah* of the Bais Yaakov of Boro Park, a *maggid shiur* of Daf Yomi for close to twenty years, and by enabling me to publish several works, namely *Sefer Ikvei Aharon* and *Peshar Davar* on various Talmudic tractates, as well as seeing the fifth printing of the Hebrew version of this Haggadah, *"Ki Yisholcha Bincha."*

To say that I am indebted to my parents is an extreme understatement. All that I am and all the values that I received are from my parents ע״ה. Their exemplary lives merited a special book, *House Calls to Eternity,* published by Mesorah. Both my father, R' Aharon ben R' Yaakov Shmuel ז״ל, and my mother, Doctor Frumet Sarah (Selma) Wehl ע״ה, personified with great self-sacrifice their devotion to Torah and mitzvos.

Pesach had special meaning for both my parents. Even at a venerable age, my father maintained his intense preparations for Pesach. He was determined to fulfill the mitzvos of matzah and *maror* even when it was quite difficult for him to do so. My mother, whose fame as a medical genius and whose herculean efforts to keep the Shabbos while serving her patients are legendary, was consulted at all hours of the day and night with problems arising from the restrictions of the Pesach holiday. By their example, they and my parents-in-law, Rabbi Yehuda Dov Galinsky ז״ל and his Rebetzin Leah ע״ה, who established Yeshivah Shaarei Tzedek in Coney Island, conveyed to us the true meaning of freedom and provided us with a deeper understanding of what Torah-true Judaism demands.

As mentioned, we are indebted to *Hashem Yisbarach* for having saved us from the burning flames of the Holocaust, and we are grateful to the messengers He sent to help us.

First and foremost, we acknowledge the memory of our dear uncles (brothers of my father ז״ל), Uncle Martin (R' Meir ben R' Yaakov Shmuel הי״ד) and Uncle Nechemia (R' Nechemia Yosef ben R' Yaakov Shmuel הי״ד), who selflessly sacrificed their exit numbers and gave them to our parents and me to enable us to leave Germany. May *Hashem Yisbarach* avenge their death among all the martyrs who have sacrificed their lives sanctifying God's Name.

Secondly, and with no less appreciation, we recall with profound gratitude three wonderful people who signed affidavits to enable us to come to this country. Captain William Cohen, whose heart carried a concern for all of world Jewry, was privileged to give affidavits to more than fifty people, providing them with the ability to start a new life in this country. His strong feelings as a proud Jew carried through to his last days as a devoted member of the Washington Heights Congregation, where he became a close friend of its Rabbi, Rabbi Gedaliah Finkelstein.

Likewise, we acknowledge with thanks the efforts of our wonderful Aunt Renate Wehl ע״ה and our cousin Paul Herzog, who provided sustaining affidavits.

The publication of this Haggadah demands a special mention of gratitude to several individuals without whom this work would have been impossible. The beauty and clarity of this translation is due to the outstanding talents and determined efforts of three profound Torah scholars. Their organizational skills as well as their ability to plumb the depths of the various commentaries cited in the Hebrew version of this work, כי ישאלך בנך – הגדה של פסח, are self-evident. Rabbi Yaakov Blinder, and his colleague in this endeavor who wishes to remain anonymous, deserve our accolades for a job well done. The efforts and the hours they dedicated to this project as well as the suggestions and ideas of Rabbi Avrohom Biderman of the ArtScroll/Mesorah staff have enriched this Haggadah and have shaped its final form.

Rabbi Sheah Brander's expertise and talent are borne out by the artful presentation of this esthetically pleasing work.

How can we adequately express our appreciation to ArtScroll/ Mesorah and the two giants who have literally transformed the American Torah scene through their inspiring effort and vision? As noted, we already had the privilege of working with Rabbi Meir Zlotowitz and Rabbi Nosson Scherman on the well-received biography of my parents, *House Calls to Eternity.* All members of the ArtScroll staff have every reason to be proud of their accomplishments and efforts on behalf of Jewish learning and practice throughout the world.

My dear friend and *chavrusa* of many years, Rabbi Binyamin Zeffren, deserves recognition for his help at a critical time in the publication of this *sefer.*

To the members of my family — and in particular to my *eishes chayil*

— who have endured the pains, trials and tribulations of publishing my works and whose goals have been to help provide me with the atmosphere to enable me to learn and teach Torah, all I can say is that I hope we will be privileged to see true Torah *nachas* from all our children and grandchildren.

In conclusion, I pray to *Hashem Yisbarach* that despite my personal shortcomings, He grant me the privilege of fulfilling King David's "one request" — "To sit in the House of Hashem all the days of my life," and that I and all of the house of Israel have the privilege to witness the fulfillment of the request in the Haggadah — that we may eat of the sacrifices and Pesach offerings that will be offered upon the Altar of the new Temple, where we will thank Him with a new song for our redemption and the liberation of our soul, speedily in our days. Amen.

לשנה הבאה בירושלים הבנוי'

Yaakov Wehl

Brooklyn, NY
אדר תשנ"ז

NOTE TO READER:

The laws and customs cited in this Haggadah are based on the following Halachic sources: *Shulchan Aruch, Chayei Adam, Shulchan Aruch HaRav, Kitzur Shulchan Aruch, Aruch HaShulchan, Mishnah Berurah, Haggadah Moadim U'zmanim, Haggadah Kol Dodi,* and *Haggadah Vayaged Moshe.*

The author requests that the readers of this Haggadah consult these original sources whenever possible.

In addition, all question of law and practice should be addressed to a competent Orthodox Rabbi.

Throughout this Haggadah citations from *Maharal* are not based on his original works but on *Haggadas Maharal.*

The author would appreciate any comments, suggestions or corrections that you may have.

THE
HAGGADAH
WITH
ANSWERS

— הִלְכוֹת בְּדִיקַת וּבִיעוּר חָמֵץ ⊰
Laws of the Search for
and Burning of Chametz

1. One should perform the search for *chametz* on the night before Pesach, as soon as it becomes dark. Starting one half-hour before dark, one may not eat or begin any kind of work before the search.

2. Even if one has an established period of Torah study at this time, he should not begin it until after the search. If a person began to study Torah before nightfall, there is a difference of opinion as to whether he must interrupt his studies in order to start the search at nightfall.

3. One should recite the *Maariv* prayer before the search.

4. Before the search the *brachah*, אֲשֶׁר קִדְּשָׁנוּ . . . עַל בִּעוּר חָמֵץ — "Blessed are You . . . Who has commanded us concerning the removal of *chametz*," should be recited. Although we do not actually burn the *chametz* until the next morning, the search itself is for the purpose of eliminating the *chametz*.

5. One may not speak between the *brachah* and the beginning of the search. All conversation which does not concern the search should be avoided until the end of the search.

6. All rooms into which *chametz* may have been brought must be checked, including cellars, attics, shops, etc. Any containers where *chametz* is stored must be checked as well. The entire house should be thoroughly cleaned before the search begins, so that the search may be carried out effectively.

7. Even though the entire house was cleaned and rid of *chametz* before the search, a *brachah* must be made before the search is performed. This is because the *brachah* addresses the destruction of the *chametz*, a process which culminates on the day of the fourteenth, as some *chametz* remains for eating that day.

8. One must check all the corners, nooks and crannies of those rooms which require searching. One also needs to check the pockets of clothing.

9. It is customary to place several (many people use 10) pieces of *chametz* around the house before the search, so that the *brachah* should not be in vain (in case no other *chametz* is found). This is not technically necessary, however, as the *brachah* is recited with the intent that one will burn any *chametz which he may find.* Care should be taken that none of the pieces are lost and that the pieces do not crumble and thus spread *chametz* all around.

A superficial search to merely gather up the pieces of bread that were placed around the house is inadequate.

10. *Chametz* that is left over to be eaten or sold should be placed (before the search) in a safe place, so that it does not find its way back into places that have been purged of *chametz*. The same goes for whatever *chametz* was found during the search.

11. After the search the *chametz* should be annulled with the pronouncement of the כָּל חֲמִירָא. It must be understood that this declaration is not a prayer, but a statement of annulling the *chametz*. If one does not understand the Aramaic formula he should recite it in a language which he understands. The כָּל חֲמִירָא recited at night, following the search, applies only to *chametz* of which he is not aware, since one wants to retain the *chametz* he will be burning, eating or selling.

12. On the day before Pesach *chametz* may not be eaten after a quarter of the daytime has passed. After a third of the daytime, one may not even derive any benefit from the *chametz*. Thus, the burning of the *chametz* and the recitation of the final annulment, which follows the burning, must be done before this time. This annulment applies to *any* *chametz* still in a person's possession.

⋘§ בְּדִיקַת חָמֵץ — *The Search for Chametz*

The *chametz* search is initiated with the recitation of the following blessing:

בָּרוּךְ אַתָּה יהוה, אֱלֹהֵינוּ מֶלֶךְ הָעוֹלָם, אֲשֶׁר קִדְּשָׁנוּ בְּמִצְוֹתָיו, וְצִוָּנוּ עַל בִּעוּר חָמֵץ.

Blessed are You, HASHEM, our God, King of the universe, Who has sanctified us with His commandments and commanded us concerning the removal of *chametz*.

Upon completion of the *chametz* search, the *chametz* is wrapped well and set aside
to be burned the next morning, and the following declaration is made.

The declaration must be understood in order to take effect; one who does not
understand the Aramaic text may recite it in English, Yiddish, or any other language.

Any *chametz* that will be used for that evening's supper or the next day's breakfast
or for any other purpose prior to the final removal of *chametz* the next morning
is not included in this declaration.

כָּל חֲמִירָא וַחֲמִיעָא דְּאִיכָּא בִרְשׁוּתִי, דְּלָא חֲזִתֵּה
(נ״א דְּלָא חֲמִתֵּה) וּדְלָא בְעַרְתֵּה וּדְלָא
יְדַעְנָא לֵה, לִבָּטֵל וְלֶהֱוֵי הֶפְקֵר כְּעַפְרָא דְאַרְעָא:

Any *chametz* which is in my possession which I did not
see, and remove, nor know about, shall be nullified and
become ownerless, like the dust of the earth.

⊷ בִּיעוּר חָמֵץ — *Burning the Chametz* ⊷

The following declaration, which includes all *chametz* without exception,
is to be made after the burning of leftover *chametz*.

The declaration must be understood in order to take effect; one who does not
understand the Aramaic text may recite it in English, Yiddish, or any other language.

When Passover begins on Saturday night, although the *chametz* is burned
Friday morning, this declaration is made on Saturday morning.

Any *chametz* remaining from the Saturday morning meal
is flushed down the drain before the declaration is made.

כָּל חֲמִירָא וַחֲמִיעָא דְּאִיכָּא בִרְשׁוּתִי, דַּחֲזִתֵּה וּדְלָא
חֲזִתֵּה, (נ״א דַּחֲמִתֵּה וּדְלָא חֲמִתֵּה,)
דִּבְעַרְתֵּה וּדְלָא בְעַרְתֵּה, לִבָּטֵל וְלֶהֱוֵי הֶפְקֵר כְּעַפְרָא
דְאַרְעָא.

Any *chametz* which is in my possession, which I did
or did not see, which I did or did not remove, shall
be nullified and become ownerless, like the dust of the
earth.

עֵרוּב תַּבְשִׁילִין

It is forbidden to prepare on Yom Tov for the next day even if that day is the Sabbath. If, however, Sabbath preparations were started before Yom Tov began, they may be continued on Yom Tov. *Eruv Tavshilin* constitutes this preparation. A matzah and any cooked food (such as fish, meat, or an egg) are set aside on the day before Yom Tov to be used on the Sabbath, and the blessing is recited followed by the declaration [made in a language understood by the one making the *eruv*].

If the first days of Passover fall on Thursday and Friday,
an *Eruv Tavshilin* must be made on Wednesday.

In Eretz Yisrael, where only one day Yom Tov is in effect, the *eruv* is omitted.

בָּרוּךְ אַתָּה יהוה אֱלֹהֵינוּ מֶלֶךְ הָעוֹלָם, אֲשֶׁר קִדְּשָׁנוּ בְּמִצְוֹתָיו, וְצִוָּנוּ עַל מִצְוַת עֵרוּב.

בַּהֲדֵין עֵרוּבָא יְהֵא שָׁרֵא לָנָא לַאֲפוּיֵי וּלְבַשּׁוּלֵי וּלְאַטְמוּנֵי וּלְאַדְלוּקֵי שְׁרָגָא וּלְתַקָּנָא וּלְמֶעְבַּד כָּל צָרְכָּנָא, מִיּוֹמָא טָבָא לְשַׁבַּתָּא [לָנָא וּלְכָל יִשְׂרָאֵל הַדָּרִים בָּעִיר הַזֹּאת].

עֵירוּבֵי חֲצֵרוֹת

On the Sabbath, it is forbidden to carry from one person's private domain to that of another person — or to a shared private domain — unless all the areas become "merged" through *eruvei chatzeiros*.

The *eruv*-foods are held while the following blessing and declaration are recited.
[If the *eruv* is made for the entire year, the bracketed passage is added.]

בָּרוּךְ אַתָּה יהוה אֱלֹהֵינוּ מֶלֶךְ הָעוֹלָם, אֲשֶׁר קִדְּשָׁנוּ בְּמִצְוֹתָיו, וְצִוָּנוּ עַל מִצְוַת עֵרוּב.

בַּהֲדֵין עֵרוּבָא יְהֵא שָׁרֵא לָנָא לְאַפּוּקֵי וּלְעַיּוּלֵי מִן הַבָּתִּים לֶחָצֵר, וּמִן הֶחָצֵר לַבָּתִּים, וּמִבַּיִת לְבַיִת, וּמֵחָצֵר לֶחָצֵר, וּמִגַּג לְגַג, כָּל מַאי דִצְרִיךְ לָן, וּלְכָל יִשְׂרָאֵל הַדָּרִים בַּשְּׁכוּנָה הַזּוֹ/בָּעִיר הַזֹּאת [וּלְכָל מִי שֶׁיִּתּוֹסֵף בָּהּ, לְכָל שַׁבְּתוֹת הַשָּׁנָה, וּלְכָל יָמִים טוֹבִים].

ERUV TAVSHILIN

It is forbidden to prepare on Yom Tov for the next day even if that day is the Sabbath. If, however, Sabbath preparations were started before Yom Tov began, they may be continued on Yom Tov. *Eruv Tavshilin* constitutes this preparation. A matzah and any cooked food (such as fish, meat, or an egg) are set aside on the day before Yom Tov to be used on the Sabbath, and the blessing is recited followed by the declaration [made in a language understood by the one making the *eruv*].

If the first days of Passover fall on Thursday and Friday,
an *Eruv Tavshilin* must be made on Wednesday.

In Eretz Yisrael, where only one day Yom Tov is in effect, the *eruv* is omitted.

Blessed are You, HASHEM, our God, King of the universe, Who has sanctified us with His commandments and has commanded us concerning the commandment of *eruv*.

Through this Eruv may we be permitted to bake, cook, insulate, kindle flame, prepare for, and do anything necessary on the festival for the sake of the Sabbath [— for ourselves and for all Jews who live in this city].

ERUVEI CHATZEIROS

On the Sabbath, it is forbidden to carry from one person's private domain to that of another person — or to a shared private domain — unless all the areas become "merged" through *eruvei chatzeiros*.

The *eruv*-foods are held while the following blessing and declaration are recited.
[If the *eruv* is made for the entire year, the bracketed passage is added.]

Blessed are You, HASHEM, our God, King of the universe, Who has sanctified us with His commandments and has commanded us concerning the commandment of *eruv*.

Through this *eruv* may it be permitted for us to carry out or to carry in from the houses to the courtyard, and from the courtyard to the houses, from house to house, from courtyard to courtyard, and from roof to roof, all that we require, for ourselves and for all Jews who live in this area/city [and to all who will move into this area, for all the Sabbaths and festivals of the year].

הדלקת הנרות

The candles are lit and the following blessings are recited.
When Yom Tov falls on the Sabbath, the words in parentheses are added.

בָּרוּךְ אַתָּה יהוה אֱלֹהֵינוּ מֶלֶךְ הָעוֹלָם, אֲשֶׁר קִדְּשָׁנוּ
בְּמִצְוֹתָיו, וְצִוָּנוּ לְהַדְלִיק נֵר שֶׁל (שַׁבָּת וְשֶׁל)
יוֹם טוֹב.

Some women do not recite the following blessing now, but wait until *Kiddush*.

בָּרוּךְ אַתָּה יהוה אֱלֹהֵינוּ מֶלֶךְ הָעוֹלָם, שֶׁהֶחֱיָנוּ
וְקִיְּמָנוּ וְהִגִּיעָנוּ לַזְּמַן הַזֶּה.

It is customary to recite the following prayer after the kindling.
The words in brackets are included as they apply.

יְהִי רָצוֹן לְפָנֶיךָ, יהוה אֱלֹהַי וֵאלֹהֵי אֲבוֹתַי, שֶׁתְּחוֹנֵן
אוֹתִי [וְאֶת אִישִׁי, וְאֶת בָּנַי, וְאֶת בְּנוֹתַי,
וְאֶת אָבִי, וְאֶת אִמִּי] וְאֶת כָּל קְרוֹבַי; וְתִתֶּן לָנוּ וּלְכָל
יִשְׂרָאֵל חַיִּים טוֹבִים וַאֲרוּכִים; וְתִזְכְּרֵנוּ בְּזִכְרוֹן טוֹבָה
וּבְרָכָה; וְתִפְקְדֵנוּ בִּפְקֻדַּת יְשׁוּעָה וְרַחֲמִים; וּתְבָרְכֵנוּ
בְּרָכוֹת גְּדוֹלוֹת; וְתַשְׁלִים בָּתֵּינוּ; וְתַשְׁכֵּן שְׁכִינָתְךָ בֵּינֵינוּ.
וְזַכֵּנִי לְגַדֵּל בָּנִים וּבְנֵי בָנִים חֲכָמִים וּנְבוֹנִים, אוֹהֲבֵי
יהוה, יִרְאֵי אֱלֹהִים, אַנְשֵׁי אֱמֶת, זֶרַע קֹדֶשׁ, בַּיהוה
דְּבֵקִים, וּמְאִירִים אֶת הָעוֹלָם בַּתּוֹרָה וּבְמַעֲשִׂים טוֹבִים,
וּבְכָל מְלֶאכֶת עֲבוֹדַת הַבּוֹרֵא. אָנָּא שְׁמַע אֶת תְּחִנָּתִי
בָּעֵת הַזֹּאת, בִּזְכוּת שָׂרָה וְרִבְקָה וְרָחֵל וְלֵאָה אִמּוֹתֵינוּ,
וְהָאֵר נֵרֵנוּ שֶׁלֹּא יִכְבֶּה לְעוֹלָם וָעֶד, וְהָאֵר פָּנֶיךָ
וְנִוָּשֵׁעָה. אָמֵן.

LIGHTING THE CANDLES

The candles are lit and the following blessings are recited.
When Yom Tov falls on the Sabbath, the words in parentheses are added.

Blessed are You, HASHEM, our God, King of the universe, Who has sanctified us with His commandments and commanded us to kindle the flame of the (Sabbath and the) festival.

Some women do not recite the following blessing now, but wait until Kiddush.

Blessed are You, HASHEM, our God, King of the universe, Who has kept us alive, sustained us, and brought us to this season.

*It is customary to recite the following prayer after the kindling.
The words in brackets are included as they apply.*

May it be Your will, HASHEM, my God and God of my forefathers, that You show favor to me [my husband, my sons, my daughters, my father, my mother] and all my relatives; and that You grant us and all Israel a good and long life; that You remember us with a beneficent memory and blessing; that You consider us with a consideration of salvation and compassion; that You bless us with great blessings; that You make our households complete; that You cause Your Presence to dwell among us. Privilege me to raise children and grandchildren who are wise and understanding, who love HASHEM and fear God, people of truth, holy offspring, attached to HASHEM, who illuminate the world with Torah and good deeds and with every labor in the service of the Creator. Please, hear my supplication at this time, in the merit of Sarah, Rebecca, Rachel, and Leah, our mothers, and cause our light to illuminate that it not be extinguished forever, and let Your countenance shine so that we are saved. Amen.

৶ঌ *Preparations Before the Onset of the Holiday*

1. The table should be set so that one will be ready to begin the Seder immediately at nightfall, without delay.

2. The table should be set with the finest and most elegant utensils one owns. Although the rest of the year this is not encouraged, in commemoration of the destruction of the Temple, on Pesach it is considered to be a demonstration of freedom.

3. The roast egg or shankbone of the Seder plate should preferably be prepared before nightfall of the Yom Tov. If it is prepared on the Yom Tov festival, care must be taken to eat these items on the first day of Yom Tov. (While the egg may be eaten during this meal, we do not eat roasted meat at the Seder meal.)

4. While preparing the roast shankbone, one should be careful not to say at any point that he is "roasting a bone for Pesach," as this may be considered "sanctifying" the bone, rendering it forbidden for consumption.

There should be some meat on the bone.

The bone should not be discarded in a disrespectful manner, for it was used in the performance of a mitzvah. Rather, it should be eaten during the Yom Tov day meal. As mentioned, it must not be eaten at the Seder, since we do not eat roasted meat during the Seder meal.

5. It is preferable to prepare the salt water before Yom Tov, especially if Yom Tov falls out on Shabbos.

6. If the *maror* is a food which must be checked for insects, the vegetable should be checked before Yom Tov, in order to avoid the prohibition of בּוֹרֵר (*separating*) and to allow sufficient time for a proper inspection.

If the *karpas* is a vegetable which requires separation, it should be prepared before the holiday.

7. If horseradish is used for *maror*, the *Chayei Adam* recommends grinding it before Yom Tov and leaving it uncovered for a while so that it is not too strong to eat. The *Gra*, however, used to prepare the horseradish at night (or cover it carefully if it was ground during the day), to insure that it would be sufficiently strong. The manual grinding of the horseradish is permitted on Yom Tov (though not on Shabbos). However, *Kitzur Shulchan Aruch* calls for a deviation from the normal manner of grinding if it is being done on Yom Tov. Thus, many prefer to grind the *maror* before Yom Tov and cover it tightly.

8. It is preferable that the *charoses* be prepared before Yom Tov. If Pesach occurs on the Sabbath and the *charoses* was not prepared in advance, there is disagreement whether one may add wine and use his finger, rather than a spoon, to stir the mixture, or if even this is prohibited unless he makes the *charoses* of a very loose consistency. A competent Halachic authority should be consulted.

9. The *charoses* should be thick, as it is meant to recall the mortar which the Jewish slaves used in their building. Some liquid should then be poured into it, to commemorate the Jewish blood that the Egyptians spilled. The *charoses* should be made from the fruits which are used in *Tanach* to symbolize the nation of Israel, such as figs, nuts, dates and pomegranates. Nowadays it is customary to make it out of apples and almonds, which also have their own symbolic value. One should add a liquid with some pungency, such as wine, to recall the fact that the teeth of our ancestors were set on edge by their difficult travails in Egypt. Some dry, chunky spices (such as cinnamon or ginger) that resemble straw, which was used in making bricks, should also be added.

10. According to *Rema*, the Seder plate should be arranged so that the items used first are closest to the leader of the Seder, in order that he need not reach past any item as he stretches his arm for another item. Thus the *karpas* should be closest, together with the salt water, then the matzah, then the *maror, chazeres* and *charoses*. *Mishnah Berurah* suggests that it is not improper to reach past the roasted egg or shankbone, as they are not used to fulfill a mitzvah, but are only commemorative.

The *Ari* had an alternative arrangement for the Seder plate, based on kabbalistic ideas.

11. Ideally, the matzos used at the Seder should be *matzah shemurah* — matzah that has been supervised from the time of the cutting of the wheat. Enough *matzah shemurah* should be available for all the participants (see *Shulchan Aruch Orach Chaim* 453:4).

⋖§ הַסֵּדֶר — *The Seder*

⋖§ קַדֵּשׁ — *Reciting Kiddush*

1. *Kiddush* should be recited and the Seder begun as soon as possible after synagogue services. Although *Kiddush* may generally be recited before dark, this should not be done on Pesach, as the Pesach offering was eaten only at night (*Exodus* 12:8): The other mitzvos of the Seder, such as drinking the four cups of wine (of which *Kiddush* is the first) follow this rule as well.

2. It is customary for the leader to wear a *kittel* at the Seder.
One should distribute nuts, sweets, and the like to the children, so that they will be prompted to ask questions in general, and especially the four questions of the Haggadah.

3. The participants should have their cups of wine poured by an attendant or another one of the assembled, as this is a symbol of freedom.

4. It should be made clear to all those present that they should drink at least most of the wine of each of the four cups. It is preferable that each person drink the entire cup. This is particularly true of the fourth cup, which requires that a *brachah acharonah* be recited.

5. As the participants drink the wine, they should intend to fulfill the mitzvah of *Kiddush* as well as the mitzvah to drink the four cups of the Seder. Some recite a verbal declaration to this effect before starting *Kiddush*.

6. Men and women alike are obligated to drink the four cups as well as to fulfill all the other mitzvos of the Seder.

7. On Friday night, *Kiddush* begins with *Vayechulu;* on Saturday night, the blessing over the fire and *Havdalah* blessing are appended to *Kiddush,* before *Shehecheyanu.*

8. *The Kol Dodi Haggadah* cites *Yaavetz* who says that when one recites the *Shehecheyanu* blessing, he should bear in mind that it also applies to the many mitzvos of the Seder. Women who have already recited this blessing at candlelighting should not repeat it in *Kiddush.*

9. The wine must be drunk while reclining on the left side. If one drank the first cup without reclining he should not drink a replacement cup while reclining, unless he had in mind before drinking the *Kiddush* wine that he might drink more wine after *Kiddush.*

10. Although in our culture even people of leisure do not eat while reclining, the accepted halachah is that we recline. In fact, some authorities note that since we make many departures from the ordinary at the Seder in order to arouse the curiosity of the children, it is even more important to recline.

11. The requisite amount of wine must be drunk at one time. Preferably this means the cup should not be taken away from the mouth until it is finished. The maximum amount of time lapse is the amount of time it takes the average person to drink a *revi'is*. If the drinking took longer than this amount of time, it depends on which cup one just drank. If it is the first cup, he only drinks a replacement cup of wine if he intended at the time of the blessing that he might drink additional wine. In the case of the second cup, he must drink a replacement cup unless he intended *not* to drink wine during during the meal. If it is the third or fourth cup, he does not drink a replacement cup. If the duration was even longer — the amount of time that it takes the average person to eat a *pras* of bread (see below under matzah) — one must drink another cup of wine in any event.

12. One should not drink any wine or other alcoholic drink between the first and second cups of the Seder, but he may consume other drinks (*Mishnah Berurah*). The opinion of *Shulchan Aruch HaRav* is that one should not drink those beverages which areconsidered חֲמַר מְדִינָה, *chamar medinah* (a beverage accepted in that locality as a social drink, used for toasts, etc.). *Aruch HaShulchan* says that all drinks except water should be avoided. Nowadays, it is customary not to drink at all between the first two cups, so if one wishes to drink even water it is best to have that in mind when he recites Kiddush.

13. The minimum amount of wine for the first cup (particularly on Friday night) is 5.1 fluid ounces according to *Chazon Ish*, or approx. 4.5 according to *R' Moshe Feinstein.* The other three cups may contain as little as 3.3 fl. oz.

14. A child who is old enough to participate in the Seder should also be given a full cup of wine, but he does not have to drink any more than a cheekful.

וּרְחַץ — *Washing the Hands*

1. After *Kiddush* one should wash his hands as though for bread, but without saying the *brachah*. Two reasons are given for the washing of the hands at this point. One reason is that, strictly speaking, one must wash his hands before eating any food which has been dipped in any liquid. Although throughout the year the general custom does not follow this rule, on the Seder night we do wash our hands. The other reason is that this is simply another change done to pique the children's curiosity.

2. There are two customs regarding this handwashing. In some homes, only the leader washes his hands; in others, all the participants do so as well. It would seem that the different customs are based on the two reasons. If we wash just to encourage the children to ask, only the leader need wash his hands. If, on the other hand, the basis for the custom is the rule regarding dipped foods, then all should wash their hands.

3. It is preferable for those participants who did not wash their hands to use a fork or spoon when eating the *karpas*.

כַּרְפַּס — *Dipping the Vegetables*

1. The *karpas* may be any vegetable over which the blessing *ha'adamah* is recited. The word *karpas* is the name of a particular vegetable. It was originally customary to use this vegetable because its letters, when rearranged, spell ס׳ פרך — *sixty [times ten thousand people worked at] backbreaking labor*. Each family should follow their own custom regarding which vegetable to use for *karpas*.

2. A piece of *karpas* smaller than a *kezayis* should be eaten by each participant at the Seder.

3. The *karpas* is dipped in salt water, which should be made before the advent of the festival. If the Seder is held on Friday night and salt water was not prepared in advance, vinegar (kosher for Passover) should be used instead. If no vinegar is available, a small quantity of salt water may be prepared in an unusual manner, (i.e., pouring the water into a vessel and then adding salt). According to some opinions, even when the Seder is not held on Shabbos, this ruling applies.

4. When saying the *ha'adamah* blessing on the *karpas* vegetable, one should have in mind that this *brachah* also covers the *maror* which will be eaten later.

5. Customs differ regarding whether the *karpas* should be eaten while reclining or not.

6. Even if one ate a *kezayis* of the vegetable, he should not recite a *borei nefashos* afterwards, as the *maror* still needs to be eaten as part of the *ha'adamah* of the *karpas*, as mentioned earlier.

7. The reason for the eating of *karpas* is to encourage children to inquire into the unusual practices performed at the Seder meal.

◦§ יַחַץ — *Breaking the Matzah*

---

1. After eating the *karpas,* the middle matzah is broken. The larger piece is set aside to be eaten as the *afikoman* later. At this time, one should put aside enough *afikoman* matzah (adding additional matzah to the broken piece) for each of the participants to have a *kezayis* [heard from *R' Tuviah Goldstein*]. The smaller piece, which preferably should also be the size of a *kezayis,* is returned to the Seder plate.

2. It is customary to wrap up this piece of matzah in a cloth, perhaps as a commemoration of the verse "Their leftover [dough] was bound up in their garments, upon their shoulders." Some have the custom of actually placing the matzah over their shoulder for a moment. One should be careful that the cloth should not have been starched with a *chametz* derivative. It is customary to put the wrapped matzah under the cushions used for reclining.

3. A piece is set aside for the *afikoman* because the *afikoman* matzah is in place of the Pesach offering, which was eaten at the end of the meal.

4. The middle matzah is the one which is broken because this is the matzah over which the *al achilas matzah* is recited.

◦§ מַגִּיד — *Telling the Story of the Exodus*

---

1. Before beginning the recitation of the Haggadah one should intend to fulfill the obligation to retell the story of the Exodus.

2. The Seder plate with the matzah (or the matzah itself) should be raised by the leader of the Seder as "*Ha lachma anya* — This is the bread of affliction" — is recited.

3. After this, many have the custom to remove the Seder plate or the matzos from the table or to move it to the far end of the table, as though they have already finished with it. This is so that the children should be prompted to ask why, unlike every other occasion, we are not eating soon after *Kiddush*. Others merely cover the matzah.

4. The second cup of wine is now poured to encourage the children to question our actions. A child then asks "The Four Questions." If no child is present, another participant should ask the questions. Following the questions, the matzah is returned to its place and uncovered, as the retelling of the Exodus is connected to the matzah before us. The recitation of the Haggadah begins with *Avadim hayinu.*

5. One should not recite the Haggadah while reclining, but in a demeanor of seriousness and reverence.

6. Women must also recite the Haggadah, or hear it from others who recite it. It is commendable to translate each section of the Haggadah for those who may not understand the Hebrew.

It is of particular importance that the section "Rabban Gamliel used to say" — which enumerates the three Biblical commandments of the Seder — be recited by, and explained to, all.

7. The *Sh'lah* writes that during the recitation of the paragraph *Vehi she'amdah la'avoseinu,* the matzah should be covered and the cup of wine lifted.

8. It is customary to remove a drop of wine from the cup as one enumerates "blood, fire and columns of smoke," the names of the ten plagues, and R' Yehudah's abbreviation of the plagues — a total of sixteen drops. Many take out these drops with the forefinger, in commemoration of the verse, "It is the finger of God," while some spill the wine directly from the cup. Others use the fourth finger, and some the little finger.

9. Before beginning the section "Rabban Gamliel" it is customary to replenish the cups of wine. As noted, this section should be recited by all and translated into a language that they understand.

10. When saying, "מַצָּה זוֹ — Matzah — Why do we eat this unleavened bread? . . .," the matzah should be raised up or pointed to. Similarly, when we say the paragraph regarding *maror,* we lift or point to the *maror.* Nothing should be indicated, however, when saying, "Pesach — Why did our fathers . . ."

11. When the paragraph beginning "לְפִיכָךְ — Therefore" is recited, the matzah is covered, and the participants raise their cups of wine until they drink the second cup.

12. There is a difference of opinion as to whether the declaration of intent (הִנְנִי מוּכָן וּמְזוּמָן) should be said before the second cup or not.

13. The second cup of wine should be consumed while reclining. If one forgot to recline, he should drink a replacement cup of wine while reclining.

⊰§ רָחְצָה — *Washing the Hands*

---

1. It is of utmost importance that at this point there be an adequate supply of matzah for all the participants. Many do this by providing each person with their own 2¹/₂ matzos. Others bring additional whole and broken matzos to the table and intend that their blessings apply to all of these matzos.

2. The hands are washed for bread, and this time the blessing is recited. The reason a new washing is required is because of the long delay since the first washing, during which time a person did not fully concentrate on what he touched. If one is certain that his hands have not touched anything inappropriate, he should "soil" them purposely, so that he be able to make a blessing on the washing of his hands.

3. Some maintain that the declaration of intent (הִנְנִי מוּכָן וּמְזוּמָן) for eating the matzah should be recited after washing the hands, while other authorities believe it is preferable to say it beforehand so as to avoid interruption between the washing and the eating of the matzah. The same holds true for announcing the words מוֹצִיא and מַצָּה.

⊰§ מוֹצִיא מַצָּה — *Reciting Two Blessings over the Matzah*

---

1. The leader should hold all three matzos in his hand and say the *brachah Hamotzi*.

2. He should then let go of the bottom matzah and recite the *brachah al achilas matzah* while holding the remaining two matzos.

3. The blessings *al achilas matzah* and *al achilas maror* cover the *korech* "sandwich" as well. Therefore, no unnecessary interruption should be made from the time one makes the blessings on the matzah until after that sandwich has been eaten. While saying the blessing *al achilas matzah,* one should intend that this blessing is also for *korech* and the *afikoman.*

4. After reciting the blessings, one should break off a *kezayis-*size piece from both the top and the middle matzah and eat them together, while reclining. The matzah is not dipped in salt on the Seder night.

5. It is preferable that the two *kezaysim* be in one's mouth all at once, although they need not be swallowed at one time. If this is difficult, the piece from the whole (top) matzah should be eaten first, and then the piece from the broken (middle) matzah. At any rate, there should not be a long delay between the beginning of the *swallowing* of the matzah and the end of the *swallowing* of the requisite amount of matzah. The maximum delay allowed is the time it takes an average person to eat a *"pras"* of bread, which has been estimated at somewhere between two and nine minutes. Most authorities agree that in view of the fact that the mitzvah of matzah is of Biblical origin, as stringent a view as possible should be used. To insure proper fulfillment of this obligation, a competent halachic authority should be consulted.

6. If someone ate only one *kezayis* (instead of the required two), he has, *post facto,* fulfilled his basic obligation.

7. The leader should recite the *hamotzi* blessing on behalf of all the participants. There are varying customs regarding the recitation of the blessing *al achilas matzah.* If every participant has his own set of matzos, each one may certainly recite the *brachah* individually.

8. The matzah must be eaten while reclining. If someone forgot to recline, he must eat another *kezayis* while reclining. It should be chewed and not swallowed in chunks.

9. The minimum amount of matzah that should be eaten to satisfy the requirement of these two *kezaysim* is the volume of 1.5 fl. oz., or matzah which covers an area approximately 7x6¼".

10. The matzah should be eaten before halachic midnight. If someone was not able to eat it before this time, he should eat the matzah without the blessing *al achilas matzah.*

11. If someone is unable to chew the matzah it may be soaked in water, although it must not be soaked for 24 hours, nor may it be soaked until it has completely dissolved. It may also be ground into matzah meal and eaten.

12. In view of the fact that there is a divergence of opinion regarding which matzah of the Seder discharges the Biblical obligation, it is best to say, "I intend to perform the mitzvah of matzah as prescribed by the Torah and as defined by its sages and commentaries."

⋖§ מָרוֹר — *Eating the Bitter Herbs*

---

1. At this point the *charoses* should be softened by adding some wine or vinegar if necessary. (This is halachically problematic on Shabbos; see above.)

2. A *kezayis* of *maror* is taken. According to some, it is totally immersed in the *charoses;* others, however, dip only a bit of the *maror* into the *charoses.* According to many authorities, the *maror* should be shaken so that most of the *charoses* comes off.

3. After the *maror* has been dipped in the *charoses*, the blessing *al achilas maror* is recited and the *maror* is eaten. We do not recline when eating the maror.

4. It is preferable that the entire *kezayis* of *maror* be eaten at one time. Even if one cannot do this, there may not be a lapse greater than (according to various opinions) 2-9 minutes, from the time one begins swallowing the *kezayis* of *maror* and the time he finishes swallowing it. As noted previously, a competent halachic authority should be consulted for a personal decision.

5. One *must* chew the *maror*, and not swallow it whole, so as to feel the bitterness of its taste. (While it is preferable that the matzah be chewed, this is not essential, as tasting it is not fundamental to the mitzvah.)

6. When reciting *al achilas maror*, one should bear in mind that this blessing covers the *maror* of the *korech* "sandwich" as well.

As noted, there should be no unnecessary interruption until after *korech*.

7. The *maror* must not have soaked in water for 24 hours.

8. According to *R' Moshe Feinstein* צ″ל, the minimum amount of *maror* that must be consumed is the volume of 1.1 fl. oz. if ground horseradish is used. (In cases of difficulty, this figure may be lowered to .7 fl. oz.) If romaine lettuce is used, leaves covering an area of 80 square inches or stalks which cover 15 square inches should be eaten. These measurements may be made on Yom Tov.

בוֹרֵךְ 8‏ — *Eating the Sandwich of Matzah and Maror*

1. A *kezayis* of matzah should be taken from the bottom of the three matzos, and a sandwich made with a *kezayis* of *maror* between two pieces of matzah. It should be dipped into *charoses*.

2. It is customary to say the declaration of "In remembrance of the Temple . . ." before eating the *korech* sandwich.

3. The sandwich should be eaten while reclining. If one forgot to recline, he need not eat another sandwich.

4. One should try to have the entire sandwich in his mouth at one time. The time from when one begins to swallow the sandwich until he finishes may not be longer than the time it takes to eat a *pras* (see above).

5. According to *R' Moshe Feinstein* זצ״ל, the minimum amount of matzah for *korech* is a piece 28 inches square. The minimum amount of *maror* is the same as that cited for *maror,* above.

שֻׁלְחָן עוֹרֵךְ 8‏ — *The Meal is Served*

1. It is preferable that one recline throughout the entire meal.

2. In most communities there is a strict custom not to eat any roasted meat, even a pot roast, at the meal.

3. While eating the meal one should be careful not to eat too much, so that he will have at least some appetite for the *afikoman*.

4. In many places there is a custom to eat eggs at the Seder meal.

5. Some have the custom to refrain from dipping any foods into liquids, dips, etc., other than the two times called for in the Haggadah.

6. As noted above, the blessing for the mitzvah of matzah applies to the *afikoman* as well. There should be no unnecessary or idle conversation at the Seder meal. *Divrei Torah* and expounding on the Exodus enhance the Seder meal.

צָפוּן 8‏ — *Eating the Afikoman*

1. After the meal is completed the *afikoman* is eaten. One should preferably eat two *kezaysim* of matzah, but a minimum of one *kezayis* must be eaten.

2. The *afikoman* must be eaten while reclining. If one forgot to do so, he should eat another *kezayis* of matzah while reclining, unless this is difficult for him.

3. While one must be sated, he should preferably still have a good appetite when eating the *afikoman*. For this reason, one should be careful not to fill oneself excessively at the meal. If the *afikoman* is eaten when one is in such a bloated state that the eating is repulsive to him, he has not discharged his obligation.

4. The *afikoman* should be eaten before halachic midnight.

5. If someone forgot to eat the *afikoman* and washed מַיִם אַחֲרוֹנִים or said, "Let us recite Grace After Meals," he should eat the *afikoman* then, without reciting another *hamotzi* on the matzah (although this is not the rule at other meals). If he did not remember that he overlooked the *afikoman* until after having said Grace After Meals, see *Shulchan Aruch Orach Chaim* 477 and *Mishnah Berurah* there.

6. If the matzah set aside for the *afikoman* was misplaced, any other *kezayis* of *matzah shmurah* may be substituted.

7. The minimum amount of matzah that should be eaten to satisfy the requirement of these two *kezaysim* is the volume of 1.5 fl. oz., or matzah which covers an area approximately 7x6¼".

⚜ בָּרֵךְ ⚜ — *Reciting Grace After Meals*

---

1. The cups used for the wine should be rinsed out if they are dirty.

2. The third cup of wine is poured, the hands are washed for *mayim achronim* and *bircas hamazon* is recited.

3. Following Grace After Meals, the third cup of wine is consumed, while reclining. If someone forgot to recline he should not drink another cup of wine to compensate.

4. No wine or other alcoholic beverage should be consumed following the third cup of wine. Other drinks are permitted, provided they are not חֲמַר מְדִינָה (a beverage accepted in that locality as a social drink, used for toasts, etc.). There are many leading halachic authorities who maintain that most common drinks are חֲמַר מְדִינָה and therefore permit only water and seltzer (kosher for Passover, of course).

1. It is customary to pour an extra cup of wine. This is called "Elijah's cup."

2. There is also a custom to open the door of the house at this time, in order to recall that this is the "night of watching" (*Exodus* 12:42). It is hoped that this show of faith will help bring closer the age of the Messiah, and this is why the verses "Pour Your wrath, etc." are recited at this point.

3. The fourth cup is poured and the remainder of Hallel, starting from "*lo lanu* — Not for our sake . . .," is recited.

4. Many authorities maintain that Hallel should be finished before halachic midnight.

5. It is preferable to try to have at least three people (including women and children) at the Seder so that Hallel may be recited in responsive fashion.

6. There are various customs as to which psalms, prayers, and blessings should be recited, and in which order. According to the *Shulchan Aruch* the order is: Hallel, Psalm 136, *Nishmas* without its closing blessing, and then יְהַלְלוּךְ — the paragraph and blessing which customarily ends Hallel. The *Mishnah Berurah* cites other customs: Hallel, יְהַלְלוּךְ without its closing blessing, Psalm 136, *Nishmas* closing with either the regular closing of *Yishtabach* or the closing blessing of Hallel — מֶלֶךְ מְהֻלָּל בַּתִּשְׁבָּחוֹת.

7. According to most customs, the fourth cup of wine is drunk after the end of Hallel and its *brachah,* before the recitation of the concluding songs. Some have the custom to drink the wine after the songs, however.

According to the prevalent custom, the poem with the refrain "It came to pass at midnight" is recited on the first night, and "And you shall say: This is in the Feast of Passover" on the second night. Some recite both poems on each night.

8. Women must also participate in the recitation of Hallel.

9. Hallel should be recited while sitting, unlike the recitation of Hallel in the synagogue throughout the year. This reflects our liberation and freedom. One should not be reclining, however, as a mood of solemnity is more appropriate.

10. One should drink the entire fourth cup. It is imperative that one have at least a full *revi'is* of this cup, in order to be able to say the blessing which follows the drinking of wine (עַל הַגֶּפֶן).

11. The cup should be drunk while reclining. If one forgot to recline, he need not drink another cup.

12. After the fourth cup of wine one may not drink any more wine the rest of the night, although drinking water is permitted. There are several reasons given for this. Some say the reason is to prevent one from becoming intoxicated and drowsy, which would render him unable to fulfill the obligation to speak about the Exodus until late into the night. According to this reasoning, it is only wine or other alcohol that is forbidden.

Another reason offered is that another cup of wine would appear as if the person is adding on to the required four cups. According to this, any *chamar medinah* is forbidden.

A third possibility is that this ruling is related to the prohibition against *eating* anything after the *afikoman* because it would eliminate the taste of the matzah from a person's mouth. According to this opinion most beverages would be forbidden. The *Shulchan Aruch* seems to prefer the last opinion, although a more lenient position may be adopted in case of need.

נִרְצָה §⊷ — *The Conclusion of the Seder*

---

1. Everyone should discuss the story of the Exodus after the Seder until he falls asleep. Some read *Shir HaShirim* after the Seder.

2. It is customary to say only the first paragraph of *Shema* before going to sleep, omitting the prayers that are said to beseech Hashem to guard over us during the night, as this is called the "night of watching," when God watches over us especially. The blessing *Hamapil* should be recited, however.

קַדֵּשׁ

Kiddush should be recited and the Seder begun as soon after synagogue services as possible — however, not before nightfall. Each participant's cup should be poured by someone else to symbolize the majesty of the evening, as though each participant had a servant.

On Friday night begin here:

(וַיְהִי עֶרֶב וַיְהִי בֹקֶר)

יוֹם הַשִּׁשִּׁי. וַיְכֻלּוּ הַשָּׁמַיִם וְהָאָרֶץ וְכָל צְבָאָם. וַיְכַל אֱלֹהִים בַּיּוֹם הַשְּׁבִיעִי מְלַאכְתּוֹ אֲשֶׁר עָשָׂה, וַיִּשְׁבֹּת בַּיּוֹם הַשְּׁבִיעִי מִכָּל מְלַאכְתּוֹ אֲשֶׁר עָשָׂה. וַיְבָרֶךְ אֱלֹהִים אֶת יוֹם הַשְּׁבִיעִי וַיְקַדֵּשׁ אֹתוֹ, כִּי בוֹ שָׁבַת מִכָּל מְלַאכְתּוֹ אֲשֶׁר בָּרָא אֱלֹהִים לַעֲשׂוֹת.[1]

On all nights other than Friday, begin here;
on Friday night include all passages in parentheses.

סַבְרִי מָרָנָן וְרַבָּנָן וְרַבּוֹתַי:

בָּרוּךְ אַתָּה יהוה אֱלֹהֵינוּ מֶלֶךְ הָעוֹלָם, בּוֹרֵא פְּרִי הַגָּפֶן:

בָּרוּךְ אַתָּה יהוה אֱלֹהֵינוּ מֶלֶךְ הָעוֹלָם, אֲשֶׁר בָּחַר בָּנוּ מִכָּל עָם, וְרוֹמְמָנוּ מִכָּל לָשׁוֹן, וְקִדְּשָׁנוּ בְּמִצְוֹתָיו. וַתִּתֶּן לָנוּ יהוה אֱלֹהֵינוּ בְּאַהֲבָה (שַׁבָּתוֹת לִמְנוּחָה וּ)מוֹעֲדִים לְשִׂמְחָה, חַגִּים וּזְמַנִּים לְשָׂשׂוֹן, אֶת יוֹם (הַשַּׁבָּת הַזֶּה וְאֶת יוֹם) חַג הַמַּצּוֹת הַזֶּה, זְמַן חֵרוּתֵנוּ (בְּאַהֲבָה) מִקְרָא קֹדֶשׁ, זֵכֶר לִיצִיאַת מִצְרָיִם, כִּי בָנוּ בָחַרְתָּ וְאוֹתָנוּ קִדַּשְׁתָּ מִכָּל הָעַמִּים, (וְשַׁבָּת) וּמוֹעֲדֵי קָדְשֶׁךָ (בְּאַהֲבָה וּבְרָצוֹן) בְּשִׂמְחָה וּבְשָׂשׂוֹן הִנְחַלְתָּנוּ. בָּרוּךְ אַתָּה יהוה, מְקַדֵּשׁ (הַשַּׁבָּת וְ)יִשְׂרָאֵל וְהַזְּמַנִּים.

Kiddush continues on the next page.

KADDESH

Kiddush should be recited and the Seder begun as soon after synagogue services as possible — however, not before nightfall. Each participant's cup should be poured by someone else to symbolize the majesty of the evening, as though each participant had a servant.

On Friday night begin here:
(And there was evening and there was morning)

The sixth day. Thus the heaven and the earth were finished, and all their array. On the seventh day God completed His work which He had done, and He abstained on the seventh day from all His work which He had done. God blessed the seventh day and hallowed it, because on it He abstained from all His work which God created to make.[1]

On all nights other than Friday, begin here;
on Friday night include all passages in parentheses.

By your leave, my masters and teachers:

Blessed are You, HASHEM, our God, King of the universe, Who creates the fruit of the vine.

Blessed are You, HASHEM, our God, King of the universe, Who has chosen us from among all nations, exalted us above all tongues, and sanctified us with His commandments. And You, HASHEM, our God, have lovingly given us (Sabbaths for rest, and) appointed times for gladness, feasts and seasons for joy, this day of (Sabbath and this day of) the Festival of Matzos, the season of our freedom, (in love,) a holy convocation in memory of the Exodus from Egypt. For You have chosen us and sanctified us above all peoples, (and the Sabbath) and Your holy festivals (in love and favor), in gladness and joy have You granted us as a heritage. Blessed are You, HASHEM, Who sanctifies (the Sabbath), Israel, and the festive seasons.

Kiddush continues on the next page.

---

(1) *Genesis* 1:31-2:3.

On Saturday night, add the following two blessings.
Two candles are held while the following blessing is recited.

בָּרוּךְ אַתָּה יהוה אֱלֹהֵינוּ מֶלֶךְ הָעוֹלָם, בּוֹרֵא מְאוֹרֵי הָאֵשׁ.

Hold up the fingers to the light of the candles to see their reflected light.

בָּרוּךְ אַתָּה יהוה אֱלֹהֵינוּ מֶלֶךְ הָעוֹלָם, הַמַּבְדִּיל בֵּין קֹדֶשׁ
לְחוֹל, בֵּין אוֹר לְחֹשֶׁךְ, בֵּין יִשְׂרָאֵל לָעַמִּים, בֵּין יוֹם
הַשְּׁבִיעִי לְשֵׁשֶׁת יְמֵי הַמַּעֲשֶׂה. בֵּין קְדֻשַּׁת שַׁבָּת לִקְדֻשַּׁת יוֹם
טוֹב הִבְדַּלְתָּ, וְאֶת יוֹם הַשְּׁבִיעִי מִשֵּׁשֶׁת יְמֵי הַמַּעֲשֶׂה קִדַּשְׁתָּ,
הִבְדַּלְתָּ וְקִדַּשְׁתָּ אֶת עַמְּךָ יִשְׂרָאֵל בִּקְדֻשָּׁתֶךָ. בָּרוּךְ אַתָּה
יהוה, הַמַּבְדִּיל בֵּין קֹדֶשׁ לְקֹדֶשׁ.

On all nights conclude here:
One should bear in mind that this blessing applies to all observances of the Seder.
Women who recited this blessing at candle-lighting should not repeat it now.

בָּרוּךְ אַתָּה יהוה אֱלֹהֵינוּ מֶלֶךְ הָעוֹלָם, שֶׁהֶחֱיָנוּ
וְקִיְּמָנוּ וְהִגִּיעָנוּ לַזְּמַן הַזֶּה.

The wine should be drunk without delay while reclining on the left side. It is preferable to
drink the entire cup, but at the very least, most of the cup should be drained.

וּרְחַץ

The head of the household — according to many opinions, all participants in the Seder —
washes his hands as if to eat bread (pouring water from a cup, twice on the right and twice
on the left), but without reciting a blessing.

כַּרְפַּס

All participants take a vegetable other than *maror* and dip it into salt water. A piece smaller
in volume than half an egg should be used. The following blessing is recited (with the
intention that it also applies to the *maror* which will be eaten during the meal) before the
vegetable is eaten. It is preferable that those who did not wash their hands at *urchatz* not
touch the vegetable with their hand, but use a utensil.

בָּרוּךְ אַתָּה יהוה אֱלֹהֵינוּ מֶלֶךְ הָעוֹלָם, בּוֹרֵא פְּרִי
הָאֲדָמָה.

On Saturday night, add the following two blessings.
Two candles are held while the following blessing is recited.

Blessed are You, HASHEM, our God, King of the universe, Who creates the illumination of the fire.

Hold up the fingers to the light of the candles to see their reflected light.

Blessed are You, HASHEM, our God, King of the universe, Who distinguishes between sacred and secular, between light and darkness, between Israel and the nations, between the seventh day and the six days of activity. You have distinguished between the holiness of the Sabbath and the holiness of a Festival, and have sanctified the seventh day above the six days of activity. You distinguished and sanctified Your nation, Israel, with Your holiness. Blessed are You, HASHEM, Who distinguishes between holiness and holiness.

On all nights conclude here:
One should bear in mind that this blessing applies to all observances of the Seder. Women who recited this blessing at candle-lighting should not repeat it now.

Blessed are You, HASHEM, our God, King of the universe, Who has kept us alive, sustained us, and brought us to this season.

The wine should be drunk without delay while reclining on the left side. It is preferable to drink the entire cup, but at the very least, most of the cup should be drained.

URECHATZ

The head of the household — according to many opinions, all participants in the Seder — washes his hands as if to eat bread (pouring water from a cup, twice on the right and twice on the left), but without reciting a blessing.

KARPAS

All participants take a vegetable other than *maror* and dip it into salt water. A piece smaller in volume than half an egg should be used. The following blessing is recited (with the intention that it also applies to the *maror* which will be eaten during the meal) before the vegetable is eaten. It is preferable that those who did not wash their hands at *urchatz* not touch the vegetable with their hand, but use a utensil.

Blessed are You, HASHEM, our God, King of the universe, Who creates the fruit of the soil.

יחץ

The head of the household breaks the middle matzah in two. He puts the smaller part back between the two whole matzos, and wraps up the larger part for later use as the *afikoman*. It is preferable that an amount of matzah adequate for all the participants be set aside. Some briefly place the *afikoman* portion on their shoulders, in accordance with the Biblical verse (*Exodus* 12:34) recounting that Israel left Egypt carrying their matzos on their shoulders, and say, בְּבְהִלוּ יָצָאנוּ מִמִּצְרָיִם, "In haste we went out of Egypt." The remaining matzah should be the equivalent of a *kezayis*.

מגיד

The Seder plate (if it contains the matzos) or the matzos are lifted for all to see as the head of the household begins with the following brief explanation of the proceedings. One should, at this point, declare his intent to fulfill the mitzvah to retell the story of our Exodus from Egypt. The Haggadah is to be recited with reverence, and thus is not recited while reclining.

1. Why is the text for this evening's discussion of the Exodus called "Haggadah"?

It is generally assumed that the name derives from the language of the verse in the Torah which obligates us to retell the story of our redemption on this night (*Exodus* 13:8). That verse reads: *"and you shall **tell** (vehigadeta) your child on that day."* Thus, "Haggadah" simply means telling (*Avudraham* and *Malbim*). However, other commentators offer several other possibilities. *Rashi* (*Exodus* 13:5) teaches that one should engage a child in the discussion of the redemption through *divrei aggadah* (stories) — words that speak to, and carry the heart — rather than halachic or philosophical approaches. Hence, the title "Haggadah," since a good deal of the text is the story of our exodus from Egypt. *Avudraham* points out that *Targum Yerushalmi* renders the word הִגַּדְתִּי (*Deuteronomy* 26:3) as *I give praise*. Thus, it is the message of tribute to the Almighty embodied in the tale of our redemption which may account for the name "Haggadah." *Maasei Nissim* states that the root of the word *haggadah* means pulling, or drawing out. The term is used here with respect to the mouth. It means to imply that there should be a continuous flow of speech regarding the Exodus on this night, and one should make an effort to bring to light as much as possible concerning this subject, as we say later in the Haggadah, *"The more one tells about the Exodus, the more he is praiseworthy."*

YACHATZ

The head of the household breaks the middle matzah in two. He puts the smaller part back between the two whole matzos, and wraps up the larger part for later use as the *afikoman*. It is preferable that an amount of matzah adequate for all the participants be set aside. Some briefly place the *afikoman* portion on their shoulders, in accordance with the Biblical verse (*Exodus* 12:34) recounting that Israel left Egypt carrying their matzos on their shoulders, and say, בְּבְהִלוּ יָצָאנוּ מִמִּצְרָיִם, "In haste we went out of Egypt." The remaining matzah should be the equivalent of a *kezayis*.

MAGGID

The Seder plate (if it contains the matzos) or the matzos are lifted for all to see as the head of the household begins with the following brief explanation of the proceedings. One should, at this point, declare his intent to fulfill the mitzvah to retell the story of our Exodus from Egypt. The Haggadah is to be recited with reverence, and thus is not recited while reclining.

2. What distinguishes this evening's mitzvah of recalling the Exodus from the obligation to do so every night of the year?

(A) On this night, it is not sufficient merely to remember the Exodus oneself. The mitzvah is to tell the story of our redemption to others *by way of question and answer* (see question 19). Indeed, if a person finds himself alone on the night of Pesach, he must conduct this question-and-answer exchange on his own, despite the lack of apparent necessity for such a procedure.

(B) During the year, one need not recount anything more than our deliverance from the land that enslaved us. Tonight, the recollection of the redemption must describe our people's transition from humble roots (either as idol worshipers or slaves[1]) to their ultimate, exalted status as a nation redeemed by God.

(C) In addition, on this night one is required to explain the reasons (or symbolic meanings) behind the mitzvos we perform at the Seder in relation to the Exodus (as we do by reciting Rabban Gamliel's declaration later on in the Haggadah).

These reasons are, however, contrary to the opinions of *Rif* and *Rashba,* quoted by *Avudraham,* who maintain that mere mention of the Exodus is enough to fulfill one's obligation on this night, although it is praiseworthy to discuss it at length on this special occasion. *Maasei Nissim,* on the other hand, insists that there must be a difference

---

1. The Dispute of Rav and Shmuel; *Pesachim* 116a. See question 26.

between *remembering* the Exodus, which we are required to do every morning and evening (and which, by definition, would allow for a cursory treatment), and *retelling* it, which is the mitzvah at hand. On this night, he asserts, it is incumbent upon every Jew to review the entire sequence of events surrounding our redemption.[1] *Sefer HaChinuch* agrees with him, noting that particular emphasis should be placed on the miracles which occurred on our behalf, and on the revenge that God exacted from the Egyptians for their oppression of us. *Maasei Hashem* adds a point previously touched upon. He feels that the recounting of the Exodus should be viewed primarily as providing a context for understanding the other mitzvos of this evening: *Pesach, matzah,* and *maror.* These mitzvos are directly related to the redemption, serving to memorialize specific physical and/or spiritual aspects of that experience.

3. Why don't we make the customary benediction that precedes the performance of mitzvos (*Who has sanctified us with His commandments, and commanded us to . . .*) before reciting the Haggadah?

Rif's position is that there is no need to make a blessing over this mitzvah since one has already discharged his obligation by uttering the words *"in memory of the Exodus from Egypt"* during *Kiddush. Rashba* comments that no benediction is required for mitzvos that do not call for a designated amount or degree of performance. In this case, a minimal amount of talk — "even one word" — is sufficient to meet the requirement. Therefore, no blessing is needed. Others, however, disagree with these opinions.

Maasei Nissim[2] proposes that our sages did not establish benedictions to be made over other blessings. As an example, he notes that while Grace After Meals is a Biblically ordained commandment, the Rabbis of the Talmud never instituted a benediction to be made prior to reciting the Grace After Meals. Likewise, he points out, the recitation of the Haggadah already incorporates a blessing at its conclusion: *Who redeemed us and redeemed our ancestors . . .* Therefore, it needs no additional benediction preceding it.

B'samim Rosh points out that the reading of the Haggadah in and of

---

1. *Bircas Avraham* suggests that this is the reason that the ruling of R' Elazar ben Azaryah immediately follows the story of the sages gathered all night in Bnei Brak — to indicate that the sages themselves surmised the importance of discussing the Exodus at length on this night from the fact that there is already a mitzvah to recall the redemption every night, and if so, there must be more to tonight's mitzvah.

2. Other commentaries offer a similar explanation.

itself constitutes great praise to the Almighty. (He suggests that this concept might also explain why we make no blessing over the mitzvah of drinking the four cups of wine. That too is covered by the blessing and praise already contained in the Haggadah text, and no other benediction is required.[3]) *Chida's* comment clarifies these two opinions. The purpose of a benediction preceding the performance of a mitzvah, he states, is to establish that what is about to take place represents the realization of Divine Will. In pronouncing a blessing or reciting praises to the Almighty, the nature of the act is self-evident, and no such prior declaration is necessary.

Bircas HaShir does not accept the notion that the blessing *at the end* of the Haggadah can substitute for the proper benediction, which should *precede* the mitzvah. He proposes that when *Rif* said that one's obligation was satisfied by recitation of *Kiddush, Rif* meant that *the Kiddush itself,* with its mention of the Exodus, serves in place of the requisite blessing. *Shibbolei HaLeket* offers a solution similar to that of *Rif.* He believes it might be the blessings of the *Shema* in the evening services preceding the Seder that absolve us of the need to make a benediction over the Haggadah. Throughout the year, these blessings frame the daily mitzvah of remembering the redemption which we perform by reciting the last sentence in *Shema.* Thus, they may serve as the blessing for our expanded commemoration on this night.

4. Why do we not recite the blessing usually associated with the commemoration of great occurrences (. . . *Who performed miracles for our ancestors . . .*) before reading the Haggadah?

Ohr Zarua, Shibbolei HaLeket and *Aruch HaShulchan* note that these very words are included in the text of the Haggadah after the recounting of the wonders we experienced: *"Therefore, it is our duty to thank, praise, pay tribute . . . and acclaim Him Who performed all these miracles for our fathers and for us."* This is followed, shortly thereafter, by a blessing over the redemption (*Blessed are You . . . Who redeemed us . . .*). Thus, no additional blessing is required.

Aruch HaShulchan, though, says that this blessing cannot be made at the Seder for a more basic reason: Since the very nature of the mitzvah of the night is to speak of God's miracles, making the

---

1. The reason that the mitzvos of matzah and *maror* still require separate blessings before their performance — despite their inclusion in the praise and blessing of the Haggadah — may be that they are Biblically ordained. By contrast, the four cups of wine are Rabbinically derived. Therefore, they need no Rabbinical addendum. (See also *Maharal's* opinion in question 20.)

הָא לַחְמָא עַנְיָא דִּי אֲכָלוּ אַבְהָתָנָא בְּאַרְעָא דְמִצְרָיִם. כָּל דִּכְפִין יֵיתֵי וְיֵכוֹל, כָּל דִּצְרִיךְ יֵיתֵי וְיִפְסַח.

blessing ". . . Who performed miracles" would, *in itself,* constitute ful-fillment of the basic Biblical requirement to recount the Exodus. Clearly, it would have been pointless for the sages of the Talmud to institute a benediction of such redundant nature, where it no longer precedes the mitzvah, but becomes the mitzvah itself. As for the blessing that concludes the Haggadah (*Who redeemed us and redeemed our ancestors . . .*), the *Aruch HaShulchan* maintains that this blessing is primarily concerned with the other mitzvos of the evening, not the recalling of the redemption, and therefore, presents no difficulty.

5. Must we actually talk in order to fulfill the mitzvah of "retelling" the Exodus?

In explaining why no blessing is prescribed before beginning the reading of the Haggadah, *Be'er Miriam* offers a unique approach. His opinion is that one can fulfill the obligation to recount the Exodus by way of thought, without actually speaking. Therefore, no benediction is called for since we only pronounce blessings over actions. While dis-agreeing with the basic premise, *Maharal* insists that although the spo-ken word is necessary to meet the requirement of the mitzvah, under-standing is equally essential, and is, in fact, the *chief* ingredient in its performance. "Retelling" the story of the Exodus from Egypt means *retelling with comprehension.* Since the primary element here is thought, not action or speech, we do not make a blessing.

⇜§ הָא לַחְמָא עַנְיָא — *This is the bread of affliction.*

6. Its nature and significance — general perspectives

While most commentaries agree that the opening paragraph of the Haggadah is not focusing specifically and/or exclusively on tonight's mitzvah of eating matzah, opinions differ on its main intent.

Shibbolei HaLeket suggests that the beginning of the Haggadah is based on those verses in the Torah that introduce the mitzvos of this night (*Exodus* 12:3 ff). There, we are told of the arrangements to be made in order to partake of the meat of the *Korban Pesach* — the Passover sacrifice, the focal point of the evening's religious observance — in groups. In order to participate, one had to be formally included in such

This is the bread of affliction that our fathers ate in the land of Egypt. Whoever is hungry — let him come and eat. Whoever is needy — let him come and celebrate Passover!

---

a group before the animal was slaughtered. It is in remembrance of this practice (which actually took place, as mentioned, earlier in the day) that the sages incorporated the proclamation, *"Whoever is needy — let him come* and take part in (the korban) Pesach" at the beginning of the Haggadah.

According to *Kol Bo,* however, this paragraph serves only to explain to the children why we have just broken one of the matzos in half, as a poor person does. Additionally, in order not to delay the Exodus from Egypt, Jews shared their own supplies of food with those neighbors who needed more time to prepare their own. This is what we recall when we extend the invitation, *"Whoever is hungry — let him come and eat"* — let those whose food is not ready come and partake of my meal, which is already fixed.

Abarbanel provides a different explanation, which also explains why this is the only major portion in the Haggadah written in Aramaic rather than in Hebrew. When the festival was celebrated in Jerusalem, people did so not only with family, but together with the needy, such as the Levite, in fulfilling the Biblical command (*Deuteronomy* 12:12). When the Jews were exiled to Babylonia, the sages instituted that they continue this tradition of inviting others to join in their meal. To this end, they formulated this paragraph which is recited in Aramaic — the language spoken in Babylonia which calls to those less fortunate to join in our meal. In that spirit, our sages saw fit to begin the Haggadah with the same clearly understood invitation to the poor that was customary in Babylonia, where the language was Aramaic — כָּל דִּכְפִין.

Bircas HaShir notes that an integral ingredient of charity is to soothe the recipient with words that ease the pain of his reliance on others. We therefore preface our hospitality with a reminder that *"this is the bread of affliction that our fathers ate in the land of Egypt"* — there is no shame in accepting this bread, for through it we relive the poverty and suffering of those days, which our ancestors experienced equally, without any class distinction. Indeed, on this night, the poor join with their hosts in enjoying the choicest food in the house: matzah, symbol of affliction, but also of ultimate redemption.

Malbim agrees that *"Whoever is hungry . . ."* was an announcement one heard throughout Babylonia on the eve of Pesach, but he adds this

הָשַׁתָּא הָכָא, לְשָׁנָה הַבָּאָה בְּאַרְעָא דְיִשְׂרָאֵל. הָשַׁתָּא עַבְדֵי, לְשָׁנָה הַבָּאָה בְּנֵי חוֹרִין.

---

insight. In order to spare the poor person from shame, it was first pointed out that הָא לַחְמָא עַנְיָא — our forefathers ate matzah, *maror,* and the *Korban Pesach* in Egypt as they were commanded to by Moses, and we do the same, as the Torah demanded of all future generations. Please join us, then, in the fulfillment of these mitzvos. Thus, the invitation is more a call for shared fulfillment of a religious obligation than an offer of charity, and the sting of dependency has been lessened.

Maasei Hashem also views this paragraph as an outgrowth of the Babylonian experience, but his approach is entirely different. He sees it as a lament before beginning the Seder, bemoaning the loss of all that was associated with the performance of this evening's mitzvos. While in Jerusalem, for example, only prearranged groups were able to come together to eat the *korban,* in *galus* one can invite anyone to tonight's meal, even people not previously designated to be present. According to this interpretation, the phrase כָּל דִּצְרִיךְ יֵיתֵי וְיִפְסַח is actually an expression of anguish over our loss (i.e., it is understood as, "[now,] whoever is needy *may* come and take part in [the festivity of] Pesach"). And so, the Haggadah begins: "this" — the portion of matzah that we will soon eat in place of the *Korban Pesach,* and indeed, the entire meal[1] — "is the bread of affliction." It is eaten in pain and with yearning, exactly the way our ancestors ate in Egypt before they were redeemed. Having mourned the past, we conclude this paragraph with the hope that in the near future we will once again be free and in our land, so that we may perform all the mitzvos properly. With these dreams, we usher in the evening's celebration.

Maasei Nissim takes the opposite view. His opinion is that the message for those that went into, and remain in, exile, is entirely one of comfort and consolation. If a person should question the propriety of celebrating the previous Exodus when we find ourselves once again in exile, he must be told that this is the bread of affliction that our forefathers ate, yet they were redeemed. It is precisely their experience which guarantees our own future redemption. Just as God chose us then to be his nation, even though we partake now of the bitter bread of exile, we are certain that the time will soon arrive when our hearts overflow with happiness, and we will declare, "Whoever is hungry — let him come and share in our joy."

---

1. The word "bread" is often used to refer to a full meal.

Now, we are here; next year may we be in the Land of Israel! Now, we are slaves; next year may we be free men!

Even though *"now we are here,"* in exile, *"next year"* we will surely be home *"in the Land of Israel."*

Finally, *Maharal* proposes that this paragraph refers specifically to the mitzvah which we are about to perform: namely, to retell the story of the Exodus. The Talmud describes matzah as being the basis of the discussion on the Seder night (see *Pesachim* 115b). We make a point, therefore, of calling attention to the matzah at the outset, so that all will remain cognizant of the central role it plays in the evening's service.

According to some of the above approaches, it is clear why this paragraph does not appear to have been part of the Haggadah text in the time of the *Beis HaMikdash,*[1] since it serves only to remind later generations of some element of those times. *Malbim,* however, seems to suggest that portions of this paragraph were announced publicly on the eve of the festival, and other portions may have been part of the Haggadah as well. He states that the phrase *"now, we are slaves"* refers to the rule of the Persians, Greeks, and Romans during the period of the Temple.

7. Why is this paragraph written in Aramaic rather than Hebrew?

Maasei Nissim and *Maasei Hashem* state that this was done to make clear that it is not part of the original Haggadah text, but something added after the destruction of Jerusalem.

Maamar Mordechai suggests that the sages in Israel authored the entire Haggadah in Hebrew, while those in Babylonia added this paragraph and חַד גַּדְיָא (an allegorical song at the end of the Hagaddah) in Aramaic — the language commonly spoken — so that people should question and debate their meaning, and, as a result, increase the discussion of the Exodus.

A number of commentaries (*Avudraham, Maharal, Shibbolei HaLeket,* and others) echo the basic theme that the phrasing of the paragraphs in the native tongue, Aramaic, was in order to involve the women, children, and unlearned people right at the start of the service, so that they would pay attention to and question the various elements of the Haggadah and Seder, in order to elicit a response. This conforms to the requirement laid down in the verse: *"And you shall tell your child on that day . . ."* (*Exodus* 13:8).

---

1. See *Rambam's* version (*Laws of chametz and matzah* 8:2).

Shibbolei HaLeket says that we are alluding to the Midrash which states that the reason we were sent into exile was because of the sin of eating *chametz* during Pesach. We therefore warn our children in their native tongue that it is matzah which holds the key to our redemption, past and future. We then declare, *"Whoever is hungry — let him come* and eat with us," since we are among those who are careful to eat only matzah. In that merit, we hope that although *"now, we are here,"* in exile, *"next year"* we will all be home, *"in the Land of Israel."*

8. Is the proper reading "ha" ("this") or "keha" ("like this" or "like that")?

Maasei Hashem interprets "This is *like* the bread of affliction" to mean that the meal we will eat this evening is not like those that our ancestors enjoyed in Jerusalem. Rather, our meal is exactly like those that our forefathers *"ate in the land of Egypt,"* mired in gloom and anguish, longing for redemption. *Rokeach* and *Avudraham* suggest that we are saying the matzah itself is just like the bread that our forefathers ate in Egypt.

Shulchan Aruch HaRav offers that those who say, "This is *like* . . .," rather than, *"This is* . . .," do so because one cannot suggest that this *is* the bread that our ancestors ate. Therefore, even though *"This is"* is the more common version of the opening line, those who say, "This is like," are not to be regarded as incorrect.

9. Why do we call matzah *lachma anya*?

In a lengthy review of this matter, *Abarbanel* cites several reasons:

(a) In the Talmud (*Pesachim* 115b), Shmuel describes matzah as "the bread that we *recite* (*onin*) many things over"; thus, *anya* is derived from the word *oneh* (to *recite*).

(b) The Egyptians never granted the Jews enough time to bake their dough into bread. The result — matzah — is thus a reminder of their *affliction* (*inuy*).

(c) It is eaten in the manner of a poor person (*ani*). Just as he rarely partakes of whole foods, we perform the mitzvah with a broken piece of matzah.

(d) Because, at the time of the Exodus, it was eaten together with the Passover sacrifice and was, in a sense, a 'poor' (*ani*) second to the main part of the meal.

(e) Because the Jews used the same measure of flour to bake their matzah as was later required by the Torah of a poor individual when bringing a sacrifice — a tenth of an *eifah*.[1]

(f) *Ramban's* reasons:

(1) Matzah is fashioned in a poor (inexpensive) way, with no ingredients but flour and water.

(2) It reminds us of how the Jews in Egypt subsisted on very meager (poor) rations.

However, *Abarbanel* has difficulties with each of these explanations and therefore offers two others:

(a) Matzah does not rise, and remains "poor" (*ani*) in texture, as opposed to bread, which rises and becomes "rich."

(b) Matzah is not easily digested, and remains in the digestive tract longer than other foods. It is therefore a practical food for a poor person (*ani*), since a little bit lasts for a long time, and is in fact what the Jews were fed by their taskmasters in Egypt.

Maharal reasons that it is called poor bread because it is comparable to a poor person. Just as the pauper has no money or possessions, but only his body, matzah too consists of only a basic dough. There is no enhancement of the dough, which would require introducing an additional ingredient to the composition of the matzah.

10. How can we say, "that our fathers ate in the land of Egypt," when the Torah tells us that the baking of the matzos took place as they left the country *(Exodus* 12:39)?

Yaavetz explains that even though the Jews left the heart of Egypt on the fifteenth of Nissan, they did not actually exit the country until several days later. Thus, the matzah they baked upon their departure was eaten while they were still on Egyptian territory. In addition, they had already eaten matzah as a religious requirement on the night of the fifteenth, before they left.

Abarbanel and the *Gra* both maintain that the Egyptians fed their Jewish slaves matzah (as was customary for prisoners and slaves in many countries, since, as mentioned, it is not digested quickly). They make it clear, however, that tonight's mitzvah of eating matzah is not intended to recall a facet of our suffering as slaves. Rather, it is based on the matzah the Jews themselves baked at the time of the Exodus.[2] This symbolized the great haste with which God brought them out of Egypt.

---

1. A tenth of an *eifah* = the volume of 43.2 eggs. Since this was the measure of manna that fell for each Jew in the wilderness (*Exodus* 16:36), it is considered to be the amount of food consumed in a day by the average person.

2. As Rabban Gamliel's declaration later points out.

Sh'lah HaKadosh phrases it this way: "How amazing it is that the Exodus should so mirror the exile. The Egyptians worked their Hebrew slaves mercilessly, never allowing them enough time to bake anything but matzah. When the hour of redemption arrived, this scenario was repeated, only in a much more joyful context for the Jews." Thus, the phrase *". . . that our fathers ate in Egypt"* is a subtle reference to haste, which the Egyptians had used to persecute the Jews but later became a salient feature of the Jew's redemption and the retribution Egypt suffered at the hands of God. This represents the characteristic of "measure for measure" that is the hallmark of Divine justice.

11. If we mean to welcome in outsiders, why isn't the declaration, "*Whoever is hungry — let him come and eat,*" made at the doorway? Are we really prepared to provide for all the needy?

The commentaries that view this invitation as merely an allusion or a reminder obviously have no difficulty here. As for the others, *Avudraham* informs us that many generations ago, the custom was, in fact, to leave the door unlocked on the night of Pesach, and loudly announce that the needy are welcome to join us. *Yaavetz* concurs with him, and they both maintain that this practice came to an end when Jews began living among a majority of non-Jewish neighbors. From then on, poor Jews were provided with their Seder needs beforehand. However, we do not tamper with the language of the Haggadah and the formula was left intact.

Chok Yaakov insists that it is still the custom among righteous people to open the door and announce, *"whoever is hungry — let him come and eat!"* However, he quotes *Raavan* as having held that the invitation is not directed towards outsiders. Rather, it is an invitation to one's own family to gather at the table and perform the evening's mitzvos.

In a similar vein, *Shibbolei HaLeket* echoes the language of *Rokeach,* and offers a novel interpretation. *"Whoever is hungry — let him come and eat,"* he suggests, does not refer to the destitute. It is an invitation to all those who have refrained from eating in the afternoon (as required by the halachah — *Shulchan Aruch O.C.* 471) in order to insure a hearty appetite for the matzah to be eaten at the Seder.

12. Why does our call for guests not precede *Kiddush,* so that they not miss the beginning of the Seder?

Bircas HaShir explains that even if our call is actually an invitation to the needy, it is said after *Kiddush* so that there should not arise a mistaken impression that the poor person can meet his obligation of drinking the first of the four cups by merely answering *"amen"* after the *Kiddush* of the head of the house. On this night, he must be given his own wine in order to fulfill the requirement of drinking the four cups of wine.

13. Why are similar invitations not extended on other *Yamim Tovim* (festivals)?

Shibbolei HaLeket suggests that since there is a Biblical requirement to eat matzah on Pesach night, we want to make certain that everyone has the means to satisfy that obligation.

Avudraham notes that the expenses involved in preparing for Pesach exceed those of other festivals. Thus, we are concerned that there are more people who will not have enough provisions to perform the Seder properly.

HaShir VeHaShevach says that even though all *Yamim Tovim* remind us of the Exodus from Egypt, they also stress other significant themes, such as the receiving of the Torah at Mt. Sinai or God's providing shelter for us in the desert. Pesach, however, deals only with the transition from our formerly low status as slaves to that of the chosen nation. If we ignore the poor and downtrodden, then we will have overlooked this essential character of the festival — redemption of the humble.

Bircas HaShir writes that the Exodus from Egypt is not merely an occurrence in the past, but an omen of the coming redemption for the Jewish people. Since our sages (*Bava Basra* 10a) attribute to the mitzvah of charity the power to draw the ultimate redemption closer, we take advantage of this auspicious occasion to perform appropriate charitable acts, in the hope of arousing heavenly mercy.

14. Since there is currently no Passover sacrifice, why do we include the added invitation, *"Whoever is needy — let him come and make [the Korban] Pesach"?* Furthermore, even when it was still offered, inviting people at this point would be senseless, since the sacrifice could only be eaten by those who were counted in as part of the group before the animal was slaughtered, earlier in the day.

As above, the commentaries that view the entire paragraph as an allusion have no problem here. If it is seen as an actual invitation though, *Yaavetz* says that the call to the hungry may apply to non-Jews, whom we are required to provide for along with poor Jews, and who are merely "hungry"' for food; the call to the needy, however, refers to Jews, who "need" to fulfill their religious obligation, and "celebrate Pesach" (the Seder). Accordingly, the word *"yifsach"* is rendered as referring to the Pesach meal, rather than the Pesach sacrifice.

Avudraham and *Maharal* suggest that *"whoever is needy"* includes those who will not truly go hungry, for they were already addressed with the words *"whoever is hungry."* Here we call to those who lack elements of the Seder to come and join us.

Chida maintains that *"whoever is needy"* means that whoever "needed" to fast on the eve of Pesach because he is a firstborn,[1] or because eating on that day would ruin his appetite at night, should now partake heartily of the Seder.

Yalkut Shimoni propounds that this phrase is a reference to the two elements of a particular law of the *Pesach sacrifice.* One who is very hungry must first eat of the meal, for it may only be eaten when one is full. On the other hand, one may not eat of the sacrifice if he is sated to the point of being disgusted by any more food. Thus, one has to be satisfied and hungry at the same time. *"Whoever is needy"* means to imply that whoever is already full, but still "needs" a drop more food to be completely full, may partake of the Passover sacrifice.

Maasei Y'dei Yotzer offers that one may now welcome *anyone* to participate in the Passover meal. In former times, one had to be careful not to use up too much food on unexpected guests; enough food had to remain for those who were included in the group eating the sacrifice to be able to eat their fill. Now, however, "whoever is needy" may join the Seder without impacting on the eating of the Passover sacrifice. "Let him come and celebrate Passover" thus means "he may come and be part of whatever celebration of Passover is taking place." We caution, however, *"Now, we are here"*; we may do this only here and now. When we return to Jerusalem, it will no longer be possible to invite guests freely, since we will then have to give consideration to the consumption of the Passover sacrifice.

15. What do the two concluding lines — הָשַׁתָּא הָכָא, "now, we are here (in exile)," and הָשַׁתָּא עַבְדֵי, "now, we are slaves" — mean to bring out? Would one of these statements not have been adequate?

According to *Yaavetz,* these statements explain why we didn't make our invitations with the door wide open, as would be appropriate for such a public call. This is because we are in exile, and are wary of our non-Jewish neighbors. *"Next year,"* though, we hope to be free to invite as we like.

---

1. It is customary that firstborn males should fast on the eve of Pesach, as a reminder that they were spared the fate of the Egyptian firstborn, who were killed that night.

Shibbolei HaLeket suggests that these are expressions of hope and prayer, meant to raise our spirits which are pained over the realization that we are unable to partake of the aforementioned Passover sacrifice.

Malbim opines that we want to arouse the curiosity of the children, who will wonder and ask why we mention the prayer of "next year in Jerusalem," which usually follows our meals and celebrations, at the start of the meal.

Baruch She'amar cites the Talmudic opinion of Shmuel that the only change the Messiah will bring in the condition of the world is the ending of our subjugation by the nations. Needy people, however, will still abound. In that case, the invitations to the poor will be just as relevant *"next year . . . in the Land of Israel,"* as *"here,"* in exile. The difference, however, is that now we are under the rule of others, but then we will be completely free.

The *Gra* applies the two statements to two distinct future redemptions — that of Eretz Yisrael and that of the Jewish people. He and *Avudraham* state that we make these statements at this point in the Seder in order to make the poor guests at the table feel equal. We tell them that now we are all slaves in exile, without distinction. Soon, we will all be free together in Israel.

Maharal feels that *"now, we are here"* is a prayer that God accept our service this evening in place of the Passover sacrifice, which we cannot bring because we are *"here,"* in exile, without the Temple. Next year in Jerusalem, though, we hope to offer the real thing. Just returning to the Holy Land, however, is not enough to realize this dream. To be truly free and able to offer the Passover sacrifice, we need a second obstacle removed as well: We must go from *"Now, we are slaves"* to being *"free men."*

16. Why do we switch from Aramaic to Hebrew for the words "l'shanah habaah," next year?

Rokeach, Kol Bo and *Yaavetz* feel that we want to avoid arousing the fears and hatred of our non-Jewish neighbors, who, upon hearing us talk of returning to Israel, might suspect us of planning a rebellion or mass flight.

Shibbolei HaLeket states that since we are offering prayers (for redemption), we use Hebrew, the language that angels understand, so that they can bring our pleas before the heavenly throne.

Bircas HaShir understands that we do not want to ruin the joy of the children (in Babylonia, where this paragraph originated, the language was Aramaic, not Hebrew), who are fascinated by the splendor and

The Seder plate is removed and the second of the four cups of wine is poured.
The youngest present asks the reasons for the unusual proceedings of the evening.

מַה נִּשְׁתַּנָּה הַלַּיְלָה הַזֶּה מִכָּל הַלֵּילוֹת?

majesty of the Seder. Lacking the maturity to appreciate our desire to return to Jerusalem, they will be saddened to hear their father speak of traveling to a faraway place.

§ מַה נִּשְׁתַּנָּה — *Why is this night different from all other nights?*

17. Why do we cover the matzos (or remove the Pesach tray from the table) and pour more wine before reading the *Mah Nishtanah*?

The Talmud instructs us to move the entire table away from where we are sitting before beginning to read the Haggadah. This is done in order to prompt the children to question the things we do differently on this night.

This also explains why we pour the wine for the second of the required four cups now, even though we will not be drinking this wine until after we finish reading the Haggadah. The child, it is hoped, will wonder why, only a few moments after making *Kiddush* and before partaking of the meal, we remove the table and prepare to drink again as if we have finished. All agree, however, that the practice now is not to remove the table. *Rashbam* explains that this is because our tables are much larger than those used at the time of the Talmud, and moving them would involve much more inconvenience. We do, however, remove the tray with the matzos and other Seder foods. *Magen Avraham* and *Shulchan Aruch HaRav* are of the opinion that we do not even remove the tray. *Aruch HaShulchan* establishes that the custom is simply to cover the matzos.

There is some dispute among the authorities as to the proper time to do this, and when things should be returned to their previous locations. The accepted opinion in *Shulchan Aruch,* however, is that the matzah and *maror* must be back on the table (or the matzah uncovered) before we begin reading the paragraph of *"We were slaves."* That is where the retelling of the Exodus commences, and the Haggadah insists that this mitzvah demands the presence of matzah and *maror* (see below, paragraph beginning *"One might think"*).

18. Is the reciting of *Mah Nishtanah* absolutely required?

As mentioned, the Talmud states that we move the table in order to

The Seder plate is removed and the second of the four cups of wine is poured. The youngest present asks the reasons for the unusual proceedings of the evening.

Why is this night different from all other nights?

pique the curiosity of the children. There is disagreement, however, regarding whether the children's resulting inquiry — "Why are you doing this?" — deems the subsequent recital of *Mah Nishtanah* — the four questions regarding our unusual practices — unnecessary. *Rashi* and *Rashbam* maintain that once the issue of deviation from the norm has been raised at the table, no further inquiry into the matter is called for, and one may proceed directly to the paragraph of *"We were slaves . . ."* The *Baalei Tosafos* insist that the purpose of moving the table is to get the child to examine *all* the unusual customs he witnesses on this night; specifically, the ones contained in "the four questions." But if all he asks is why the table was moved or why we have poured another cup of wine — questions that are not included in *Mah Nishtanah* — one must adhere to the text, and recite *Mah Nishtanah.*

Among the later commentaries, *Abarbanel* states that the sages were not referring to the questions of *Mah Nishtanah* when they sought, through unusual practices, to arouse the interest of the child. It is enough if he is stimulated to ask, "What is (all) this about?" And we respond with the story of our redemption. *Malbim* adopts the view of *Tosafos.* He agrees with *Abarbanel* that the Rabbis of the Talmud did not mean to elicit the words of *Mah Nishtanah* from the child, who can only be expected to ask questions based on his age and level of intelligence. The purpose of moving the table and pouring new wine is to open up a dialogue concerning the Exodus. But, he says, this discussion must eventually lead to "the four questions." Adults too must definitely address these questions, for they are an integral part of the Haggadah text.

19. The Torah commands us to respond to our children's questions about our observance of Pesach by describing our redemption from Egypt.[1] Why, however, did our sages *insist* on a question-and-answer format for the retelling of the Exodus?[2]

Haggadas Sofrim and *Maasei Hashem* see this Rabbinic mandate as a technique. They point out that a story told in response to curiosity and inquiry is much more effective at imparting a message, and implanting

---

1. *Exodus* 13:14 and *Deuteronomy* 6:20. Cf. *Exodus* 13:8.

2. See Talmud, *Pesachim* 116a.

שֶׁבְּכָל הַלֵּילוֹת אָנוּ אוֹכְלִין חָמֵץ וּמַצָּה,
הַלַּיְלָה הַזֶּה – כֻּלּוֹ מַצָּה.

---

it deeply into the listener's heart, than one given over without prior stimulation. Through the question the audience becomes naturally receptive, and the presenter need not rely solely on his storytelling and oratorical skills. The Rabbis felt, therefore, that the tale of our redemption, the cornerstone of our status and responsibility as God's chosen people, and a fundamental article of faith, demands this optimally effective approach for its transmission to others.

Maasei Nissim, on the other hand, views the procedure of question and answer as an essential component of the mitzvah. He reminds us that the Haggadah interprets the verse that requires us to recount the Exodus (*Exodus* 13:8) as stipulating that this is to be done specifically when there is matzah and *maror* before us. In addition, *Rashi* comments on this verse that it was on account of our future observance of these mitzvos that God brought us out of Egypt. These two observations lead *Maasei Nissim* to say that the mitzvah is not to simply recall the events surrounding our redemption, but to retell them in the context of *mitzvos* we perform on this special night, which commemorate that redemption. The intrinsic relationship between the two must be clearly articulated and understood in order to properly fulfill the obligation, "*You shall tell your child on that day, saying, 'It is because of this* (the matzah and *maror*) *that* HASHEM *did so for me when I went out of Egypt'*" (*Exodus* 13:8). Thus, the sages saw the need to have us present the events of the Exodus as a response to questions regarding the evening's unusual practices — particularly, the eating of matzah and *maror* — so as to highlight the connection between our Exodus and our observances.

20. Why is there no mention of the four cups of wine in these questions?

Bircas HaShir and *Chasan Sofer* both point out a simple reason for this: It has not taken place yet. "The four questions" all refer to things that have already been seen at the Seder table (either actually performed or set out), unlike the four cups of wine. Having wine on the table indicates nothing out of the ordinary, for even after making *Kiddush,* we often drink wine during the course of our meals. As for the premature pouring of the second cup, although this is indeed meant to generate curiosity, it still does not provide a reason for asking about "four required cups" that we drink on this night, since this has yet to occur.

1. On all other nights we may eat *chametz* and matzah, but on this night — only matzah.

Be'er Miriam notes that even if it would be recognized at this time that we will ultimately consume four cups, this would give no cause for question, since we drink on other nights too, especially at festive gatherings.

Aruch HaShulchan reminds us that all nations celebrate great events with drink, not just Jews. Therefore, even if there is reason to question the particular nature of our rejoicing on this night, mentioning 'the four cups' together with the evening's other unusual practices would be out of place.

Abarbanel feels that such a question does not belong here for a different reason. He claims that drinking wine is not an *absolute* indication of our liberated status, for even slaves and otherwise oppressed people often revel in drink. Thus, whether we are free or in servitude, there is nothing perplexing about this activity.

Maharal's position is that the only items included in *Mah Nishtanah* are those which serve, or are themselves, Biblically ordained commandments. "The four cups of wine," however — while alluded to by the Torah's use of four descriptions of deliverance — are strictly Rabbinical in origin. The third and fourth questions deal with dipping and reclining — both Rabbinic ordinances. They are in place because they relate to the performance of Biblical commands — dipping the bitter herb and reclining as we eat the matzah.

21. What do we mean when we point out that *"on this night* — [we eat] *only* (or completely) *matzah"*? Aren't other foods eaten as well?

Yalkut Shimoni states that it means matzah, to the exclusion of *chametz,* and the question is simply: What is special about this night that we insist on eating only matzah? *Chasam Sofer* adds a dimension by observing that inasmuch as the eating of matzah serves to remind us of our affliction in Egypt, limiting our "bread" to *matzah* is inaccurate. During their subjugation in Egypt, he notes, even if the Jews were generally fed matzah, *chametz* was not proscribed in *any* way. As long as *chametz* was somehow obtainable, one could just as well have eaten that. And so, the question we ask is: Why do we insist on restricting our intake this evening to matzah?

V'Zos L'Yehudah contends that the words *"only matzah"* come to rule out more than just *chametz*. The intent was that even fruit or other foods

שֶׁבְּכָל הַלֵּילוֹת אָנוּ אוֹכְלִין שְׁאָר יְרָקוֹת,
הַלַּיְלָה הַזֶּה – מָרוֹר.
שֶׁבְּכָל הַלֵּילוֹת אֵין אָנוּ מַטְבִּילִין אֲפִילוּ פַּעַם אֶחָת,
הַלַּיְלָה הַזֶּה – שְׁתֵּי פְעָמִים.
שֶׁבְּכָל הַלֵּילוֹת אָנוּ אוֹכְלִין בֵּין יוֹשְׁבִין וּבֵין מְסֻבִּין,
הַלַּיְלָה הַזֶּה – כֻּלָּנוּ מְסֻבִּין.

---

are excluded. What it means is that on this night no one can relieve
himself of the requirement to eat the prescribed portion of matzah by
partaking of other foods instead. The only way to fulfill the obligation is
with matzah. This is in contrast to the rest of the festival, when, although
fasting is forbidden, one need not eat matzah. Fruit, meat or other types
of food will suffice (see *Shulchan Aruch, Orach Chaim* regarding the
obligation to eat bread at two or three Sabbath and festival meals). Thus,
the question of the Haggadah is: Why *must* we eat matzah on this night,
as opposed to making do with anything else?

Finally, *Bircas HaShir* suggests that the question relates to the requirement to eat the portion of matzah *by itself*. This is a departure from all
year round, and even from the laws which govern the rest of Pesach,
when matzah may be eaten along with anything but *chametz*. It is this
that engenders curiosity. This approach also explains the idiosyncratic
wording of this question. The question should have been phrased: "On
all nights, we eat *either chametz or* matzah," paralleling the question
regarding our reclining while eating. Instead, it says: "*chametz and*
matzah." If, as just stated, the point of the question was that normally,
matzah may be eaten *together* with anything else, "*and*" is preferable.

**22. Do we include the word *"only"* when we mention the bitter herbs
in the second question?**

Yalkut Shimoni maintains that we do not say "only," since we do not
eat the bitter herb to the exclusion of other vegetables. We actually *do*
partake of other vegetables later on during the meal.

What, then, is the point of the question? According to *Avudraham,* the
question is: Why do we deliberately consume a bitter herb this evening,
when we usually seek to satisfy our hunger and sweeten our meals with
appetizing vegetables? Many commentaries agree with this approach to
the question.

2. **On all other nights** we eat many vegetables,
   but on this night — we eat *maror.*

3. **On all other nights** we do not dip even once,
   but on this night — twice.

4. **On all other nights** we eat either sitting or reclining,
   but on this night — we all recline.

Rashi, however, does include the word "only" in his reading, suggesting that, in a way, everything we eat tonight is *maror* (bitter). The bondage and affliction of our ancestors — the predominate theme of the Seder — remain foremost on our minds throughout our activities on this night making even the sweet food "bitter."

Ritva differs strongly with this opinion. He maintains that the term "only" is used here with respect to the beginning of our meal, and it means to distinguish that we normally try to stimulate our appetite with salads and sweet things. Tonight, however, we insist that the first item on our menu be bitter herbs, and this strange behavior must be explained.

23. What is meant by the general statement *"on all other nights we do not dip* (our foods) *even once"*? People often *do* dip foods.

Avudraham says that this question refers to the fact that we do not generally dip vegetables before beginning the actual meal, whereas tonight, we do this twice (*karpas* and *maror*). Similarly, *Rokeach's* suggestion is that it is not customary to dip foods with an accompanying blessing, because dipping is normally done in the course of a meal. This being the case, the blessing on bread at the beginning of the meal exempts us from blessings on most foods that follow. Tonight, though, we make a blessing when we dip.

24. The Mishnah (*Pesachim* 116a) includes a question which was asked when the Passover sacrifice was offered, regarding the eating of roasted meat at the Seder. Why do we substitute this question specifically with one concerning the practice of reclining?

The opinion of the *Gra* is that in the time of the Mishnah, reclining was not an unusual practice that needed to be addressed, while the eating of the Passover sacrifice, with its associated laws, was. Today, when we have no sacrifice, and we are not in the habit of reclining, the reversed situation calls for a switching of questions. *Haggadas Sofrim* makes the two questions interdependent.

The Seder plate is returned. The matzos are kept uncovered as the Haggadah is recited in unison. The Haggadah should be translated, if necessary, and the story of the Exodus should be amplified upon.

עֲבָדִים הָיִינוּ לְפַרְעֹה בְּמִצְרָיִם, וַיּוֹצִיאֵנוּ יהוה אֱלֹהֵינוּ מִשָּׁם בְּיָד חֲזָקָה וּבִזְרֹעַ נְטוּיָה. וְאִלּוּ לֹא הוֹצִיא הַקָּדוֹשׁ בָּרוּךְ הוּא אֶת אֲבוֹתֵינוּ מִמִּצְרַיִם, הֲרֵי אָנוּ

When people ate the Passover sacrifice, he says, reclining would not arouse curiosity because all sacrificial meats were eaten in that fashion.[1] Today, however, since we no longer partake of the sacrifice, we ask: What reason do we have to recline?

Yalkut Shimoni suggests that the emphasis is on the fact that *"we all"* recline. This does not mean everyone at the table reclines, for there are those who are not permitted to recline — such as a student in the presence of his rebbi. We wonder why it is that not only people in countries where it is still the custom to recline do so, but *"we all"* — Jews of all countries — follow this practice.

25. What is significant about the choice and arrangement of "the four questions"?

Abarbanel divides the questions into two groups. The first two, concerning matzah and *maror,* he views as depicting poverty, suffering and bitterness. The second two, he says, describe practices associated with free, comfortable and even luxurious living. Thus, a major unspoken theme of the *Mah Nishtanah* is the contrast between the two types of actions we engage in on this night. What is the source of this bizarre behavior? To this we respond with the tale of our rise from slavery to proud nationhood. *Abarbanel* believes that this is why there is no mention of the four cups. Neither slavery nor liberation are clearly indicated through their consumption, for wine is imbibed by the lowly and oppressed as well as the rich and comfortable. It therefore does not fit into the two groups of queries.

Chida observes that each one of these four practices would be specifically suited to one of the other special occasions during the year. For example, the dipping of the food would be appropriate for Shabbos, which is when we indulge in all manner of physical delight, especially with respect to food. The eating of *maror,* which represents the bitterness of the downtrodden, symbolizes the quality of submission,

---

1. See Talmud, *Zevachim* 91a, *Chullin* 132b and *Tosafos Zevachim* 16a s.v. "uma."

The Seder plate is returned. The matzos are kept uncovered as the Haggadah is recited in unison. The Haggadah should be translated, if necessary, and the story of the Exodus should be amplified upon.

We were slaves to Pharaoh in Egypt, but HASHEM our God took us out from there with a mighty hand and an outstretched arm. Had not the Holy One, Blessed is He, taken our fathers out from Egypt, then we, our

---

which would fit in on Rosh Hashanah when we proclaim God to be the King of the universe. He goes on to ascribe the eating of matzah to Shavuos and the practice of reclining to Succos. In short, all these practices could have been done at some other point on the calendar. Yet we reserve all these activities for the night of Pesach, instead. Why is this? That is the underlying question we are posing here.

⤶§ עֲבָדִים הָיִינוּ — *We were slaves.*

---

26. Is this a response to "the four questions" or the beginning of the retelling of the Exodus — or both?

The answer to the questions we asked in *Mah Nishtanah* lies in the tale of our redemption on this night. Whether this paragraph constitutes a mere introduction to that story, or the opening lines of the story itself, is a matter of dispute.

The Talmud (*Pesachim* 116a) teaches that we must begin this evening's discussion of the Exodus by calling to mind our past shame, and progress from there to our ultimate praise. The term "shame," however, could mean two things, the Talmud tells us. It might simply imply the obvious notion of our lowly status as slaves in Egypt. Or it may refer to our people's roots as idol worshipers in the time of the Patriarch Abraham. At issue is the perception of the Exodus as a *uniquely uplifting* experience in the history of nations. The question is: Do we limit our discussion to the immediate context of redemption from slavery and oppression, or is the recognition of the cosmic implication of the Exodus better served by enlarging the perspective on this event to have it invoke the spiritual odyssey of our people? This journey began with Abraham's life, and led to his descendants' rising to a singular status among nations — the people chosen and beloved in the service of the true God.

Avudraham tells us that although the halachah opts for the former definition of "shame" (which is why we begin with *"We were slaves"*), the latter is not rejected entirely, and we therefore include mention of our idolatrous origins later on in the Haggadah. *Malbim* agrees that these views are not mutually exclusive, and states that even according to the opinion that the recounting of the Exodus should start with the paragraph *"Originally our ancestors were idol worshipers," "We were slaves"* still serves the purpose of answering the *Mah Nishtanah's* questions and introducing the mitzvah of discussing the redemption. Thus, the Haggadah begins with this paragraph.

Maharal explains that it is vital to begin the evening's discussion with mention of our shame to make it clear that the Exodus was a premeditated act designed to raise us and lead us to become God's nation. To emphasize the hand of God coming specifically to rescue the Jews, it is necessary to first note the intolerable condition that brought this about. Thus, by first focusing on our shame, we bring out the point of our importance to, and relationship with, God, Who relieved us of that dreadful condition.

Malbim says that we mention our shame to offer starker contrast to the heights we achieved. Without recalling our prior disgrace, he says, the greatness and honor bestowed upon us through the redemption cannot be properly appreciated.

27. How does this paragraph answer the questions in *Mah Nishtanah*?

Avudraham states that all we mean to address here are the two main issues raised in *Mah Nishtanah* — the eating of matzah and *maror*. The response is simply that our forefathers were slaves in Egypt, and on this, the anniversary of their redemption, we commemorate the matzah that they ate, and the *maror* (i.e., the bitter life) that they escaped.[1] This is best accomplished by eating in the manner of royalty. As for the other questions, they are the focus later on in the Haggadah when we recite Rabban Gamliel's declaration.

Abarbanel, however, views this paragraph as addressing all four questions: In accordance with the theme he presented previously (see question 25), it seeks to explain why we do certain things on this night that seem to indicate a state of liberty, while at the same time practicing other, seemingly contradictory, customs that indicate servitude. We explain that we seek to recall and relive our birth as a nation, and that experience involves contradictory elements — *"We were slaves"* and *"HASHEM our God took us out"* — servitude and freedom.

---

1. See question 10.

Maasei Nissim offers a unique approach, explaining our performances this evening in the context of the other mitzvos of the Torah. We do the mitzvos, he says, even though we can never fully fathom their rationale. This is because we are faithful subjects of the true King. That is what we mean to bring out here. *"We were slaves to Pharaoh in Egypt"* — and certainly carried out his decrees even if we knew little or nothing of their reason. *God took us out from there* — in order that we be His nation, willing to undertake to do His bidding in similar fashion. Thus, the message, in response to "the four questions," is that we follow the practices of this evening even if we cannot plumb the depths of meaning underlying these commandments and customs. We are obedient simply because God redeemed us, and is our Master.

As for the additional sentence, "*. . . Had not the Holy One, Blessed is He, taken our fathers out from Egypt . . .,*" *Shibbolei HaLeket* and *Abarbanel* both point out that this conforms to the requirement that each person, and in every generation, view himself as having personally left Egypt. As we begin the explanation for this evening's celebration, we want to make clear to the children how relevant the Exodus is to our own status as free people, and how much we are obligated to give praise for that experience.

28. What is the significance of God's *"mighty hand"* and *"out-stretched arm"*? Is there a difference between the two?

Malbim opines that a *"mighty hand"* refers to the fact that the redemption took place against the will of the Egyptians, while an *"outstretched arm"* means that God made it perfectly clear that it was He Who was performing wonders for the sake of the Jews. There was no room to misattribute the miraculous occurrence to chance, for it was as if an arm stretched out from Heaven.[1]

Maasei Nissim makes no clear distinction between the two phrases, but explains them as follows. One of the key aspects of the Exodus is the fact that God did not cause the Egyptians to free the Jews of their own accord (which He could very well have done). Had He done so, Moses would not have had grounds to plead with God on behalf of the Jews when they sinned in the desert and rebelled against entering the land of Canaan.[2] His argument at that time was that if, after having taken His people out of Egypt with such a display of might, God would not now bring them into the land which He had promised them, the

---

1. See *Exodus* 8:15, 8:18-19, 9:7, 9:26, 10:23 and 14:25.

2. *Numbers* 14:1-4.

וּבָנֵינוּ וּבְנֵי בָנֵינוּ מְשֻׁעְבָּדִים הָיִינוּ לְפַרְעֹה בְּמִצְרָיִם. וַאֲפִילוּ כֻּלָּנוּ חֲכָמִים, כֻּלָּנוּ נְבוֹנִים, כֻּלָּנוּ זְקֵנִים, כֻּלָּנוּ יוֹדְעִים אֶת הַתּוֹרָה, מִצְוָה עָלֵינוּ לְסַפֵּר בִּיצִיאַת

---

nations would say that He was simply unable to do so. Thus, we are praising God for two things: for having had the mercy to redeem us, and for having done so in a manner that not only exhibited great concern for us on that occasion, but also paved the way for dealing with calamitous situations in the future.

29. Is there any significance in the fact that the paragraph opens with the words "We were slaves to Pharaoh (avadim)," but then switches to the term "subservient" (mishubadim)?

Malbim points out that the term *"subservient"* is used in discussing what would have happened had we not been redeemed. Thus, it is inappropriate to use *"slaves"* because it is possible that our conditions would be even worse than that of slaves. All we can say for sure is that we would have been subservient to him; i.e., that he could have done with us as he saw fit.

HaShir VeHaShevach suggests that even if we had achieved independence on our own through rebellion, while we might have broken loose of our physical bonds (as slaves), we would still have been subservient to the cultural chains of that idolatrous land. The Exodus that God effected was equally, if not primarily, spiritual in nature; it meant the birth of a nation devoted solely to His service. This is what the Haggadah is highlighting here.

Maasei Hashem's opinion is that even had the Egyptians ultimately freed us of their own volition, while we would no longer be actual slaves, we would still have been subservient to them for the kindness they displayed in releasing us. Our sense of gratitude would have obligated us to feel beholden to them. This is the point of the particular wording used here.

30. Why does the Haggadah say *"we, our children . . . would still be subservient to Pharaoh"?* Would it not have been likely that at some future point in time we would have left Egypt on our own?

Abarbanel focuses on the three possible scenarios for leaving Egypt:
(a) by the hand of God, through miracles;
(b) through rebellion;
(c) through Pharaoh's own willingness.

children, and our children's children would still be subservient to Pharaoh in Egypt. Even if we were all men of wisdom, understanding, experience, and knowledge of the Torah, it would still be an obligation upon us to tell about the Exodus from

---

The Haggadah is trying to tell us that had God himself not freed us in a supernatural fashion, neither of the other two possibilities would have come to pass. We would have remained subservient because being born into slavery would have instilled in us a weak-hearted, servile mentality that would not harbor thoughts of rebellion. And we highlight *to Pharaoh*, whose wickedness would never have allowed for us to leave with his consent. *Baruch She'amar* echoes this approach. Had God Himself not taken us out of Egypt, he says, we would never have left under natural circumstances. For whereas every country seeks and finds some excuse, however ridiculous, to expel the Jews, in this case, despite all the difficulties, Pharaoh stubbornly refused to release the Jews. His only desire was to keep them in his possession forever.

Avudraham makes the point that if, because of their spiritual deficiencies, God would not have taken the Jews out when he did — in the generation of Moses, Aaron and other spiritual giants — we, in our generation, would certainly not have been found deserving of redemption.

Maharal declares that had we not left Egypt by the hand of God, we would never have earned the spiritual status of free people. In other words, the nature of our identity as a nation would have been bound up with the concept of servitude. Even if we succeeded in gaining our freedom some other way, we would still have been "an enslaved and subservient people" by definition. It was the Godly nature of the redemption that permanently altered our internal spiritual makeup.

Abarbanel states that we gained three permanent, fundamental things from going out of Egypt. These make the Exodus significant, no matter how bitter the conditions of our current exile may be. The three things are:

(a) faith in God that He rules over the entire universe and runs nature as He sees fit, even disturbing the natural order of things for His chosen people if need be;

(b) the honor of having left the great and mighty country of Egypt against the will of its inhabitants, then conquering the Land of Israel and living there for many years;

(c) the receiving of the Torah.

מִצְרַיִם. וְכָל הַמַּרְבֶּה לְסַפֵּר בִּיצִיאַת מִצְרַיִם, הֲרֵי זֶה מְשֻׁבָּח.

Maharal strongly opposes this whole suggestion. As explained, *Maharal* insists that what we acquired of eternal significance was the distinction of *becoming an inherently free nation*. As a result, says *Maharal,* not only did we become suitable to receive the Torah — whose world is the domain of spiritually free people, who, rather than be bound by the constraints of earthly needs and desires, shape those wishes to the designs of the Torah — we transcended the very notion of being subordinate to others. Indeed, later exiles cannot be permanent, because the natural order of the world will not allow it. *By definition,* we are an independent nation that cannot *"be"* enslaved. *Maharal* compares later exiles to the sun. While the sun is occasionally blocked by a cloud formation, the natural order of things prevails; the clouds dissipate or depart, and the sun bursts forth in all its glory.

As for the words, *"we, our children . . . would still be subservient to Pharaoh,"* *Maasei Hashem* points out that all rulers of Egypt are called "Pharaoh" and that it certainly does not refer to the same king who ruled then. Interestingly, *Avudraham* quotes *Machzor Vitry* as omitting the word "Pharaoh" because it cannot mean the Pharaoh of the Exodus, and since the title has not been used in Egypt for many generations, it can no longer refer to anyone.

31. Why is it necessary to add the statement, *"Even if we were all men of wisdom . . . it would still be an obligation upon us to tell about the Exodus from Egypt"*?

Avudraham makes the simple point that having just explained to the child why we engage in certain unusual practices this evening, the obvious question now is why we do not eat the matzah and *maror* right away. To explain this, we respond that it is first necessary to go into detail concerning the Exodus which we have mentioned, and offer praise and thanks to God. Only then is it proper to perform the mitzvos which commemorate the experience. And, we tell the children, we must do this even if we are scholars; even if we are righteous and well intentioned and do not lack the proper thoughts and motivation when we perform those mitzvos; even if we are old and thoroughly familiar with the story. For this is a mitzvah — just like the other mitzvos of the evening.

Bircas HaShir suggests that *". . . knowledge of the Torah"* means

Egypt. The more one tells about the Exodus, the more he is praiseworthy.

---

something else. One might have thought that since the ultimate purpose of the redemption was to bring us to Mt. Sinai and present us with the Torah, perhaps it is preferable for those who are constantly involved with the study of Torah and are well versed in its contents to immerse themselves in Torah study on this evening. Would that not be, in a sense, the greatest tribute to the achievement of the Exodus? To counter this reasoning, we exhort the participants at the Seder: *"Even if we were all men of . . . knowledge of the Torah, it would still be an obligation upon us to tell about the Exodus from Egypt."* *Malbim* comments that, in view of the fact that our children and grandchildren would still be subservient to Pharaoh, the thrust of the mitzvah is to convey the story of the redemption to the next generation. He points out that the Torah phrases the mitzvah as an obligation to transmit the story of the Exodus to our children. Thus, while we ourselves may be familiar with it or already knowledgeable in its subtler points, it must still be discussed.

32. What do we mean by saying "*The more one tells about the Exodus, the more he is praiseworthy*"? If there is a mitzvah to retell the Exodus, then one should be praiseworthy for performing that mitzvah, even without exceeding the obligation; and if we are commending the person for going beyond the basic requirement, is it not true of all mitzvos? When should this additional discussion be held?

Avudraham takes the position that to fulfill the obligation, one need only make mention of the Exodus. Even one word would be sufficient. But it is considered proper and praiseworthy for everyone to go beyond the minimum requirement on this special occasion. Thus, the Haggadah is describing for us the true form the mitzvah should take, and the word *"praiseworthy"* is meant in the same sense that the fulfillment of all mitzvos is considered meritorious. In this opinion, there is no distinction between this and other mitzvos. *Abarbanel* offers a similar approach.

Maasei Hashem has a variant reading of this phrase. He suggests that we are saying that this story is not like others. Other stories are only retold if the listeners are not yet familiar with them. This story is recalled even if we know it, understand it and fully appreciate its message. That is because *"vechal hamesapeir beyetzias Mitzrayim harei zeh meshubach,* whoever tells the story of the Exodus from Egypt (this is *Maasei Hashem's* reading) gives an indication of praise." This is to be

מַעֲשֶׂה בְּרַבִּי אֱלִיעֶזֶר וְרַבִּי יְהוֹשֻׁעַ וְרַבִּי אֶלְעָזָר בֶּן
עֲזַרְיָה וְרַבִּי עֲקִיבָא וְרַבִּי טַרְפוֹן שֶׁהָיוּ

understood as follows: Had the Egyptians released us of their own volition, it would have been embarrassing for us (i.e., it would appear that we are not really free men, but slaves who were discharged by our master). Telling the story indicates we are not ashamed of its message. It indicates the praise of our release — that we were worthy of redemption, and were liberated by God, against our master's will. In effect, according to *Maasei Hashem,* the Haggadah is really explaining *why* it is a mitzvah to retell this story even if we already know it well: because it is praiseworthy, and we must give over to our children, and anyone not yet familiar with it, the pride and praise inherent in the tale of the Exodus.

Yalkut Shimoni's opinion is that increasing the discussion at the Exodus is not just a *quantitatively* different performance of a mitzvah. To speak of the redemption at length is an indication of the degree to which one senses and enjoys the status of freedom from the alien culture of Egypt, and hence, a declaration of one's subjugation to God's will. Speaking at length about the Exodus is thus *an entirely different statement,* and therefore, it is considered praiseworthy. Similarly, *Otzar HaTefillos* suggests that additional discussion is not just a good thing to *do.* Rather, it reflects the stature of the speaker, showing that he has a deeper perception of the miraculous nature of the Exodus and knows how to express proper praise.

Be'er Miriam concurs with this approach and offers a second reason to explain why the word "praiseworthy" is used instead of the word "good" or "proper." In contrast to most other settings, where, according to the Talmud, it is considered inappropriate, or even repulsive, to engage in extreme tribute to God,[1] on this night it is not only "good," it is praiseworthy. *Yalkut Shimoni* quotes *Maharal* that we are permitted to utter so much praise only because it is our intent to express gratitude, not merely to recite an endless stream of glorification. Once our motive is gratefulness, praise is not only permissible but praiseworthy.

When should this increased discussion take place? *Rashbam, Kol Bo* and *Abarbanel* all say it should only take place after we have eaten the evening meal, so that the children should not fall asleep and miss

---

1. *Berachos* 45b. The reason for this is that God's praise is immeasurable. Any attempt to list it must inevitably come up short, and is thus a slight to His honor, for it would appear that one has said all that can be said about Him.

It happened that Rabbi Eliezer, Rabbi Yehoshua, Rabbi Elazar ben Azaryah, Rabbi Akiva and Rabbi Tarfon were

participating in the Seder (see *Pesachim* 109a).

§ מַעֲשֶׂה בְּרַבִּי אֱלִיעֶזֶר — *It happened that Rabbi Eliezer . . .*

33. What is the purpose of this story?

Most commentaries agree with the *Gra* that this story proves two things:

(a) Even scholars and great men must recount the Exodus.

(b) It is praiseworthy to increase this discussion, as they did, going all night and into the morning.

Be'er Miriam notes that it says, *"until their students came and said to them . . .,"* implying that the students were not present during the discussion. Thus, we see that even a group made up strictly of scholars must still engage in this mitzvah. (*HaShir VeHaShevach* suggests that the students were not present in order that they should be able to recline during their Seder, for a student may not recline in the presence of his rebbi.)

Rokeach assumes that if not for the students, the Rabbis would have continued even though the time for prayers had come. This is a striking indication of the importance of elaborating on the topic of the Exodus. He and *Chida* suggest that the students were suggesting to their teachers:

(a) This mitzvah may be performed just as well later on, but the reciting of *Shema* in the morning must be done during its limited, prescribed time frame.

(b) The reading of *Shema* also contains a remembrance of the Exodus, so that one can accomplish both goals with this one act.

Chida offers an additional observation. He notes that most of these sages at the Seder were descendants of people who were not actually enslaved in Egypt (Kohanim, Levites and proselytes). The point of the story is to illustrate that even they felt it incumbent to increase the discussion of the Exodus.

Netziv understands that this story establishes that one may even increase the discussion beyond its time frame without worrying about transgressing the law of *bal tosif* — the prohibition of adding on to any mitzvah of the Torah. He explains that R' Eliezer's opinion (in *Mechilta*)

מְסֻבִּין בִּבְנֵי בְרַק, וְהָיוּ מְסַפְּרִים בִּיצִיאַת מִצְרַיִם כָּל
אוֹתוֹ הַלַּיְלָה. עַד שֶׁבָּאוּ תַלְמִידֵיהֶם וְאָמְרוּ לָהֶם,
רַבּוֹתֵינוּ הִגִּיעַ זְמַן קְרִיאַת שְׁמַע שֶׁל שַׁחֲרִית.

אָמַר רַבִּי אֶלְעָזָר בֶּן עֲזַרְיָה, הֲרֵי אֲנִי כְּבֶן שִׁבְעִים
שָׁנָה, וְלֹא זָכִיתִי שֶׁתֵּאָמֵר יְצִיאַת מִצְרַיִם

---

is that just like the mitzvah of matzah must be performed before
midnight, the mitzvah of retelling the Exodus extends only until
midnight. According to R' Eliezer, one who eats matzah past midnight
with the intent to fulfill the obligation of eating matzah transgresses *bal
tosif*. Yet the Rabbis, including R' Eliezer, continued their talk until
morning. This is because there is a separate, year-round mitzvah to
remember the redemption by day and at night, and that mitzvah is not
restricted to midnight. That would also explain why the Haggadah
follows this story with the paragraph of R' Elazar ben Azaryah, which
proves that there is a mitzvah to remember the Exodus every night.

As for the problem of how the sages were allowed to deprive
themselves of sleep when the mitzvah of rejoicing on the festival
prohibits paining oneself in any way, *Maharal* assures us that they were
so absorbed in the mitzvah that they did not even feel their weariness.
The time passed quickly as a result of their intense desire to perform this
mitzvah on a supreme level, and the loss of sleep was not a deprivation.

Abarbanel posits that the Jews did not sleep on the "protected night"
when they left Egypt. Thus, remaining awake could be viewed as part of
the Seder performance. In fulfillment of their obligation to see
themselves as having left Egypt, the Rabbis began the night with the
mitzvos of the Seder — matzah and *maror* — just as our ancestors did
in Egypt, then remained awake in discussion, "involved the redemption," as it were, reflecting the experience of the Jews' Exodus from
Egypt.

34. Why is it important to mention that this Seder took place in the city of Bnei Brak?

Abarbanel quotes an opinion that the sages were eating with the
people or students of the city of *Brak*, but he disagrees with this view.
Instead, he claims the term "Bnei Brak" does not refer to the city, but to
the furnishings upon which they were reclining. These were called *berak*

reclining (at the Seder) in Bnei Brak. They discussed the Exodus from Egypt all that night, until their students came and said to them: "Our teachers, it is [daybreak] time for the reading of the morning Shema."

Rabbi Elazar ben Azaryah said: I am like a 70-year-old man, but I could not succeed in having the Exodus from Egypt

---

(shine) because they were covered with luxurious, shiny silk.

Maasei Hashem says the Haggadah simply means the city near the Mediterranean coast where R' Akiva was the prime authority. *Maharam Padua* derives from this incident that in the place of a person's authority, even his teacher should accord him honor; for although R' Eliezer was R' Akiva's teacher, he allowed R' Akiva to recline in his presence, behavior normally viewed as inappropriate.

Maharal's view is that the name of the place tells us that the Rabbis were not just trading Torah observations. If that was their goal, each one would have done so in his own study hall. Here, they were gathered in Bnei Brak (the city of R' Akiva). This was for the sake of participating in the mitzvah together, an act which would lead to much conversation on the subject. The story thus illustrates how praiseworthy it is to delve into and discuss our redemption at length.

אָמַר רַבִּי אֶלְעָזָר בֶּן עֲזַרְיָה ﷽ — *Rabbi Elazar ben Azaryah said:*

35. What is the purpose of this paragraph?

Chida states that the Haggadah is presenting us with additional proof that even if we are knowledgeable in Torah, we are required to discuss the redemption on the night of Pesach. According to the sages who disagree with R' Elazar ben Azaryah, the phrase, *"all the days of your life,"* means to include the era following the arrival of the Messiah in the mitzvah of remembering the redemption. The prophets (*Isaiah 11:9*) have described this period as one in which knowledge and awareness of God will flourish among all people. Even so, insist the Rabbis, it will be necessary for us to recall our liberation from Egypt. Thus, we see that this commemoration is not restricted to the ignorant or unfamiliar, but must be performed by the learned as well.

Maharal's view is that the concept of this mitzvah applying — according to varying opinions, each day; each day and each night; and even, in

בַּלֵּילוֹת, עַד שֶׁדְּרָשָׁהּ בֶּן זוֹמָא, שֶׁנֶּאֱמַר, לְמַעַן תִּזְכֹּר אֶת יוֹם צֵאתְךָ מֵאֶרֶץ מִצְרַיִם כֹּל יְמֵי חַיֶּיךָ.[1] יְמֵי

---

the opinion of the sages, in the days of the Messiah (when the events surrounding our previous experiences will have been eclipsed by the wonders that will usher in "the end of days") — gives an indication of the *eternal significance* of the Exodus from Egypt, and how much we must dwell on its details this evening. *Abarbanel's* approach is similar, but he adds that the very fact that R' Elazar ben Azaryah *strove* to establish the halachah as requiring one to remember the redemption every night of the year is evidence enough of the consequential nature of this mitzvah. It is the significance of the mitzvah of recalling the Exodus that the Haggadah seeks to convey.

36. What did R' Elazar mean when he said, *"I am like a 70-year-old man"*?

Maharal suggests that although the Talmud seems to imply that he was only 18 at the time (see *Berachos* 28a), it should not be understood literally. What it means is that when he was 18, his hair had already begun turning white, so that by the time he turned 50, he appeared to be a man of 70. *Malbim* and *Shibbolei HaLeket,* however, understand that he was indeed only 18, but on the day he was elected *Nasi,* leader of the people, he miraculously aged so that he appeared to be 70 years old.

Abarbanel explains that in honor of the leadership role to which he was appointed, God filled him with a complete knowledge of Torah, as though he were an experienced sage. *Rambam's* view is that the long-term effect of his diligent Torah studies taxed his physical strengths to their limits, and caused him to age beyond his years.

37. What is the purpose of R' Elazar's statement that he did not initially succeed in establishing the halachah as he thought it should be decided?

According to *Abarbanel,* he was lamenting the fact that although rich in Torah knowledge, he was unable to produce an argument in support of his viewpoint that could alter the opinion of his colleagues. *Rambam's* approach is similar. He adds that R' Elazar labored in Torah to an extraordinary degree, and associated with many great people. He was understandably disappointed, therefore, that he was still unable to convince the others of this halachah in accordance with his view.

mentioned every night, until Ben Zoma expounded it: It says: "So that you will remember the day of your departure from the land of Egypt all the days of your life."[1] "The days

---

(1) Deuteronomy 16:3.

Baruch She'amar directs us to the second half of this statement for the emphasis of R' Elazar's comment. "See how great it is to come to the true understanding of a verse in the Torah!" R' Elazar was saying. "I am well versed, like a 70-year old; yet a young unknown (Ben Zoma), who goes only by the name of his father, was privileged to find a Biblical source for this ruling, not I."

Avudraham and *Malbim* interpret R' Elazar's remark in the following manner: Even though I was accepted as *Nasi,* and was even granted a heavenly sign of approval over my appointment by my miraculously aging, the Rabbis still refused to set down the halachah as I saw it.

V'Zos L'Yehudah declares that R' Elazar ben Azaryah is speaking in admiration of Ben Zoma. He means to say: How great is this young man who was successful at accomplishing what I, with my stature, position and Divine approval, could not! We learn from here the scrupulous integrity of our sages, and how they respected and honored each other.

38. What was the custom before Ben Zoma produced his proof? Did people recall the Exodus at night or not?

Raavad's opinion is that the third paragraph of *Shema,* which contains the reference to the Exodus, was recited as part of the evening services prior to the establishment of the halachah in R' Elazar ben Azaryah's favor. However, this was only Rabbinically instituted, not Biblically ordained, and the subject of the debate between R' Elazar and his colleagues was whether there is a Biblical source for this requirement or not.

Rashba argues strongly that they definitely did *not* include the last portion of *Shema* at night, and the sages here are in disagreement over whether such an obligation to remember the redemption at night exists *at all* — not whether it is Biblical or Rabbinical in origin.

As for R' Elazar ben Azaryah's own practice, *Minchas Chinuch* (mitzvah 78) makes clear that before the final redaction of the Talmud, in certain limited circumstances, individual sages of the Mishnah or Talmud whose positions were opposed by their peers still followed their

חַיֶּיךָ הַיָּמִים, כֹּל יְמֵי חַיֶּיךָ הַלֵּילוֹת. וַחֲכָמִים אוֹמְרִים, יְמֵי חַיֶּיךָ הָעוֹלָם הַזֶּה, כֹּל יְמֵי חַיֶּיךָ לְהָבִיא לִימוֹת הַמָּשִׁיחַ.

---

own opinions in their personal performance of mitzvos and fulfillment of religious responsibilities. Here too, we can assume that R' Elazar ben Azaryah was careful to recall the Exodus every night of the year even before his view was established as the halachic requirement.

39. Even though Ben Zoma now concurred with R' Elazar ben Azaryah, should the halachah not follow the majority of the Rabbis, who argued against them?

Malbim and *Rokeach* state that until then, R' Elazar was a lone opinion maintaining that there was a Biblical requirement to recall the Exodus at night. R' Elazar, together with Ben Zoma, however, represented a united viewpoint which demanded serious consideration. *Malbim* points out that the simple reading of the verse certainly more closely reflects Ben Zoma's interpretation — that *"all the days of your life"* comes to include the nights — than it does the Rabbis' opinion— that *"all"* refers to the days of the Messiah. In addition, the verse is phrased in the singular, not the plural, implying that it is addressing the individual and his responsibility to remember the Exodus at night, as opposed to speaking to the nation as a whole.

40. The verse *"so that you will remember . . ."* is contained in a section of the Torah that discusses the festival of Pesach. What indication is there that this verse pertains to the mitzvah of remembering the Exodus every day of the year?

Abarbanel states that the verse is obviously not referring to the mitzvah of recalling the redemption on Pesach because it says you should keep in mind *"all the days of your life."*

Maharal states that recalling the Exodus every day of the year carries no significance unless it is rooted in the remembrance that takes place on Pesach night, the anniversary of the redemption. It is only against the background of the recollection of the Passover that additional reminders throughout the year have meaning. (This must be compared to the farcical notion of someone speaking longingly, every day of the year, about some special occasion, but when that day finally arrives, he

of your life" indicates the days. "All the days of your life" indicates the nights. The other Sages say: "The days of your life" indicates the world in its present state. "All the days of your life" includes the days of *Mashiach*.

---

makes no mention or indication of any significant occurrence.) Thus, the mitzvah to remind oneself of the redemption every day of the year is deliberately presented in the section that deals with the observances on Pesach night which commemorate the Exodus, for it is the observances of this evening which provide a context for the proper performance of the daily requirement.

41. According to Ben Zoma, had the verse omitted the words "*All* [from which Ben Zoma learned the requirement to recall the Exodus also at night] *the days* [which according to Ben Zoma would have limited the obligation to a daytime recitation]," would we have known the requirement to recall the Exodus each night?

Maharsha advises us (*Berachos* 12b) that without these words, it would not have been clear whether the mitzvah applies at night also, or not. Although the redemption began at night, with the slaying of the firstborn and Pharaoh's begging the Jews to leave, their actual departure from Egypt did not occur until the following day. Thus, we would be unsure if the obligation would extend to the time of the start of the redemption.

42. According to the sages, who maintain that there is generally no obligation to recall the Exodus at night, why is there a mitzvah to discuss the redemption specifically on the night of Pesach?

Maharal explains (and others follow a similar line of thought) that even though the Jews' departure from the land of their enslavement took place by day (which is why the sages consider daytime the only required time to recall the Exodus during the year), and the previous wonders and miracles, including the final blow to the Egyptians on the night of the fifteenth, only paved the way for that main event, it is appropriate on *this* night to recount the experience of the Exodus. This is because the Torah established that our commemoration take place on the anniversary of when the miracle of redemption occurred, and this took place at night.

בָּרוּךְ הַמָּקוֹם, בָּרוּךְ הוּא. בָּרוּךְ שֶׁנָּתַן תּוֹרָה לְעַמּוֹ יִשְׂרָאֵל, בָּרוּךְ הוּא. כְּנֶגֶד אַרְבָּעָה בָנִים

בָּרוּךְ הַמָּקוֹם . . . כְּנֶגֶד אַרְבָּעָה בָנִים דִּבְּרָה תוֹרָה ⤳ — *Blessed is the Omnipresent . . . Concerning four sons does the Torah speak.*

---

43. What is the purpose of the introductory paragraph, "*Blessed is the Omnipresent*"?

Abarbanel offers three explanations:

(a) This is another verification of the fact that it is praiseworthy to elaborate on the discussion of the Exodus at the Seder. We see that the Torah prepared a separate presentation for each of four different types of children, so that each one might come to know the details of the redemption according to his respective level. Once the Haggadah presents this final proof, it launches into its story: "*Originally our ancestors were idol worshipers.*"[1]

(b) Once we have established the importance of detailed discussion regarding the Exodus, this paragraph comes to describe how the discussion of the Exodus should proceed. Is it advisable to delve into the explanation of verses in the Torah dealing with the redemption, or should one dwell on the mitzvos of the evening, and the fine points of their laws? The answer offered here is that the Torah demands *haggadah* — simply *telling* the story — as the proper procedure, but it speaks to four different children. The implication is thus that we must present each person with a version suitable to his level, as illustrated by the Torah's replies to the inquiries of the different children.

(c) According to the opinion of Shmuel that "*We were slaves . . .*" marks the start of our recounting of the Exodus,[2] we have recalled our shame at having been slaves, and, as dictated by the Talmud, we follow with the mention of our praise — having been drawn into the service of God: "*Blessed is the One Who has given the Torah to His people Israel.*" The Haggadah then proceeds with its story, utilizing the Torah's answers to the questions of the four sons as the basis for a discussion of the Exodus. This accomplished, it begins anew with Rav's approach to the tale of the redemption, starting with "*Originally our ancestors were idol*

---

1. This is, of course, according to the opinion of Rav that מִתְּחִילָה — "*originally*" — constitutes the true start of the tale of the Exodus. See question 26.

2. See question 26.

Blessed is the Omnipresent; Blessed is He. Blessed is the One Who has given the Torah to His people Israel; Blessed is He. Concerning four sons does the

---

worshipers. . ." — the paragraph that recalls our shameful roots as idol worshipers.[1]

Malbim says that the Haggadah's intent is to provide a source from the Torah for the requirement to tell the story of the Exodus on the night of Pesach. That source is the verse (*Exodus* 13:8) *"And you shall tell your child on that day . . .,"* which is associated with the child who is not at the level of asking on his own. This, *Malbim* points out, is a *deliberate* juxtaposition, as it is meant to indicate that the mitzvah is not restricted to a situation where it functions as a response to a previous inquiry, but includes, and even demands, *initiating* talk of the Exodus. The other verses in the Torah that discuss transmitting the story do so only within the framework of *responding to questions* about the redemption or the practices associated with its commemoration, and therefore cannot serve as valid derivation of an obligation beyond that context. Once we mention this verse, however, we cite the others as well, clarifying how the Torah proposes addressing four different types of children.

44. If this paragraph means to discuss the four sons, why does it have to begin with a special praise to God?

Malbim states that since we mention that the Torah spoke of four kinds of children, we are careful to give praise and thanks for the giving of the Torah before proceeding further. In a similar vein, *Shibbolei HaLeket* claims that this is a form of the blessing pronounced before beginning the study of Torah. We insert it here because we are about to expound on verses in the Torah. *Shibbolei HaLeket* and *Yaavetz* suggest that this is a minor form of a blessing over the mitzvah of retelling the Exodus that we are about to begin.

45. Why are there four separate expressions of praise found here?

Kol Bo and *Yaavetz* declare that each of these expressions represents one of the four sons about to be discussed, and the specific manner of God's manifestation on earth which corresponds to the spiritual and/or intellectual level of that particular child.

Maasei Nissim claims that we are praising God for having redeemed

---

1. See question 26.

דִּבְּרָה תוֹרָה: אֶחָד חָכָם, וְאֶחָד רָשָׁע, וְאֶחָד תָּם, וְאֶחָד שֶׁאֵינוֹ יוֹדֵעַ לִשְׁאוֹל.

the *entire* nation of Israel from bondage. He divides the people into four distinct groups, paralleling the four sons:

(a) those whose spiritual and intellectual level is such that they perceive the beneficence and sovereignty of God's omnipresence on their own, as the Patriarch Abraham did (this is the wise son);

(b) those who cannot achieve such realization on their own, but are stimulated by the Torah to do so (this is the simple son);

(c) those who cannot arrive at any awareness on their own, but merely follow the example of those who preceded them and do not deviate from that standard (this is the son who is unable to ask);

(d) those who deny or ignore the rule of God's sovereignty over the universe (this is the wicked one).

The *Gra's* opinion, however, is that the words, "*Baruch Hamakom* — Blessed is the Omnipresent," do not refer to God Himself, as they usually do. Rather, they are to be translated literally: "Blessed is the place (*hamakom*)," meaning, in this case, the *Beis HaMikdash.* (*Abarbanel* quotes an opinion that it means Mt. Sinai, which is where the Jews received the Torah, but he rejects that view.) The next phrase, "*Blessed is He*," represents the glory of God which emanates from there. The third line is obviously expressing praise over the giving of the Torah, while the final "*Baruch Hu*" alludes to the fact that, in truth, God's spirit resides within "the four cubits of halachah," i.e., the labor of Torah study which results in halachic application (*Maharshal, Berachos* 8a).

46. What is the meaning behind the arrangement of the four sons, who appear here in a totally different order than they do in the Torah?

The Torah presents four *types of questions,* which happen to reflect the characters of these four children. These must be relevant to the surrounding text, and thus the verses appear in an order which is not related to the children per se. The Haggadah, on the other hand, focuses on four *types of children,* and arranges them according to their *nature as people,* beginning with the wise one. *Maharal* explains that since the wise son and the wicked son maintain opposing perspectives they belong together, for their contrasting approaches

Torah speak: A **wise** one, a **wicked** one, a **simple** one, and one **who is unable to ask.**

---

highlight their differences. The Haggadah then follows with the other two children.

Maharal goes on to explain the relationship between each question, which derives from the particular nature of the person asking it, and the context within the Torah in which it is cited:

(a) The wicked child wants no part in anything that might serve God. Therefore, when he seeks to question (or ridicule) our sacred activities, he focuses on the observances of Passover, which the Torah specifically terms a *service* (to God).[1] This is why his question is found in the section of the Torah which introduces the practices associated with Pesach (*Exodus* 12:26).

(b) The child who is incapable of asking has to rely on us to stimulate him and present him with the story of the Exodus. For this reason the verse referring to his situation is spelled out in the portion of the Torah that elaborates on the mitzvah of matzah (loc. cit. 13:8), which is, as explained, the basis for such discussion.

(c) The simple child asks on his own, but only when he senses unusual or irregular occurrences. Thus, his question follows the mitzvah to decapitate a firstborn mule which was not redeemed, a commandment which would strike the child as odd.

(d) The wise child needs no stimulation of any sort. He readily desires to learn and understand as much as he can about each and every mitzvah. That is why his question addresses all mitzvos and is found in a part of the Torah that, likewise, speaks about all mitzvos (*Deuteronomy* 6:20).

Avudraham says simply that the four children are arranged in descending order of intellectual level or depth of questioning (in his view, the wicked son too is wise as well; however, he uses his intelligence improperly). *Maasei Hashem* and *Shibbolei HaLeket* voice a similar opinion. They stress that it was important to end off with the verse, *"And you shall tell your child,"* which is associated with the unquestioning child, for this verse is a preface to the ensuing discussion of the details of the Exodus.

---

1. *Exodus* 12:25 and 13:5. When the wicked son refers to our observance as *avodah,* the term used by the Torah to mean "service," he refers to an alternative interpretation of the word "labor." See *Abarbanel's* view in question 53.

חָכָם מָה הוּא אוֹמֵר? מָה הָעֵדֹת וְהַחֻקִּים וְהַמִּשְׁפָּטִים אֲשֶׁר צִוָּה יהוה אֱלֹהֵינוּ אֶתְכֶם?[1] וְאַף אַתָּה אֱמָר לוֹ כְּהִלְכוֹת הַפֶּסַח, אֵין מַפְטִירִין אַחַר הַפֶּסַח אֲפִיקוֹמָן.

---

47. What is meant by the question that precedes each child's paragraph (e.g., "*the wise son* — what does he say")?

Malbim and *Otzar HaTefillos* explain that this is the Haggadah speaking. It is clarifying which of the four questions and answers found in the Torah regarding the redemption should be ascribed to each type of child.

⋞ חָכָם — *The wise son*

---

48. What is it that distinguishes the wise son's question as wise?

As mentioned previously, *Maharal* describes the wise son as the child who needs no prodding to question the guidelines and deeper meanings of all mitzvos. This son's words make it clear that he already understands that even the most minute details of the mitzvos carry tremendous import and reflect profound truth, and this is what makes him stand out as wise.

Abarbanel points out that this son was careful to divide the practices of Pesach into distinct categories: testimonies (*eidos*) — observances which are testimonial in nature; decrees (*chukim*) — laws for which there is no discernible rationale; and ordinances (*mishpatim*) — those requirements that seem reasonable and appropriate even from a non-Torah perspective. His perspicacity illustrates his refined grasp of the nature of mitzvos. *Maasei Hashem* takes this approach a step further by explaining that what the wise son really wants to know is why the decrees or ordinances of Pesach require the *additional* performance of the testimonial commandments, namely, the recounting of the Exodus. Generally, testimonial mitzvos serve as a confirmation of some event or element of Jewish identity. In our case, the performance of mitzvos such as eating matzah and maror should already bear adequate recognition of, and testimony to, God's having delivered us from Egypt.

49. Why is the wise son not criticized for describing the mitzvos of Pesach as applying to "*you*" (and by inference, not himself) just as the wicked son is?

Most commentaries explain that this is because the wise son attributes the commandments to "*our God.*" In other words, although he declares

The wise son — what does he say? "What are the testimonies, decrees, and ordinances which HASHEM, our God, has commanded you?"[1] Therefore, explain to him the laws of the Passover offering: that one may not eat dessert after the final taste of the Passover offering.

_____

(1) *Deuteronomy* 6:20.

_____

that God commanded *"you"* to perform these mitzvos, he does not mean to exclude himself from subservience to the yoke of heavenly rule. He makes this clear by saying that it was *"our God"* Who did the commanding.

Why does he insert the word *"you"* into his query? *Kol Bo* and *Maharal* answer that the Torah presented this question as being posed by the child of a person who actually left Egypt. In that context, the word *"you"* simply means "you who were *personally* commanded by God regarding these mitzvos." *Malbim* agrees with this approach, making a distinction between the word *"lachem — to you,"* which the wicked son uses, and the word *"eschem— you,"* which is the wise son's expression. *"To you"* implies that the command was directed to you, rather than to me; *"you,"* on the other hand, merely describes who it was who heard God's instruction. (*Maharal* adds that "to you" in the wicked son's question also carries with it a tone of ridicule. He is challenging us with the words: "What is it *'to you'*? What do you gain from this service?")

Shibbolei HaLeket's opinion is that the word *"you"* in the wise son's question is nothing more than a reference to the law that we do not slaughter an animal to be used as a *Korban Pesach* for a minor. Thus, the child excluded himself from the notion of personal obligation when asking about the mitzvos connected with Pesach.

Chasam Sofer offers an entirely different perspective. He claims that the crucial distinction between the questions of the two sons is the timing. The wise son, he says, does not probe the rationale behind mitzvos during their actual performance, for while it is proper to delve into the meaning and the complex interrelationships of the Torah's directives, one's readiness to fulfill God's command must remain independent of any such understanding. The impetus for carrying out the responsibilities placed upon us by the Torah must be rooted in our acceptance of God's will as unconditionally binding, not based on the satisfaction of our intellect with the scheme of those obligations. The wicked son cannot make peace with this subjugation of one's freedom. For him, the determining factor in any undertaking is whether it is sensible *to him.* And so he questions us while we engage in

רָשָׁע מָה הוּא אוֹמֵר? מָה הָעֲבֹדָה הַזֹּאת לָכֶם?¹ לָכֶם
וְלֹא לוֹ, וּלְפִי שֶׁהוֹצִיא אֶת עַצְמוֹ מִן הַכְּלָל,

the fulfillment of our duties: "What is this labor (or service) to you? What does it mean? If it provides some immediately apparent and practical benefit, that's fine. But if not, why are you doing it?" Thus, the two inquiries differ in a fundamental way.

50. What is the meaning of the phrase "ein maftirin achar hapesach afikoman," generally translated as, "one may not eat dessert after the final taste of the Passover offering"?

The words "ein maftirin" mean "we do not end or finish." This refers to the fact that instead of ending tonight's meal with the usual sweet treats, when we conclude the meal we will once again partake of a portion of matzah — or, in the times of the Temple, a piece of meat from the Passover offering.

Rashi and Abarbanel state that the word afikoman is a conjunction of two words which together mean "take out." It is referring to the desserts normally brought out following a meal. The point being that on Passover night, unlike the rest of the year, we do not announce "the sweets are to be brought out" after eating the required portion of matzah (or meat). The foods that are brought to the table in order to "wash down" the main portion of the meal must be consumed prior to the eating of the afikoman.

Otzar HaTefillos interprets the word afikoman to mean "take away all food from the table." According to this understanding, the word is actually an announcement in itself. The entire phrase is read as: "We do not finish the meal with anything following the matzah (or the Passover offering). Instead, we announce that everything should be removed from our presence, lest someone mistakenly consume additional food."

51. Why does the Haggadah present a different response to the wise son's question than the one dictated by the Torah ("We were slaves . . .")?

Most commentaries agree that the Haggadah's response here is supplemental to the basic answer of "We were slaves . . ." which has already been used to begin the discussion of the Exodus. Indeed, the language of the Haggadah is: "and 'also,' you should say to him," indicating that we mean to add this to "We were slaves." Otzar HaTefillos and Abarbanel explain that aside from a general explanation for the observances on this night, we want to provide the child with an understanding of the specific practices he has questioned, and so the Haggadah instructs us to "also speak to him about the laws of Pesach" (see question 5).

The wicked son — what does he say? "Of what purpose is this work to you?"[1] "To you," thereby excluding himself. By excluding himself from the community of believers,

---

(1) *Exodus* 12:26.

Bircas HaShir suggests that the Haggadah means something altogether different. Our statement is intended to console the child who is disillusioned over the fact that without the Temple there is no Passover offering, and so a key element of our celebration is missing. He may perceive our observance as an incomplete one, at best. To this, we respond that our words make up for the sacrifices we cannot offer, and together with the portion of matzah that we eat at the Seder in place of the *Korban,* what we do tonight is *just like (kehilchos) (the observance of) the laws of Pesach (HaPesach).* As proof that this is true we cite that we do not allow anything to follow the eating of the *afikoman* — the matzah that we eat in place of the sacrifice — just as we were prohibited from eating after eating from the offering. (This is one reason why the Haggadah specifically cites this halachah of Pesach over all others. [See next question.])

52. Why does the Haggadah single out this particular law of Pesach in response to the question of the wise son?

Almost all the commentaries maintain that the Haggadah does not mean to limit our answer to this one halachah. Rather, the intent is that one should discuss all the laws of Pesach, up to the very last one (last, in this case, means the last one that is relevant to the Seder). *Baruch She'amar* even notes that this is the first time that the word *until (ad)* appears in the Haggadah. The Haggadah, he says, alludes that you should teach your wise son all the mishnayos in the chapter of the Talmud that deals with this subject, *until,* and including, the last one. And *Malbim* points out that the Haggadah says *"like the laws of the Pesach"* (*kehilchos HaPesach*). The message is that just as you tell the child all the laws of Passover, you should also teach him the laws that apply after the meal.

◆§ רָשָׁע — *The wicked son*

---

53. Why does the Haggadah view the phrase, *"Of what purpose is this work to you,"* as the question of a wicked child?

Abarbanel offers three reasons:

(a) In introducing this phrase, the Torah stated, "It will be when your

כָּפַר בְּעָקָר – וְאַף אַתָּה הַקְהֵה אֶת שִׁנָּיו וֶאֱמָר לוֹ,
בַּעֲבוּר זֶה עָשָׂה יהוה לִי בְּצֵאתִי מִמִּצְרָיִם.[1] לִי וְלֹא לוֹ,
אִלּוּ הָיָה שָׁם לֹא הָיָה נִגְאָל.

children *say* to you" (*Exodus* 12:26), rather than referring to it as a question. In other words, it is an arrogant, provocative statement, not a sincere question.

(b) There is no mention of God as the source of the mitzvos being questioned. The person doing the asking is obviously not willing to acknowledge the Divine origin of the Torah.

(c) He refers to the mitzvos in question not as "testimonies," "decrees," or "ordinances," but as *"ha'avodah hazos lachem"* — which can be understood as meaning "this service which you have established." The wicked son means to imply two things: first, that the mitzvos were established "by you," and are not Godly in origin; and that not only are they humanly inspired, but their goal is not Divine service, as they are not testimonies or ordinances. He asserts that self-interest and personal gratification are the driving forces behind our performance of these rituals — i.e., the *Korban Pesach* serves as a convenient excuse to partake of a good piece of roasted meat, while the four cups of wine offer an opportunity to imbibe. Thus, he indicates that he is indeed the wicked son.

Malbim's approach is similar, except that according to him the point of the word "*avodah*" in the wicked son's question is that he views mitzvos as "labor," a heavy load and an imposition on his lifestyle. (*Ritva* quotes the Talmud Yerushalmi as explaining this son's complaint to be focused on our interference with the rejoicing of the festival by delaying the evening's meal with the Seder performance.) *Malbim* also notes that the wicked son has excluded himself from the collective identity of his people by limiting the notion of responsibility to God that is a primary ingredient of that identity; "to you," and not himself. Furthermore, in response to his question, the Torah states: *"And you should say that this is a Pesach sacrifice to God."* However, it does not stipulate that this must be said *to him.* Indeed, the Haggadah does not respond to him with this line because these words are intended *for oneself,* in order to counteract any subversive effect his blasphemous suggestion might have. To the son himself, the Haggadah offers quite a different response. This is because his question makes it clear that we are dealing with a wicked person; for him there are no answers — because he is not interested in a response. And so for him, the Haggadah instructs us to *"blunt his teeth,"*

he denies the basic principle of Judaism. Therefore, blunt his teeth and tell him: "It is because of this that HASHEM did so for me when I went out of Egypt."[1] "For me," but not for him — had he been there, he would not have been redeemed.

---

(1) *Exodus* 13:8.

---

and let him know that, as he himself already declared, he has no place among the people who were redeemed by God. (See the next question.)

54. Why does the Haggadah offer the wicked son a response different from the one the Torah presents?

Ritva points out that this question is expressed in the Torah in plural form: "*. . . when your 'children' will say to you . . .*" (*Exodus* 12:26). This indicates, he says, that there are two types of children who might ask such a question: the wicked child, and the child who is totally unfamiliar with the concept of service to God. The latter was the spiritual state of the children who actually left Egypt, because they had spent their formative years surrounded by the depraved culture of that idolatrous land. These children were not responsible for their perspective, and deserved a considerate response: "It is a Pesach offering to HASHEM, Who passed over the houses of the Children of Israel in Egypt when He smote the Egyptians, but He saved our households." For the wicked son, on the other hand, there is the Haggadah's response.

The *Gra, Maasei Nissim* and others echo the opinion of *Malbim* (quoted in the previous question) that the answer found in the Torah was never meant to be told to the wicked person himself. Rather, the people he has confronted should say this to themselves in order to strengthen their own faith and resolve in the face of his challenge to their convictions. They stress, however, that we do not address the wicked person because it is *not proper* to engage in debate with someone whose views are heretical. This may be in contrast to *Malbim*, whose words may imply that it is the futility of responding that accounts for our reluctance to answer his question.

55. Why does the Torah express the question of the wicked son as coming from "your children," in the plural — rather than from "your child," in the singular?

Abarbanel offers two reasons for this. First, there are several heretical elements contained in his question, and so it is as if there are numerous children challenging us. Secondly, he notes that the portion in the Torah where this verse is found is phrased in plural form because it is speaking to the entire nation. It would thus be incongruous to interrupt the paragraph with a verse or two in singular form.

Bircas Avraham suggests that a wicked person will often gather people around him in order to provide his misguided views a wider audience, and lend potency to his attack. In this way he soon has others echoing his corrupt ideas; rather than being a lone voice challenging our religious commitment, there is an entire community of "children" clamoring against tradition. *Sh'lah HaKadosh* understands that the setting for the questions of the children has all of them present at once. The wise son, of course, opens the discussion with his question, for he is the first to speak at any gathering. But as soon as he begins to make his point, the wicked child interrupts with what *he* considers to be "words of wisdom." Thus, the reality of the situation is that at the time that the wicked son asks his question, there are two children talking simultaneously.

56. In what way has the wicked son excluded himself from the group?

Avudraham, Malbim and others adopt the simple approach that it is his use of *"to you"* in describing the mitzvos of Passover and their obligatory nature that places him apart from his brethren.

Interestingly, *Yalkut Shimoni* suggests that this son never removed himself from his people. He understands that the Haggadah's comment "By excluding himself (*atzmo*)" refers to God, Who is often referred to in the Talmud as *Atzmo* (e.g. *Gittin* 56b). Thus, the wicked son's chief evil, as stated by numerous commentaries, is his refusal to acknowledge the Divine source of the mitzvos. By removing God from the context of his question, this child has, *ipso facto*, removed himself from fellowship in the privileged status of his nation. Had he been in Egypt, he would not have merited redemption.

57. What does *ve'af atah* (literally: *and you also*) imply?

Sh'lah HaKadosh interprets this to mean that in addition to the answer you are going to give the wicked son, "you should also" blunt (damage) his teeth. (Most commentaries view this figuratively; i.e. deal him a psychological blow. See the next question.) Others, including *Malbim*, understand that we are being told that aside from the response found in the Torah, "you should also" offer the reply presented here. Finally, there are those who translate the words literally, meaning that just as the wicked child's intent in posing his challenge was evil, "you too" should answer in kind with words (or actions) that deliver a scathing message.

58. What is the Haggadah advising us to do to the wicked son's teeth, and why?

Avudraham suggests two possibilities:

(a) By ridiculing basic tenets of his religion, this son has estranged himself from his people and entered the category of those who are prohibited from partaking of the *Korban Pesach* (*Exodus* 12:43, see *Rashi*). Forced to stand by and watch our celebration, he will grind his teeth in fury and envy until they are dull (*Otzar HaTefillos* gives a similar explanation).

(b) The Haggadah means that we should irritate and anger him by declaring that it was he that the Torah intended to exclude when it stated "HASHEM did so *for me*," in describing our obligation to commemorate the Exodus. The implication of the verse is thus that there were intended beneficiaries of God's miracles leading to the Exodus, and these were those who, because of their wickedness, were, or would have been, excluded from the experience.

Malbim's remarks are similar, but he stresses the need to respond in kind to the wicked person. One's teeth are dulled by things a person takes into his mouth himself, not from some outside force. Thus, the Haggadah is telling us that in our reply we turn the very strategy the wicked person employed, in question, against him. He sought to deny his affiliation with the people whose obligation to God he finds too encumbering, so we should assure him that he does not belong to the ranks of those redeemed by God.

HaShir VeHaShevach understands that the Haggadah means we should literally "hit his teeth." This reaction is called for because, through his question, the wicked child illustrates that he is bound to his earthly desires, and is unwilling to embrace a way of life that rejects their senseless pursuit. Such a person needs to have his teeth knocked out, so that his interest in and involvement with food, drink and other physical enjoyments will diminish, allowing him to focus more on life's truths, and perhaps draw him closer to the Torah and its ways.

Chesed L'Avraham tells us that when dealing with a wicked person, it is foolish to respond to his questions directly, for he will just continue his assault with new challenges to our convictions. The only way to "blunt his bite" is to let him know that we have no intention of engaging in debate with him. We stand firm in our faith, and will ultimately experience the spiritual fruit of our labors. He, disassociated from his people and the beneficial effect they might have upon him, and, naively secure in his corrupt ways, will eventually pass from the scene and face Divine judgment for his evil deeds.

Finally, *Bircas HaShir* injects a philosophical note into this scenario. The wicked son's argument, he explains, is that the whole concept of mitzvos is degrading, for it presumes that a person is somehow incomplete without them. The notion that perfection is achieved through the performance of mitzvos is antithetical to his perspective on life. He insists that the closer something is to being *inherently* complete, the more superior it is to that which is less so. The wicked child notes that most living creatures, and certainly inanimate objects, come into existence whole, without any need for refinement. To imagine that human beings must labor to achieve their full spiritual potential is to place them at the bottom rung on the ladder of creation. Therefore, to the evil person the idea of mitzvos is preposterous. In fact, however, nothing could be further from the truth. Gold and diamonds are unquestionably superior to mere sand, yet the former need much work in the form of sifting, polishing, refining and cutting in order to realize their value. And even the wicked son cannot deny that, physically, human beings are born incomplete; unable to walk, talk and master their resources. Teaching them these skills takes much time and effort. Animals, on the other hand, are generally ready to fend for themselves shortly after birth.

An outstanding illustration of the human's need to grow to completion is the teeth, remarks *Bircas HaShir*, for these vital parts of the body are not even in view when a child is born. This, then, is the message the Haggadah wants us to transmit to the wicked person. Illustrate to him the fallacy of his philosophy by incapacitating his teeth. If he feels that a person is created complete, let him go on without his teeth, which he did not possess when he began life. In this way he may come to recognize the error of his approach.

59. Whom is the Haggadah telling us to address when it instructs us: "*and tell him*"?

Kol Bo, Chizkuni and *Avudraham* concur with *Rashi's* comment on this verse (*Exodus* 13:8), and state that the response should be directed to the wicked child himself. We are to tell him: God did for *me* and not for *you*. Had *you* been there, *you* would not have merited redemption. As noted, however, the *Gra, Maasei Nissim* and others insist that nothing is to be said to this son. The answer offered is intended for the others gathered at the table (see the next question), and should be repeated exactly as it appears in the Haggadah, referring to the wicked child in the third person: God did for *me* and not for *him*. Had *he* been there, *he* would not have been redeemed.

60. Why does the Haggadah use the same answer for the wicked son as for the son who is unable to ask? What is the relationship between these two children?

Sifsei Chachamim (*Exodus* 13:8) states that if the Torah makes a point of using the words *"for me"* when addressing the child who is unable to ask, it obviously means to exclude someone from the redemption. That person, however, cannot be this child, for even if he has no specific merits, he still has done nothing wrong. Surely then, he merits redemption along with the rest of the nation. It must be that the Torah means to exclude the wicked son even as speaking to the son who is unable to ask.

Haggadas Sofrim feels that it is the choice of the word *"vehigadeta — And you shall tell —"* used to describe how one should give this reply, which indicates that the wicked child is also being addressed here. This word, as opposed to the word *ve'amarta — And you shall say —* is usually identified with strong or harsh talk, very uncharacteristic of the way we would speak to a small child who is incapable of posing his own questions. Thus, we must also be addressing the wicked person with these words.

The *Gra's* understanding of this association (as quoted by *Iyun Tefillah*) is that the proper time to address the child who is unable to ask is precisely when the wicked person is waiting for an answer to his question. At that point, one should turn to the young child and tell him exactly what the Torah directs us to say: *"It is because of this* (the mitzvos the wicked son is questioning) *that God did so for me when I went out of Egypt."* The word *me* should be emphasized, says the *Gra*. It should be explained to the child that *me* is to the exclusion of *him* — the wicked person.

Abarbanel and *Sh'lah HaKadosh* point out that the "child who is unable to ask" presents a problem to the "father." Not having posed any question, we have no way of knowing what his level of religious observance is. Maybe he is not the simple, unquestioning child we take him to be; perhaps the real reason he has not inquired about the evening's practices is because they are of no significance to him. Perhaps he secretly harbors some heretical ideas which he does not wish to expose to scrutiny. This being the case, we are actually dealing with a potential "wicked son." It is most appropriate, then, that these two children share a common message in the Haggadah, one which deals with the philosophy they may share. Similarly, *Maharal* says that the verse, with its restrictive implication, serves as a warning to the son who is unable to ask that he not follow the path of the wicked son, lest he too

תָּם מָה הוּא אוֹמֵר? מַה זֹּאת? וְאָמַרְתָּ אֵלָיו, בְּחֹזֶק יָד
הוֹצִיאָנוּ יהוה מִמִּצְרַיִם מִבֵּית עֲבָדִים.[1]

---

forfeit his status as one worthy of experiencing God's redemption.

Maharal adds that by not presenting any interest in the mitzvos of Pesach, the child who is unable to ask establishes that he feels no connection to those mitzvos. In a sense, then, he is in the same category as the wicked son, who has severed his link to the mitzvos. The message of the verse is that it is only because of our future observance of these mitzvos that we were privileged to take part in the Exodus. Regarding the wicked son, the response contained in this verse is: for *me* and not for *him*. Had he been there, he would not have been redeemed. This applies equally to the child who is unable to ask, except that for him, we hope that by explaining the basics of Pesach we are *creating* a relationship between him and the mitzvos.

61. How can we say that had the wicked son been there, he would not have been redeemed, when the *erev rav* — the mixed multitude of foreign people who later instigated many of the sins in the desert — and even the perennial evildoers, Dathan and Abiram, left Egypt along with the Jews?

Bircas HaShir tells us that even the wicked people of the generation of the Exodus performed the mitzvos required at the time of the redemption. In that merit, they participated in the wondrous experience of redemption. This evil son, however, does not want any part in the mitzvos of Pesach. Undoubtedly, then, he would have been left behind when the Jews left the country.

The *Gra* maintains that he would have perished during the three days of darkness that enveloped Egypt prior to the Exodus (*Exodus* 10:22, see *Rashi*).

⮜§ תָּם — *The simple son*

---

62. What is the meaning of the word *tam* (translated here as "simple")?

Rashi explains that the question of the *tam* is presented by a child whose intellectual grasp is shallow and unsophisticated (*Exodus* 13:4). In *Genesis* (25:27) *Rashi* defines a *tam* as *one who is not cunning*. *Targum Yonasan* interprets that particular reference as a person who is *complete*

The simple son — what does he say? "What is this?" Tell him: "HASHEM took us out of Egypt, from the house of slaves, by strength of hand."[1]

_____

(1) *Exodus* 13:14.

_____

(*tam*) in his service of God. The *Gra* seems to echo this concept in describing the *tam* of the Haggadah as someone who follows a path of *completeness* (meaning simplicity of faith in God).

63. How does the Haggadah know that the question, *"What is this,"* belongs to the simple son?

Rokeach, Shibbolei HaLeket and *Malbim* state that the lack of depth or sophistication in this question indicates that we are not dealing with a wise child. Nor is this the challenge of a wicked son, who is surely capable of confronting us with a more substantive query. Obviously then, it is the question of a simple child with no profound or hidden agenda. *Malbim* feels that the proof of this child's sincerity lies in the Torah's presentation of the question: "And it shall be when your child will ask you, *'What is this?'*" It is simply a question awaiting an answer, unlike the challenge of the wicked son.

64. What indication does the Haggadah have that the question of the simple son is focusing on the observances of Passover? In the Torah (*Exodus* 13:11-14) it appears in relation to the mitzvah of redeeming a firstborn animal.

Abarbanel explains that when Moses was commanded by God to teach the mitzvah of redeeming the firstborn, he first reviewed the laws of Passover (*Exodus* 13:3-7) and then he addressed the redemption of the firstborn. The reason for this is that redeeming the firstborn belongs to the same category of mitzvos as those connected with Pesach; it is another reminder of the awesome events surrounding the Exodus, in this case, the sparing of the Jewish firstborn at the same time that those of the Egyptians were being slain. In fact, notes *Abarbanel,* the two separate paragraphs in which these mitzvos are spelled out begin with the same words (*Exodus* 13:5,11), to illustrate that there is actually only one topic under discussion. Thus, when the simple son poses his question following the mitzvah of redeeming the firstborn, he is actually expressing interest in the whole gamut of Pesach observances which he has just heard emphasized. This is why the Haggadah presents his query as referring to the laws of Pesach.

וְשֶׁאֵינוֹ יוֹדֵעַ לִשְׁאוֹל, אַתְּ פְּתַח לוֹ. שֶׁנֶּאֱמַר, וְהִגַּדְתָּ לְבִנְךָ בַּיּוֹם הַהוּא לֵאמֹר, בַּעֲבוּר זֶה עָשָׂה יהוה לִי בְּצֵאתִי מִמִּצְרָיִם.[1]

יָכוֹל מֵרֹאשׁ חֹדֶשׁ, תַּלְמוּד לוֹמַר בַּיּוֹם הַהוּא. אִי

---

65. In what ways does the passage that deals with the simple son differ from those that address the wise son and the wicked son?

Abarbanel points out that the responses to the first two sons were preceded by the words: . . . *v'af atah — and you should "also."* The answer to the simple child, however, is simply the one specified in the Torah. This is because there is nothing *outstanding* about his question, either in depth or in wicked intent. It is a simple inquiry into the nature of our actions on Pesach, and so we reply with the Torah's simple explanation: God took us out of Egypt with a great display of might and miracles, and this is what we are celebrating.

‎§ שֶׁאֵינוֹ יוֹדֵעַ לִשְׁאוֹל — The child who is unable to ask

---

66. What is meant by the expression: *att pesach lo* — literally, "you open for him"?

The commentaries agree that this means we should create an *opening* for him to enter into discussion of the redemption, and thereby arrive at an understanding of its basic points. *Malbim* and *Shibbolei HaLeket* stress that one must engage the child in conversation in such a manner that he eventually *does* pose a question of his own. This should be followed by a fully detailed explanation of the Exodus.

67. Why does the word "you" appear in the feminine form (אַתְּ, *att*) rather than the masculine (אַתָּה, *attah*)?

Be'er Miriam observes that since we are dealing with a child who is incapable of formulating his own question, he is likely at an age where he is still very dependent on his mother. For this reason, the instructions regarding the proper method of explaining the Exodus are addressed to her instead of the child's father. She is the one who will be most effective at transmitting the story to this particular child. *Baruch She'amar,* however, suggests that the use of the feminine form of the word is not to be taken literally. He views it as an allusion to the fact that one should teach the

As for **the son who is unable to ask,** you must initiate the subject for him, as it is stated: "And you shall tell your son on that day, saying, 'It is because of this that HASHEM did so for me when I went out of Egypt.'"[1]

One might think that the obligation to discuss the Exodus commences with the first day of the month of Nissan, but the Torah says: "You shall tell your son on that day." but

---

(1) *Exodus* 13:8.

---

child the story of the Exodus *in its entirety,* this deriving from the fact that *att* (אַתְּ) is comprised of the first and last letters of the Hebrew alphabet.

68. What is the meaning of the added word *leimor* — "saying," in the verse which presents the response to the child who is unable to ask?

Malbim states that it means that you should convey the story of the redemption in a way that will cause you to have to "say" more, i.e., the child should be stimulated to come up with questions concerning the practices of Pesach, that will then be satisfied by the explanation, "It is because of him . . ."

Sh'lah HaKadosh claims the word refers to the child, not you. He says it means that one should elaborate on the Exodus to the point where the child himself is sufficiently knowledgeable to answer the wicked son's challenge on his own, *saying: "It is because of this . . ."*

69. To what is *"It is because of this"* referring?

Rashi and *Ibn Ezra* interpret this verse to mean that we merited the miraculous redemption brought about by God in anticipation of our future observance of the mitzvos of Passover *(Exodus* 13:8). *Ramban,* however, feels that the verse should be understood as follows: "It is because of this thing that God did for me when I went out of Egypt." I carry out the mitzvos of Pesach.

◆§ יָכוֹל מֵרֹאשׁ חֹדֶשׁ — *One might think that the obligation to discuss the Exodus commences with the first day of the month of Nissan.*

---

70. To whom is this paragraph directed, and what is its purpose?

Ritva claims that the Haggadah wants to explain the verse just cited to the child who is unable to ask. This paragraph, however, is not

בַּיּוֹם הַהוּא, יָכוֹל מִבְּעוֹד יוֹם, תַּלְמוּד לוֹמַר בַּעֲבוּר זֶה. בַּעֲבוּר זֶה לֹא אָמַרְתִּי אֶלָּא בְּשָׁעָה שֶׁיֵּשׁ מַצָּה וּמָרוֹר מֻנָּחִים לְפָנֶיךָ.

---

addressed to him. *Abarbanel* maintains that this paragraph does speak to this child, and constitutes an attempt to present the details of the Exodus on his unsophisticated level. To do this, we call his attention to the matzah and *maror* — items whose place in the scheme of the story of the redemption are easily understood.

Maasei Hashem says that this passage is directed to the father. He explains that unlike the other children who inquire about the unusual practices they observe at the Seder, the child who is unable to ask questions says nothing, indicating that this evening's special nature is beyond his level of perception. Thus, one might have thought that the procedure of describing the Exodus to him, at the Seder, is pointless. Therefore, the Haggadah reminds us that it is incumbent upon every father to give over the story of the Exodus *specifically at the Seder,* not at any time beforehand, even to the unquestioning child (see the next question).

In a similar vein, *Yalkut Shimoni* points out that the younger children generally go to sleep when it gets dark, before the Seder begins. In that case, it would have seemed advisable to tell these children the story of the redemption during the afternoon, before they are put to bed. The Haggadah counters with its insistence that the time for performing the mitzvah is *at the Seder,* when the matzah and *maror* are in front of us.

71. Why might one have presumed that the mitzvah of retelling the story of the Exodus applies from the start of the month of Nissan?

Rashi, Shibbolei HaLeket and *Maasei Nissim* voice a common theme. They suggest that since the Talmud states we should begin studying and reviewing the laws of Pesach on the first day of Nissan,[1] just as Moses taught these laws to the Jews of Egypt on that day, one could have believed that the discussion of the Exodus falls under the same requirement. The purpose would be to "open" the subject up for the child by making him familiar with the story so that he could raise questions.

Ritva points out that we could have been misled by the language of the

---

1. This is a matter of debate in Talmud, *Pesachim* 6b. The accepted opinion holds that the laws of Pesach should be reviewed beginning thirty days prior to the festival. However, *Maasei Nissim* claims that this requirement is a Rabbinical addition to the Biblically rooted obligation to begin on the first of Nissan.

the expression "on that day" could be understood to mean only during the daytime; therefore the Torah adds: "It is because of this that HASHEM, did so for me when I went out of Egypt." The pronoun "this" implies something tangible, thus "You shall tell your son" applies only when matzah and *maror* lie before you — at the Seder.

Torah itself. Several verses prior to the one in question, the Torah commands us regarding the mitzvah of matzah: *And you shall perform this service in this month* — Nissan (*Exodus* 13:5). The Torah seems to have established the *month* as the contextual frame for this mitzvah, rather than the specific day. After two more verses discussing matzah, the Torah then commands: *"And you shall tell your child* [the story of the redemption]" (*Exodus* 13:8). It would stand to reason, says *Ritva,* that the time frame mentioned — the month of Nissan — is the appropriate time to fulfill the obligation to retell the story of the Exodus. As the Haggadah notes, it is only when the verse continues with the words: *"on that day"* — i.e., the first day of Pesach — that we come to know the proper chronological setting for this mitzvah.

72. Why would one have thought that this mitzvah can be performed in the afternoon, before the festival has begun?

Rashi, Ritva and *Maasei Nissim* suggest that since the slaughtering of the Passover offering — which signals the start of the observances commemorating the Exodus — took place in the afternoon (see *Exodus* 12:6), one could have mistakenly believed that the mitzvah of discussing the redemption is equally applicable at that time. It is only when the verse in question concludes with the words *"because of this,"* referring to the matzah and *maror,* that we realize that the Seder *night* is the exclusively prescribed occasion for the performance of this mitzvah (see the next question).

73. How do the words *"because of this"* establish that the mitzvah of recounting the Exodus applies specifically to the Seder night?

As mentioned previously,[1] there is a dispute among the commentaries whether this statement means to imply that the observances of Passover were a primary factor in our having been redeemed, or that the redemption is the reason behind our performance of those mitzvos.

---

1. See question 69.

מִתְּחִלָּה, עוֹבְדֵי עֲבוֹדָה זָרָה הָיוּ אֲבוֹתֵינוּ, וְעַכְשָׁו קֵרְבָנוּ הַמָּקוֹם לַעֲבוֹדָתוֹ. שֶׁנֶּאֱמַר, וַיֹּאמֶר יְהוֹשֻׁעַ אֶל כָּל הָעָם, כֹּה אָמַר יהוה אֱלֹהֵי יִשְׂרָאֵל, בְּעֵבֶר הַנָּהָר יָשְׁבוּ אֲבוֹתֵיכֶם מֵעוֹלָם, תֶּרַח אֲבִי אַבְרָהָם וַאֲבִי

According to the first opinion, in order for the verse to read coherently, the first part, which commands us to speak of the Exodus, can only be taking place when one can actualize the second half by pointing to the matzah and *maror,* and declaring: *"because of this . . ."* According to the second approach, the proof is from the end of the statement: "Because of what God did for me when I left Egypt I do *these* things."

74. How do we explain the words *"on that 'day'"* now that the Haggadah has proven that the mitzvah to discuss the redemption must take place at night?

Malbim points to the familiar verse: "And there was evening, and there was morning; one day" (*Genesis* 1:5), as evidence that "day" does not necessarily exclude nighttime. On the other hand, had the verse not contained the phrase, *"because of this"* — indicating that the mitzvah applies only at night — we would certainly have interpreted it to mean, literally, *"on that 'day.'"* Indeed, there is a good reason why the night of Pesach is *deliberately* termed "day" in the Torah, for as the *Gra* points out, on no other night of the year are there obligations that must be carried out only then, and not by day. So, in a sense, the night of Pesach very much is a *day*! Additionally, *Chida* claims that on the night of the redemption, the Jews in Egypt experienced bright sunshine, as if it was midday, and that is why the verse says: *"on that 'day.'"*

75. What purpose was there in the Torah stating *"on that day"*?

Bircas HaShir and *Malbim* are of the opinion that without these words, the phrase *"because of this"* might have been interpreted as referring to the Passover offering, which was sacrificed on the afternoon of the fourteenth, and we would have assumed that the mitzvah to speak of the redemption should be performed during the day, prior to the Seder. Now that both expressions are included, however, the intent of the verse is clear.

Maasei Nissim suggests that if not for the words *"on that day,"* one might have believed that the phrase *"because of this"* tells us that the mitzvah should be performed beginning on the first of Nissan, which is

Originally our ancestors were idol worshipers, but now the
Omnipresent has brought us near to His service, as it is
stated: "And Joshua said to all of the people, So says HASHEM
the God of Israel: Of old, your forefathers dwelt beyond the
river — Terach, the father of Abraham and the father of Na-

---

when we start reviewing the laws of Pesach (see question 71). The
point of the verse would then be understood to be that one should tell
the child: "because of these mitzvos that we are now studying,
and will soon perform, God did wonders for me when I went out of
Egypt." Thus, *"on that day"* is necessary to establish that the setting for
this verse is the first day of Pesach, and that we are focusing the child's
attention on the mitzvos we are in the process of carrying out at the
Seder.

⊷§ מִתְּחִלָּה — *Originally our ancestors were idol worshipers.*

---

76. What is the purpose of this paragraph?

As mentioned previously,[1] the Haggadah is now presenting an alternative aspect of our history, highlighting our ascent from the ignominy of
idol worship to the pinnacle of human attainment, as servants of the true
God. This is in accordance with the Talmud's demand that the evening's
discussion of the Exodus begin with our shame, and end with our praise.

In explaining why this procedure is crucial to the performance of the
mitzvah, *Maharsha* (*Pesachim* 116a) sees an important ethical lesson
represented in our odyssey and our contrasting situations. An essential
part of any celebration, he says, whether it be related to good fortune or
to great personal achievement, is the need to recall one's less enviable
status prior to the event being celebrated. Focusing on humbler times
places current rejoicing in proper perspective, and serves to insure that
a person does not get carried away with his own success.

Aruch HaShulchan takes the unique position that the procedure of
ending with praise required by the Talmud does not mean *our* own
praise, but *God's*! After recalling our shameful roots, steeped in idolatry,
we are to praise God for the benefits we attained from the ordeal of the
Egyptian exile. This exile served as a crucible of spiritual purification,
ridding us of the deeply ingrained potential for evil which remained from

---

1. See question 26 for background on this matter.

our ignominious roots, much as the intense heat of the kiln purifies gold, silver and other metals.

77. Why was it necessary to cite verses from the Book of *Joshua* attesting to our transition from idol worshipers to Divine servants, when the actual sequence of events is spelled out in the Torah itself?

Malbim points out that it would have been impossible to review the *full* chain of events that appears in the Torah from the time we are introduced to the Patriarch Abraham, until the revelation at Mt. Sinai. Such discussion, he says, would take days, not hours. Instead, the Haggadah deliberately selected two sets of verses — those in the Book of *Joshua,* and the section of the Book of *Deuteronomy* referred to as *bikkurim* (soon to be expounded upon) — which, in terse fashion, allude to the entire account of our people's metamorphosis. (The set of verses in *Joshua* describes the emergence of the Patriarchs from idolatrous surroundings, and the arrival of their offspring in Egypt, while the verses in *Deuteronomy* detail the suffering and subsequent miracles experienced by the Patriarchs' descendants.) *Abarbanel* sees the verses from the Book of *Joshua* as being of particular relevance, in that they list three beneficent gestures of God toward Abraham. These highlight the notion of *"but now, God has brought us near to His service"* (see the next question). These three acts were:

(a) the separation of Abraham from his detrimental environment, along with Divine revelations and the infusion of Godly faith and spirit;

(b) the blessing of progeny;

(c) guaranteeing Abraham a land to be inherited by future generations.

Shibbolei HaLeket also reads a special significance into the Haggadah's choice of these verses. He claims that they demonstrate the great affection God displayed for our people by picking Isaac over all of Abraham's other children,[1] and then Jacob over Esau, to be the heirs to the blessings and guarantees that Abraham received.

78. To what point in time is the Haggadah referring when it says *"but now the Omnipresent has brought us near to His service"*?

Iyun Tefillah and *Malbim* interpret this to simply mean "later on." According to them, the Haggadah is simply presenting the two end-points of our journey — from shame to praise — without attempting to

---

1. The verses in question mention that God granted Abraham a multitude of children.

place either of these episodes in any chronological context other than relative to one another. *Abarbanel,* on the other hand, sees "now" as specifically referring to the choosing of Abraham by God to be the ancestor of a great nation devoted solely to Divine service, as Abraham himself was.[1] In fact, this is what we set out to prove by citing the verses from the Book of *Joshua*.

Maasei Hashem introduces a unique perspective regarding these words. His approach is that when the Haggadah answers the questions of *Mah Nishtanah* with the paragraph of *"We were slaves,"* one might believe that the fact that we had been enslaved in Egypt is a description of our former shame. This is not the case, however. The Haggadah here is stating *"Originally,"* long before our subjugation in Egypt, *"our ancestors were idol worshipers"*; and this is our shame. *"But now,"* when we became slaves to the Egyptians, *"the Omnipresent has brought us near to His service."* How? Because through our enslavement and subsequent redemption, God's sovereignty became known and manifest. Thus, this paragraph comes to tell us that it was before Egypt that we had our "shame." Our servitude, however, was ultimately a vehicle for proclaiming God's mastery over the world, so the slavery itself became an act of Divine service.

Chida suggests the obvious: The phrase, *"but now the Omnipresent has brought us near to His service,* is a reference to the giving of the Torah on Mt. Sinai. The reason the Haggadah uses the word *"now"* to describe this event, he explains, is because one is obligated to relate to the Torah eagerly and with a sense of freshness as though it were just presented to us today.[2]

79. What do we learn from the details presented in this passage?

According to *Malbim,* the verse mentions that Terach was Abraham's father, and that Nachor was Abraham's brother, to indicate that Abraham recognized God on his own, without his father having trained him to do so. Terach himself worshiped idols, and his other son Nachor remained in his idolatrous homeland, continuing to practice the corrupt ways of the family. In a similar vein, *Malbim* says, the verse states that God took *"your father Abraham"* away from that land. The repetitive language (the verse could have said "your father" or "Abraham") teaches

---

1. See *Genesis* 12:1-3, 15:4-7, and 17:1-8.
2. See *Rashi's* comments to *Deuteronomy* 6:6 and 11:13.

אַבְרָהָם מֵעֵבֶר הַנָּהָר, וָאוֹלֵךְ אוֹתוֹ בְּכָל אֶרֶץ כְּנַעַן,
וָאַרְבֶּה אֶת זַרְעוֹ, וָאֶתֶּן לוֹ אֶת יִצְחָק. וָאֶתֵּן לְיִצְחָק אֶת
יַעֲקֹב וְאֶת עֵשָׂו, וָאֶתֵּן לְעֵשָׂו אֶת הַר שֵׂעִיר לָרֶשֶׁת
אוֹתוֹ, וְיַעֲקֹב וּבָנָיו יָרְדוּ מִצְרָיִם.[1]

us that our Patriarchs begin with Abraham. The generations that
preceded him are not viewed as the source of our national identity.

Abarbanel sees the mention of Terach, and the fact that Abraham's
family originated from *beyond the river* [i.e., Ur Casdim], as having a
philosophical connotation. In this verse, he explains, Joshua was re-
minding the Jews who entered the land of Canaan that the roots of our
people go back *"beyond the River,"* and it is *that* land that should have
been our legacy. But Abraham separated from Terach and the rest of the
family, depriving himself of his natural inheritance. Instead, God
promised him the land of Canaan. Joshua was highlighting that without
God's graciousness, we would have remained a people without a land.
This was one of the three special acts of kindness that God displayed
towards Abraham (thus *"bringing us near to His service"*).

**80. Why does the verse make special mention of Isaac? Isn't he
included in *"I multiplied his offspring"*?**

Malbim points out that, indeed, Isaac, as the primary child,[1] must be
distinguished from Abraham's other children. It is he who bore the
guarantees, blessings and responsibilities that derive from being chosen
by God to fulfill a Divine plan, and it is he who transmits them to the next
generation. *Abarbanel* goes so far as to suggest that even *"I multiplied his
offspring"* does not refer to the other children of Abraham, because they
are so inconsequential. Rather, the verse is to be understood as "I
multiplied his offspring by giving him Isaac." (See the next question.)

**81. Why does the verse make a point of mentioning Isaac's son, Esau,
and his inheritance, if it did not do so regarding Abraham's son, Ishmael?**

Maasei Hashem suggests that Joshua was establishing that the Jews,
descendants of Jacob, were *the true seed of Abraham* to whom God had
promised the inheritance of the land of Canaan (*Genesis* 15:8). The
covenant that God made with Abraham stipulated that those offspring
would have to endure many years of servitude in a foreign land before
gaining their inheritance (*Genesis* 15:14). Therefore, Esau, who was

---

1. See *Genesis* 21:12, and Talmud, *Nedarim* 31a.

Abraham from beyond the river, and I led him throughout all the land of Canaan, and I multiplied his offspring, and I gave Isaac unto him, and I gave Jacob and Esau unto Isaac, and I gave unto Esau Mount Seir to inherit, but Jacob and his sons went down to Egypt."[1]

---

(1) *Joshua* 24:2-4.

---

already given a land of his own by God, and had been living in tranquility for many generations, never having been enslaved by another nation, was obviously *not* the offspring spoken of in the covenant. *"But Jacob and his sons went down to Egypt,"* and suffered through much hardship. Clearly, then, they are the descendants to whom God was referring. *Maasei Hashem* asserts that the Haggadah is using this point to prove that the experience in Egypt reflects our glory, not our shame. The statement that *Jacob and his sons went down to Egypt* indicates that this was the family designated by God to carry out His will on earth, the legacy of the offspring of Abraham.

As for the other children of Abraham, there was no need to dwell on them because it was clear they were not the offspring specified in the covenant when God told Abraham (*Genesis* 21:12): *"since through Isaac will offspring be considered yours."* The only remaining question was whether Jacob or Esau carries the distinction of being the preferred seed of Abraham. The answer to that is the subject of the verses quoted by the Haggadah. Other commentators (among them *Abarbanel* and *Shem MeShmuel*) point out that the purpose of the giving of Mt. Seir to Esau was to distance and separate him from Jacob, so that Jacob and his descendants might inherit the Chosen Land of Eretz Yisrael.

82. The verse states that Jacob and his sons *"went down to Egypt,"* implying that they did so of their own volition. If, as the Haggadah tells us later, they went "compelled by Divine decree," should it not have said they were *"sent* down to Egypt"?

Maharal explains that although they indeed *had* to end up in Egypt — for God had decreed that suffering and the subsequent birth of the Jewish nation must occur in that land — the *manner and immediate cause* of their descent was most befitting, and the trip was undertaken quite willingly.[1]

---

1. They went there to reunite with their missing brother, Joseph, who had become a minister to Pharaoh, and would sustain them during years of hunger. (See Talmud, *Shabbos* 89b.)

בָּרוּךְ שׁוֹמֵר הַבְטָחָתוֹ לְיִשְׂרָאֵל, בָּרוּךְ הוּא. שֶׁהַקָּדוֹשׁ בָּרוּךְ הוּא חִשַּׁב אֶת הַקֵּץ, לַעֲשׂוֹת כְּמָה שֶׁאָמַר לְאַבְרָהָם אָבִינוּ בִּבְרִית בֵּין הַבְּתָרִים, שֶׁנֶּאֱמַר, וַיֹּאמֶר

---

§⋙ בָּרוּךְ שׁוֹמֵר הַבְטָחָתוֹ — *Blessed is He Who keeps His pledge.*

---

83. What is the purpose of this paragraph?

Malbim explains that before we proceed any further with analysis relating to the Exodus, the Haggadah presents us with crucial background information — the Covenant Between the Parts that God made with Abraham regarding his offspring and their future. This covenant places the Egyptian exile and its outcome in perspective as part of a larger, Divine master plan. He adds that the reason that the paragraph begins with a blessing is because we recall the assurance God gave Abraham that He would rescue us, and the favorable manner in which He ultimately fulfilled that guarantee.

Rashi and *Shibbolei HaLeket* view this expression of gratitude to God as a response to the phrase, which describes the start of the exile, *"but Jacob and his sons went down to Egypt."* The Talmud (*Berachos* 54a) teaches that we are obligated to praise God for unfavorable events just as we are for clearly beneficial circumstances. To discharge this obligation, the Haggadah offers a "blessing" of praise for the above-mentioned development in our history.

84. What is the meaning of "keeper" (*shomer*) in this paragraph?

If the Haggadah means to offer praise to God for fulfilling His pledge that we would eventually be delivered from Egypt, the word *shomer* translates as "safeguarding" or "watching over," as it normally does. According to this interpretation, the point is that God kept watch over His words, making certain to carry them out.

Bircas HaShir, however, claims that the word *"shomer"* is used here to denotes "waiting."[1] He says the Haggadah is emphasizing how God was deliberately slow in implementing his guarantee to present us — the children of Jacob — with the land of Canaan as an inheritance, in contrast to Esau and his descendants, who inhabited their homeland at a much earlier stage.

---

1. See *Rashi's* comment to *Genesis* 37:11.

Blessed is He Who keeps His pledge to Israel; Blessed is He! For the Holy One, Blessed is He, calculated the end [of our bondage] in order to do as He said to our father Abraham at the Covenant Between the Parts, as it is stated: "He said

---

85. To which "pledge" is the Haggadah referring?

Malbim reads the entire paragraph as expressing a single thought. He explains that this blessing is giving thanks for the manner in which God computed the four hundred years that Abraham's descendants were to spend in a foreign land before being redeemed and led into the promised land of Canaan, as foretold in the covenant God made with Abraham (*Genesis* 15:13). That calculation was reckoned by God as beginning from the time of Isaac's birth, instead of when Jacob and his family settled in Egypt.[1] This, says *Malbim,* represents a very literal translation of the term "your offspring" (i.e., Isaac, not later generations), which God used to describe those who would begin to endure the exile. Being that this reckoning reduced by 190 years the time we *actually* had to spend in Egypt, we offer praise to God.

Abarbanel and *Maasei Hashem* assert that we are praising God for maintaining his guarantee *"to Israel"* — an alternate for the name Jacob (*Genesis* 32:28, 35:10). We are grateful for the fact that it is us, the descendants of Jacob, to whom God was referring when he chose Abraham, and not the offspring of Abraham's or Isaac's other offspring. (*Maasei Hashem* notes that we are grateful for the experience of Egypt itself! This conforms with his opinion that the exile was, in a sense, a privilege.[2])

Aruch HaShulchan also focuses on the word *"to Israel,"* but with a different emphasis. He understands that we are expressing gratitude for God's keeping the guarantee He gave directly to Jacob prior to his descent to Egypt. At that time, God assured Jacob that he would eventually lead him and his descendants back out of that country (*Genesis* 46:4).

Ritva feels that the Haggadah's reference is to the guarantee that we would ultimately leave Egypt with many possessions.

86. What is the purpose of the additional words *"Blessed is He"* which follow the first statement of praise?

The *Gra* explains that for every action there is a process of thought

---

1. *Rashi, Genesis* 15:13, *Exodus* 12:40.

2. See his opinion in question 78. Also see question 81, the view of *Aruch HaShulchan* in question 76, and the second approach of *Abarbanel* in question 88.

לְאַבְרָם, יָדֹעַ תֵּדַע כִּי גֵר יִהְיֶה זַרְעֲךָ בְּאֶרֶץ לֹא לָהֶם, וַעֲבָדוּם וְעִנּוּ אֹתָם, אַרְבַּע מֵאוֹת שָׁנָה. וְגַם אֶת הַגּוֹי אֲשֶׁר יַעֲבֹדוּ דָּן אָנֹכִי, וְאַחֲרֵי כֵן יֵצְאוּ בִּרְכֻשׁ גָּדוֹל.[1]

---

which brings about that action. Thus, we are praising God for the action itself, and the "thought" (in a Godly sense, of course) which brought that action to realization. *Maharal* feels that these words are simply an added blessing which we insert after making mention of God.[1] Similarly, *Malbim* tells us that after the head of the table declares, *"Blessed is He Who keeps his pledge to Israel,"* those assembled call out in response, *"Blessed is He."* *Iyun Tefillah* claims that the first statement of praise refers to the fact that God watched over us in Egypt (especially that our lineage should not be defiled by the Egyptians), while these words apply to the rest of the paragraph — the matter of God's method of calculating the four hundred years of exile.

87. To which bondage are we referring when we thank God for *"calculating the end of our bondage"*?

The Haggadah is now detailing God's fulfillment of His commitment to follow our exile with redemption. However, whether the Haggadah means to emphasize the Exodus from Egypt or our future redemption through Messiah is a matter of dispute.

Avudraham and *Malbim* read this statement in the past tense. We are noting that God *calculated* the termination of the *Egyptian* bondage in a way which departed from the simple understanding of His words, much to our benefit.

Shibbolei HaLeket, on the other hand, quotes his brother that we should understand these words as referring to our current exile. He explains that we are discussing the covenant God made with Abraham. In making the covenant, our sages tell us God revealed to the Patriarch all the future suffering of his descendants as well as their ultimate redemption. Thus, when we dwell on the fulfilled promise of the Exodus from Egypt, we also hail God's *present reckoning* as He draws closer the day of the ultimate redemption. Thus, we praise God for keeping His assurance to redeem us from Egypt, and we find solace in our current situation, strengthened in our belief in the supreme fulfillment of God's age-old promise to our forefather Abraham.

---

1. *Maharal* states this in reference to the four praises in the paragraph of *Baruch HaMakom.*

to Abram, 'Know with certainty that your offspring will be aliens in a land not their own, they will serve them and they will oppress them for four hundred years; but also upon the nation which they shall serve will I execute judgment, and afterwards they shall leave with great possessions.' "[1]

---

(1) *Genesis* 15:13-14.

---

88. Did the Egyptian exile serve as a punishment for a sin of Abraham's, or was it a necessary part of the process leading to the inheritance of the land of Canaan?

Abarbanel writes at great length in order to clarify this matter. He begins by citing a Talmudic dispute (*Nedarim* 32a) over the reason why Abraham deserved the punishment (the word of the Talmud) of having his descendants sent into exile. Three opinions are cited:

(a) R' Abahu feels that the Patriarch was deserving of punishment for having used scholars — who should have been left to their studies — to assist him in his battle against the four mighty kings who had taken his nephew, Lot, prisoner (*Genesis* 14:14).

(b) Shmuel's view is that the decree came in retribution for Abraham's asking God for "By what shall I know that I will inherit [the land of Canaan]?" (loc. cit. 15:8).

(c) R' Yochanan attributes the Divine sentence to the Patriarch's relinquishing control over the people captured in the war against the kings, since he could have drawn these people closer to God and His service.[1]

Abarbanel, however, questions: If the blame was strictly Abraham's, why was the punishment to be visited upon his *descendants,* not himself? In addition, these reasons do not explain why Egypt specifically was to be the country of exile.

Abarbanel quotes *Ramban* who stated (*Genesis* 12:10) that it was improper for Abraham to expose his wife, Sarah, to the danger of sin when he claimed that she was his sister, not his wife, when they went to Egypt. In fact, says *Ramban,* traveling to Egypt to escape the prevailing famine in and of itself displayed a lack of trust in God, Who had directed him to journey to the land of Canaan. While these reasons may explain why Egypt was the land chosen to subjugate Abraham's progeny, they still do not explain why future generations were made to suffer for their

---

1. See *Genesis* 14:21 and *Ran's* explanation of the verse. See also *Rashi, Genesis* 12:5.

ancestor's deeds. Furthermore, *Ran* notes that Abraham's move to Egypt is viewed as *testimony* (see *Rashi, Genesis* 12:10).

Ran suggests that the purpose of the Egyptian exile was to instill the characteristics of humility and subservience in Abraham's offspring. This was to prepare them to receive the Torah, which demands these qualities for a person to properly absorb and carry out its teachings.[1] However, this view is also rejected by *Abarbanel,* on the grounds that even so noble a purpose would not have warranted *suffering* without any misdeed or sin being done.

Abarbanel proposes three of his own approaches to resolve why it was necessary for the descendants of Abraham to experience exile, and specifically, in Egypt:

(a) The ordeal served as retribution for Jacob's children having sold their brother Joseph as a slave (see *Genesis* 37:28). They were responsible for Joseph's living in Egypt along with the children born to him there, so they were punished by being forced down to Egypt themselves, and having their offspring remain there.

(b) The purpose of the Egyptian experience was to proclaim, through the events surrounding the miraculous redemption, the truth of God's existence. Viewed in this context, the exile was actually a great privilege for the descendants of Abraham, since they merited to serve as the medium for that revelation. They also benefited from all the goodness — such as the Torah, the land of Canaan and serving as His Chosen People — that God wished to bestow on the people chosen to suffer for and serve Him.

(c) In fact, the entire series of circumstances experienced by the Jews in Egypt was brought about through their own volition. The exile was not meant as a punishment, nor was it inherently necessary in order to publicize God's dominion. It was "simply" the result of the actions taken by Jacob's children — i.e., the selling of Joseph to Egypt, and his subsequent insistence that the family join him there — which set in motion the events leading to the conditions of exile and slavery.

Maharal, however, focuses on the three opinions cited in the Talmud. He explains that since Abraham was the root from which our nation came forth, any "deficiencies" in his service were transmitted to all future generations. Thus, any action to correct the situation could be done to his descendants as well.

According to *Maharal,* therefore, the exile, enslavement and torture of

---

1. It is interesting that in the closing paragraph of *Shemoneh Esrei* we ask God to "let my soul be like dust (humble) to everyone" and we follow this by "open my heart to Your Torah."

the Jews was a direct consequence of Abraham's actions. The reason that Abraham himself was not subjected to the suffering is that had Abraham been part of the Egyptian exile, Ishmael and Esau would have been as well. Then they, too, would have shared in the greatness which followed the redemption. The exile and the Exodus were reserved by God for the children of Jacob because it was they who were singularly destined to be the recipients of the Torah and the beneficiaries of the glory to be enjoyed by those charged with its Divine mission.

89. Did the Jews actually spend *"four hundred years"* in Egypt as slaves before they were finally redeemed?

They certainly did not. *Rashi* tells us[1] that the reckoning of the four hundred years foretold to Abraham in the Covenant Between the Parts began with the birth of Isaac. The calculation proceeds as follows: When Isaac was sixty, Jacob was born (*Rashi, Genesis* 25:6). Jacob was one hundred and thirty years old when he went down to Egypt with his family (*Genesis* 47:9). Thus 190 of the 400 years the Jews were to have spent in Egypt were actually before Jacob and his family descended. This leaves two hundred and ten years which, *Rashi* says, is the total amount of time the Jews dwelt in Egypt.[2] *Ramban* (*Exodus* 12:40) and *Abarbanel* concur with this calculation although the latter cites, but rejects, the opinion of *Ralbag. Ralbag* agrees that the Jews spent only 210 years in Egypt. However, he maintains that the actual calculation began from the birth of *Jacob,* but God mercifully deducted sixty years from the preordained period of exile.

Maasei Hashem claims that this calculation is alluded to by the praise the Haggadah means to point out which begins earlier in the paragraph: "For the Holy One, Blessed is He, calculated the end of our bondage — (*hakeitz* — הַקֵּץ). He notes that the word קֵץ — the end [of our bondage] is 190. In other words, we are praising God for having taken "the 190" — the 190 years from birth until the actual descent of the Jews to Egypt — into consideration when He calculated the appropriate time for termination of the exile.

---

1. *Genesis* 15:13, *Exodus* 6:18, 12:40.

2. *Rashi* illustrates how one cannot possibly conclude that the Jews actually spent 400 years in Egypt. Kehath, the son of Levi, was one of those who traveled down to Egypt with Jacob (*Genesis* 46:11). He lived 133 years (*Exodus* 6:18). His son Amram, the father of Moses, lived 137 years (*Exodus* 6:20). And finally, Moses was 80 years old when he appeared before Pharaoh with the message that God wanted his people set free (*Exodus* 7:7). Even if we add up these numbers in full, we will only have 350 years. Of course, we must deduct from this calculation the many years which overlapped from one to the other.

The matzos are covered and the cups lifted as the following paragraph is proclaimed joyously. Upon its conclusion, the cups are put down and the matzos are uncovered.

וְהִיא שֶׁעָמְדָה לַאֲבוֹתֵינוּ וְלָנוּ, שֶׁלֹּא אֶחָד בִּלְבָד עָמַד עָלֵינוּ לְכַלּוֹתֵנוּ. אֶלָּא שֶׁבְּכָל

90. What is the significance of *"but also"* in God's assurance to Abraham that He would execute judgment against the oppressors of His descendants?

Rashi (*Genesis* 15:14) understands this as a reference to *all* the kingdoms that would subject the Jews to exile. God was guaranteeing that not only the Egyptians, but the others *too* would suffer for their crimes of oppression. *Ramban* and *Abarbanel,* however, view this as a continuation of the previous statement. God was declaring that just as he intended to send Abraham's children into exile as punishment (see questions 88) *so too* would He judge the nation to whom they would be subjugated, and he would administer severe punishment to that nation for its wickedness. *Ramban* goes on to explain that although it was God's express will that the Jews be subjected to exile and enslavement, the nation that effected this condition would not be absolved of guilt by the claim that they were merely implementing a Divine decree (see the next question).

91. Why were the Egyptians deserving of punishment if they were merely instruments realizing the Divine Will that the Jews endure many years of exile and servitude?

Ramban (*Genesis* 15:14) states that Pharaoh and his people went too far in their subjugation of the Jews. Instead of treating them as ordinary servants, as God's decree called for, they embittered their lives with undue oppression of all sorts. Worse than that, the Egyptians actually sought to wipe out the descendants of Abraham entirely, with schemes that included casting all newborn males into the river. Their excessively cruel conduct, says *Ramban,* is what invited Divine retribution. Similarly, *Ramban* notes, although the heavenly court on Rosh Hashanah may have sentenced a person to death, those who murder him lawlessly are not exonerated. While they did, in fact, function as tools in meting out justice, their motives were impure and were not based on law, and they are guilty of murder. The Egyptians certainly did not have the covenant between God and Abraham in mind when they dealt with the Jews in such harsh fashion, and they therefore fully deserved the destruction they ultimately experienced. *Ramban,* though he disagrees,

The matzos are covered and the cups lifted as the following paragraph is proclaimed joyously. Upon its conclusion, the cups are put down and the matzos are uncovered.

It is this that has stood by our fathers and us. For not only one has risen against us to annihilate us, but in every

---

also mentions the view of *Rambam* (*Laws of Teshuvah* 6:5) who asserts that each individual Egyptian was guilty for his personal oppression of the Jews. While God had indeed indicated that enslavement and persecution of the Jews would take place on the part of a "nation," this foreknowledge and foretelling of events did not compel any particular Egyptian to carry out these acts. Each Egyptian participated in the Jews' subjugation of his own desire and volition. Had he chosen, he could have refrained from joining the masses, for God merely stated that the people *as a whole* would engage in enslavement.

וְהִיא שֶׁעָמְדָה ﷺ — *It is this that has stood*.

---

92. Why do we lift the cup of wine while reciting this paragraph?

Maharal explains that the second cup of wine corresponds to the word *vehitzalti* — and I will rescue you — which the Torah uses to describe God's role in the Exodus.[1] Thus, it represents the characteristic of His protective embrace, which not only saved us from destructive forces in the past, but continues to shield us from the many faces of evil that rise up against us to this day. This paragraph highlights the constant protection which God had afforded us throughout the ages. Thus, it is appropriate that we raise our cups, in the spirit of the verse, *I will lift up the cup of salvations* (Psalms 116:13), in order to commemorate the protective hand of God symbolized by this cup. *Aruch HaShulchan*, also citing the above verse, states that wherever we recall God's salvation, we do so with wine in hand. Wine, he explains, is the primary medium for the expression and celebration of great joy, as the verse declares: *For wine gladdens the heart of man* (Psalms 104:15).

Yalkut Shimoni offers a homiletic interpretation. Our sages, he notes, prohibited the consumption of non-Jewish wine to prevent socialization with non-Jews and, ultimately, intermarriage and assimilation. Thus, we lift up our cup of wine and say, *"It is this"* — the decree of our sages forbidding non-Jewish wine — *"that has stood by our fathers and us"* — preventing our destruction through assimilation.

---

1. See *Exodus* 6:6.

דּוֹר וָדוֹר עוֹמְדִים עָלֵינוּ לְכַלּוֹתֵנוּ, וְהַקָּדוֹשׁ בָּרוּךְ הוּא מַצִּילֵנוּ מִיָּדָם.

93. What is the Haggadah referring to when it says: *"It is this that has stood by our fathers and us"*?

Most commentaries agree that *"It is this"* is a reference to the words we have just quoted: God's assurance to Abraham at the Covenant Between the Parts that we would be rescued from the Egyptians' grasp and that they would ultimately suffer for oppressing us. At the time of the covenant, God revealed to the Patriarch *all* the future exiles and tribulations his descendants would have to endure, and promised that the fate of *all* who rise up against us would be the same as that of the Egyptians. *That guarantee,* says the Haggadah, is what has protected and preserved all succeeding generations of Jews.

There are, however, some notable departures from this generally accepted interpretation.

Aruch HaShulchan believes that the Haggadah is addressing the subject of our people's uniqueness. He points out that generally a nation ruled by another tends, over time, to lose its distinct identity and blend into the surrounding culture. Not so with the Jews, however. We have temporarily come under the sovereignty of many an alien civilization, yet have always managed to retain our separate status. The secret, he says, is rooted in the covenant between God and Abraham. Abraham was told to cut several animals in half, and place one half of each of the animals together; thus, it was as though they became one. The bird, however, represented the Jewish people. It was not divided at all, and it remained distinct.[1] This was meant to assure Abraham that the Jewish people would never forfeit their singular identity, regardless of the variety of cultural influences they would encounter during millennia of exile. And *that* (that aspect of the covenant), declares the Haggadah, is what has preserved us all these years.

Haggadas Sofrim echoes this idea, stating that it is the very fact that *"in every generation they rise against us"* that has kept us intact as a nation. Our persecution forces us to recognize our true identity, and to realize that until the arrival of the Messiah and our return to the Holy Land, we remain strangers no matter how well we fit into the surrounding environment.

---

1. See *Genesis* 15:10 along with *Rashi's* comments.

generation they rise against us to annihilate us. But the Holy One, Blessed is He, rescues us from their hand.

Bircas Avraham understands *"It is this"* to refer to the exile in Egypt and our subsequent redemption. These reinforce our faith in God and reassure us that no matter who rises up against us, if we will but repent from our sins and cry out to God, as our ancestors did in Egypt (*Exodus* 2:23,14:10), He will surely keep His word to Abraham and deliver us. Indeed, in this sense, the plots of our enemies are to our advantage, in that they remind us who we are and draw us nearer to God. In fact, *Chesed L'Avraham* notes, when the Haggadah says *"But the Holy One, Blessed is He, rescues us from their hand,"* it means that our salvation comes about through *their own hand.* By oppressing us, they motivate us to repent; and by inflicting suffering, they help us atone for past sins (Talmud, *Berachos* 5a).

In a similar observation, *Yalkut Shimoni* remarks on God's often causing the source of our rescue to come from the enemy himself! For example, Moses grew up in Pharaoh's own home (*Exodus* 2:10-11 and *Rashi*) and Haman was himself responsible for Esther becoming queen to Achashveirosh (*Esther* 1:16-19), the circumstance which later proved to be his downfall (*Esther* 7:6-10).

Finally, *Iyun Tefillah* suggests that *"It is this"* refers to the words God spoke to Jacob as the latter began his journey down to Egypt. God assured Jacob that he would accompany him on his descent into that foreign land and remain with him throughout his stay there. *That* guarantee — that God's presence is with us in our exile — declares the Haggadah, is responsible for our survival in every generation.

94. Why does the Haggadah use the unusual phrasing, *"For not only one has risen ... but in every generation they rise against us ..."*? It would have been simpler to state: "For God has always rescued us from those who rose against us."

Avudraham and *Maasei Hashem* say that God deliberately allows new foes of the Jewish nation to arise in every era. This provides Him with an opportunity to come to our aid to demonstrate and publicize His rule over the world, and the special relationship that exists between Him and His people. *Maasei Hashem,* as mentioned previously, maintains that the Egyptian exile was actually a privilege inasmuch as we served as tools for the manifestation of God's rule. He notes that the Exodus, and its proclamation of God's sovereignty, would have been forgotten long ago by the nations, if not for the fact that in every generation the Jews relive,

צֵא וּלְמַד מַה בִּקֵשׁ לָבָן הָאֲרַמִּי לַעֲשׂוֹת לְיַעֲקֹב אָבִינוּ, שֶׁפַּרְעֹה לֹא גָזַר אֶלָּא עַל הַזְּכָרִים, וְלָבָן בִּקֵשׁ לַעֲקוֹר אֶת הַכֹּל. שֶׁנֶּאֱמַר:

to a greater or lesser degree, this saga of persecution and exile followed by redemption. That, he feels, is what the Haggadah means to highlight here.

95. How can we say that "in every generation they rise against us"? Haven't there been periods when we lived in peace and security among the nations?

Chida explains this statement in a unique fashion. There are two ways, he says, in which the nations of the world present a challenge to Jewish perpetuity. One way is for them to oppress or attempt to destroy us, physically and/or spiritually. The other more insidious method is for them to embrace us as equals, and shower us with the favor of uniform rights and privileges. In such situations, we run the risk of joining their mundane and corrupt existence, and forfeiting our distinct identity as a "kingdom of priests and a holy nation" (*Exodus* 19:6). This danger is as great as — perhaps even greater than — persecution. Thus, the Haggadah is making a point of God's safeguarding us from both types of calamity.

❧ **צֵא וּלְמַד** — *Go and learn.*

96. What is the purpose of this paragraph?

Avudraham sees this as a continuation of the statement that God has come to our rescue throughout the ages. The Haggadah illustrates this fact by expounding upon the portion of the Torah known as "*mikra bikkurim*" (*Deuteronomy* 26:5-10) — the Torah portion read when one brought the first fruits of his harvest. These verses attest to God's deliverance of the Jewish people from some of those who sought to destroy them as they developed into a nation, specifically, Laban and the Egyptians.

Kol Bo's view is that the Haggadah is finally launching into the *details* of the redemption beginning with the initial descent to Egypt, which are neatly encapsulated in these verses. *Abarbanel* focuses on the Talmud's requirement (*Pesachim* 116a) to structure the evening's tale of the Exodus and tribute to God against the background of our transition from shameful roots to our ultimately worthy status. He notes that one could not choose a more appropriate text for discussion and praise. This group of verses

G o and learn what Laban the Aramean attempted to do to our father Jacob! For Pharaoh decreed only against the males, Laban attempted to uproot everything, as it says:

---

chronicles our ascent from ignominious beginnings to ultimate glory in the most succinct fashion, while including all the particulars for which we offer praise, like God's hearkening to our pleas, the plagues and other miracles inflicted upon our oppressors, and the actual Exodus. In fact, *Abarbanel* feels that the recital of these verses with the Seder plate — containing items commemorating the Egyptian experience and symbolizing our deep appreciation and glorification of God — before us is, in a sense, a reenactment of the ritual of offering first fruits.

Malbim reflects some of these thoughts, as well. He maintains that everything mentioned in the Haggadah until now, particularly the preceding section, was only an introduction to this — the main section of the Haggadah. Here, we are presented with the entire story of the Exodus in detail so that we may fulfill the Biblical requirement to retell it on this night and discuss it at length, in the praiseworthy manner prescribed earlier. As mentioned, the reason *this* portion of the Torah was chosen is because the actual sequence of events as spelled out in the Torah would take much too long to recount. In this select group of verses, however, all the fine points of the story are alluded to. *Malbim* further explains that the Haggadah goes on to cite an additional verse in support of each nuance alluded to in the exact wording of this section even though there often seems to be no inherent advantage in quoting one verse over the other. This is because the Haggadah's intent is not always to validate one particular detail, but to demonstrate that the verses of *mikra bikkurim* incorporate all the points described at length in the Book of *Exodus* or elsewhere, guiding us towards elaborate discussion of the redemption. It is for this reason that the supporting verse is generally introduced with the words *"as it says"* — underscoring the objective of analogy, rather than *"for it says"* — which indicates an effort to derive or substantiate.

97. What is the meaning of the Haggadah instruction to "Go and learn"?

Abarbanel explains that we should interrupt (*tzei* — go "out of") our preoccupation with the evil perpetrated by the Egyptians and focus on an even greater danger which was not ultimately realized but which seriously threatened our nation's existence at its very outset — Laban's designs against Jacob.

Maharal interprets the Haggadah's instruction in reference to the previ-

ous paragraph. We are being directed to appreciate the extent and invio-
lability of the assurance given to Abraham in the Covenant Between the
Parts by *exploring* how our enemies' plots to destroy us were consistently
thwarted by God.

The *Gra* points out that sometimes we are not even aware of the miracles
God performs on our behalf. In that vein, the Haggadah sends us to "go and
learn": Analyze what Laban attempted to do to Jacob. Ostensibly, he did
nothing at all. Yet, the verse states that he *"attempted to destroy my father."*
While his plan was never made clear to us, Laban's intent was to utterly
destroy Jacob and his family; and he would have done so had it not been
for God's preemptive admonition (*Genesis* 31:24). Thus, when we give
praise for Divine protection, we must also recognize that there were instances in which we were never even aware of the danger we faced.

Aruch HaShulchan agrees that despite the description in these verses,
what Laban wanted to do is unclear. In his opinion, it would require
expounding on several verses[1] to illustrate this one fact, and such lengthy
analysis is not the style of the sages who authored the Haggadah. Therefore, we are advised to "go and learn" — i.e., delve into the Torah and
discover just how Laban desired to do away with Jacob. Rather than read
the words as *"tzei u'lemad"* (צֵא וּלְמַד, *"go and learn"*), *Iyun Tefillah* suggests
that we should read the words as *tzei v'lamed* (צֵא וְלַמֵּד), "go and *teach."*
Read in this way, it is an exhortation to train our children to realize that just
as Laban's schemes were frustrated by Heavenly intervention, our continued existence, even today, is maintained only through Divine protection
against the wiles of our opponents.

98. Why does the Haggadah focus only on Laban and the Egyptians, and not on Esau and Amalek, who also stood in the way of our nation's development and sought our destruction?

Maharal observes that Laban and Pharaoh shared a common trait:
Their antagonism towards the family of Jacob was without legitimate
cause. This is why they are singled out as archenemies of the Jewish
people. Esau, on the other hand, sought revenge for the loss of Isaac's
blessings which, he felt, were rightfully intended for him and were
obtained, in his eyes, through Jacob's deceit. Thus, his hatred was
understandable. As for Amalek, *Maasei Hashem* explains that the war
with Amalek has yet to be concluded. It is an ongoing battle throughout
the generations, whose outcome will only be settled in the times of
Mashiach.

---

1. E.g., *Genesis* 31:24, 29, 43, etc.

99. In what way did Laban seek to "uproot everything"?

Both *Maharal* and *Malbim* understand the contrast presented by the Haggadah literally: The Egyptians sought to kill only the males, while Laban wanted to kill the females as well. They disagree, however, on the Scriptural basis for this fact. *Maharal* derives it from Laban's response to Jacob upon being rebuked for chasing after him. Laban declared that "The daughters are my daughters and the sons are my sons" (*Genesis* 31:43). Therefore, he argued, what harm could he possibly have wished upon them? Of course, as Laban himself alluded, these words were spoken only after God had warned him not to carry out any evil plans (*Genesis* 51:24,29). Thus, says *Maharal,* had he not been visited by God, we can assume that he would have considered neither the boys nor the girls to be "his," and would surely have killed them all.

Malbim's proof lies in the Torah's description of Laban as "*the destroyer of my father."* This, he points out, is a term which is not even applied to Pharaoh, despite the fact that the Egyptian ruler sought to wipe out all Jewish males (*Exodus* 1:22). Clearly, then, Laban's wicked designs went a step further than even Pharaoh's. His plans must have included the entirety of Jacob's family — males and females.[1]

Maasei Nissim and *Maasei Hashem* maintain that Laban sought to wipe out "everything" that Jacob inherited from Abraham spiritually. His aim was to lead the family back to idolatry, and this was only achievable if the family would remain under his influence. That is why he was reluctant to have them leave and he chased after them. *Maasei Nissim* claims this is evident from the fact that Jacob would, soon after Laban's visit, exhort those in his company to "discard the alien gods that are in your midst" before traveling to Beth-el in order to build an altar to God. Clearly, he was concerned over any lasting effects Laban may have had. *Maasei Hashem* states that the proof is to be found in the answer to another question: Why does the verse in this section connect Laban's actions to Jacob's descent to Egypt? On the surface, these two events appear unrelated, with much having transpired during the thirty-three-year interim. The explanation, he suggests, is that when the famine in Canaan forced Jacob to look to other lands for sustenance, he could easily have sent his children to Aram, the home of Laban, which

---

1. A simple reading of the Haggadah reflects *Malbim's* approach. *Avudraham* also seems to agree that Laban wanted to wipe out the entire family, though he refers us to the verse where Laban boasted to Jacob that if not for God's warning to the contrary, he could have done them much harm (*Genesis* 31:29). It is not clear from that verse, however, what particular harm Laban intended.

אֲרַמִּי אֹבֵד אָבִי, וַיֵּרֶד מִצְרַיְמָה וַיָּגָר שָׁם בִּמְתֵי
מְעָט, וַיְהִי שָׁם לְגוֹי, גָּדוֹל עָצוּם וָרָב. [1]
וַיֵּרֶד מִצְרַיְמָה — אָנוּס עַל פִּי הַדִּבּוּר.

---

was not affected by the food shortage.[1] The reason he did this was to spare his children another encounter with Laban and the dangerous influence of his heretical designs. Instead, he sent them to Egypt, an act which led to his own descent there. That is what the juxtaposition of these two events means to convey. (See the next two questions.)

100. Does the phrase "Arami oveid avi" necessarily mean "An Aramean attempted to destroy my father"?

Ibn Ezra, Sforno and *Malbim* inform us that the simple translation of the verse would be: "My father (Jacob) was a lost (or wandering) Aramean." The word *oveid* (אֹבֵד), they say, denotes the present tense of the intransitive verb "to become lost" or "to wander." The word meaning "to cause a loss" or "to eradicate" would be *"ibeid"* (אִבֵּד). Accordingly, the point of the verse is that Jacob was originally homeless, living for twenty years in the house of Laban in Aram. At that time, his family was not prepared to inherit and inhabit the land of Canaan. It wasn't until he took up residence in Egypt, grew into a large nation, and endured years of suffering that this became possible.

Rashi, Avudraham[2] and *Maharal,* however, translate the verse as the Haggadah does: *"An Aramean [attempted to] destroy my father."* *Rashi* and *Avudraham* note that literally the words say that "An Aramean destroyed my father." Although Laban did not succeed in implementing his wicked plans, the Torah views him as having carried them out nevertheless.

Maharal explains that the word *oveid* (אֹבֵד) is being used here as a defining term. It connotes that a person is "a destroyer." It was this *potential* for destruction which is the dominant feature of Laban's character with respect to his relationship towards Jacob. *Maharal* cites the example of a rock, which can be referred to as a stumbling block although no one has yet fallen over it; by its very nature and placement, however, it is there and will cause stumbling. Similarly, Laban was essentially a force for the destruction of Jacob (and would have

---

1. He bases this assertion on the fact that there is no Scriptural indication that Aram was affected. See *Ramban's* comment to *Genesis* 41:54.

2. Citing *Targum Onkelos, Deuteronomy* 26:5.

An Aramean attempted to destroy my father. Then he descended to Egypt, and sojourned there, with few people; and there he became a nation — great, mighty, and numerous.[1]

Then he descended to Egypt — compelled by Divine decree.

---

(1) *Deuteronomy* 26:5.

---

succeeded had God not intervened to protect Jacob). Thus, he merits the title "the destroyer."

101. What is the connection between Laban's persecution and Jacob's traveling to Egypt?

Maasei Nissim states that one element of the Egyptian exile was the need for the descendants of Jacob to be purged of the unwholesome influences absorbed through their ancestor's association with the wicked Laban. This was accomplished by having them endure the excruciating experience of slavery which crushed them to the core, then redeeming and reviving them with a fresh Godly spirit and purpose. Thus, the verse in *mikra bikkurim* is telling us that because of Laban's influence over Jacob, the latter was forced to eventually make his way to Egypt so that his family could recover spiritually.

In a somewhat similar vein, *Iyun Tefillah* and *Netziv* suggest that since the descendants of Abraham were destined to endure exile, as foretold in the Covenant Between the Parts, God could have had Jacob stay with Laban far beyond the twenty years that he actually spent there, and reckon that as the period of exile. This, however, would have been too severe a decree for the fledgling nation to withstand, since, as the Haggadah points out, Laban posed a greater threat than Pharaoh and his people. Thus, it was because *"an Aramean attempted to destroy my father"* that the descendants of Abraham had to go to the less dangerous exile of Egypt.

Rashi and *Avudraham* do not read any causal inference into the verse. They interpret it as a simple statement of gratitude, listing those who rose up against the Jewish nation in its infancy but did not prevail.[1]

102. What does the phrase *"compelled by Divine decree"* mean?

Rashi explains that God instructed Jacob to travel down to Egypt,

---

1. See the view of *Maasei Hashem* in question 99 for an additional solution.

וַיָּגָר שָׁם — מְלַמֵּד שֶׁלֹּא יָרַד יַעֲקֹב אָבִינוּ לְהִשְׁתַּקֵעַ בְּמִצְרַיִם, אֶלָּא לָגוּר שָׁם. שֶׁנֶּאֱמַר, וַיֹּאמְרוּ אֶל פַּרְעֹה,

although the Torah does not explicitly mention such a command. *Rashi* feels that the Torah's choice of the word וַיֵּרֶד, *he descended,* over וַיָּבֹא, *he came,* in describing Jacob's arrival in Egypt, indicates that he was sent, and that he would not have gone of his own volition.

Shibbolei HaLeket cites the verse in which God reassures Jacob, telling him not to be fearful about making the trip. He asserts that the Patriarch was loath to travel to Egypt because he foresaw that his descendants would ultimately be enslaved there. Nevertheless, he was "compelled" to go in order to be with Joseph.

Abarbanel interprets Jacob's reluctance as stemming from the fact that he desired, and felt that it was God's desire, that he reside only in the Holy Land. It was primarily this fear which God addressed in His reassurance. *Abarbanel* apparently agrees with the view of *Bircas HaShir* and *Malbim,* who contend that *"the decree"* being referred to by the Haggadah is the Divine decree of exile which was foretold to Abraham in the Covenant Between the Parts. It was the will of Heaven that Jacob's descendants end up in Egypt, and so, though they thought they were traveling there by choice, it was actually God's design to force them into exile. According to this approach, then, God did not expressly command Jacob to go. *Bircas HaShir* (quoting the *Gra*) also suggests that the notion of being *"compelled by Divine decree"* — and by decree alone — is in contrast to the metal chains in which the Talmud states that Jacob should have been brought down to Egypt.

Abarbanel mentions an additional opinion which maintains that the Haggadah's words are not to be read as one phrase, but as two separate points: *"compelled"* — Jacob was forced to travel to Egypt due to circumstance (either the sale of Joseph, and his subsequent reappearance in that country, or the famine in Canaan); and *"by Divine decree"* — God granted him permission to leave Canaan.

103. Why doesn't *"this teaches that"* appear before the phrase *"compelled by Divine decree,"* just as it precedes some of the other statements in this section? Similarly, why isn't the above statement followed by the words *"as it says"* and a supporting verse, as is the style in the following phrases?

Abarbanel tells us there are versions of the Haggadah that do not include the phrase *"onus al pi hadibbur (compelled by Divine*

He sojourned there — this teaches that our father Jacob did not descend to Egypt to settle, but only to sojourn temporarily, as it says: "They (the sons of Jacob) said to Pharaoh:

---

decree)".[1] Indeed, the paragraph in the *Sifri* which the Haggadah is quoting does not contain this exposition. *Malbim* explains that the *Sifri* was only interpreting the verse as it appears, and the simple implication of the verse is that Jacob went on his own. This is also implied by the statement that he went down to Egypt strictly on a temporary basis, intending to return home when the famine in Canaan would end. The Haggadah, however, with its aim to convey the full background of the story, inserts this piece of seemingly contradictory information. Thus, *Malbim* continues, *"this teaches"* would be inappropriate, because the statement is not being *derived* from the verse, but is being *added* by the Haggadah. This also explains why there is no supporting verse following this statement. Not being an intrinsic element of the verses in *mikra bikkurim,* it doesn't warrant looking to the original account of the story for elaboration.

104. Why does the Haggadah emphasize the fact that Jacob was *"compelled"* to go down to Egypt?

Maharal suggests that the Haggadah is highlighting that this event could not have been left to possibility, since this would have insinuated that the entire sequence of exile and redemption was nothing more than a chance occurrence. This, he explains, cannot be. Our redemption is a fundamental part of the world's development. As such, the events which led to our deliverance, including our descent into exile, were vital and inevitable, even as they are cloaked in the guise of free will. Therefore, the Haggadah stresses that although Jacob's trip apparently resulted from circumstance and free choice, the entire situation was carefully fashioned by God to insure that he travel to Egypt. In other words, while the immediate picture has Jacob in control, in the larger scheme of things, he was, indeed, *"compelled"* by God to go.

105. How does the Haggadah deduce from the words *"and he sojourned there"* (*"vayagar sham"*) that Jacob did not intend to take up permanent residence in Egypt?

Abarbanel offers two possibilities:
(a) The verse should have used the words *vayeishev sham,* "and he

---

1. See, for example, *Rambam's* text of the Haggadah.

לָגוּר בָּאָרֶץ בָּאנוּ, כִּי אֵין מִרְעֶה לַצֹּאן אֲשֶׁר לַעֲבָדֶיךָ, כִּי כָבֵד הָרָעָב בְּאֶרֶץ כְּנָעַן, וְעַתָּה יֵשְׁבוּ נָא עֲבָדֶיךָ בְּאֶרֶץ גֹּשֶׁן.[1]

בִּמְתֵי מְעָט — כְּמָה שֶׁנֶּאֱמַר, בְּשִׁבְעִים נֶפֶשׁ יָרְדוּ אֲבֹתֶיךָ מִצְרָיְמָה, וְעַתָּה שָׂמְךָ יהוה אֱלֹהֶיךָ כְּכוֹכְבֵי הַשָּׁמַיִם לָרֹב.[2]

וַיְהִי שָׁם לְגוֹי — מְלַמֵּד שֶׁהָיוּ יִשְׂרָאֵל מְצֻיָּנִים שָׁם.

settled there." Jacob himself spent 17 years in Egypt (*Genesis* 47:28) and was no less a permanent inhabitant than anyone else.[1] Since the word *vayagar* — *"and he sojourned"* — implies transience, and his stay was not temporary, it must be telling us Jacob's intent upon traveling to Egypt.

(b) The verse states that Jacob sojourned in Egypt, *"with few people."* This cannot apply to the period of the Jews' stay in the country, for we are immediately informed that they developed into a large nation even before being enslaved. It must, therefore, be referring to the time of arrival in Egypt, when he came with 70 people. It is this point in time that is described as Jacob's "sojourning" — a temporary stay. This teaches us that his arrival was with the intent of remaining only for a short while.

Malbim's view is similar to *Abarbanel's* second approach. He states that the words *"with few people"* really belong after *"Then he descended to Egypt,"* for it was at the time of his trip that Jacob's family consisted of *"few people."* Interpolating the words *"and he sojourned there"* teaches that his intention upon descending was only to dwell in the land for a short time. However, *Malbim* questions his own assumption that the word *"vayagar"* indicates a short-term stay rather than a permanent one. He asserts that the word can refer to a lengthy residence as well.[2] It is this issue, *Malbim* concludes, that the Haggadah sought to clarify by referring to the supporting verse, the statement of Joseph's brothers to Pharaoh. They explained to him that they came to *dwell* in Egypt *because* their animals could not graze in Canaan at the time. They made their stay dependent upon a specific, temporary circumstance. This establishes that their intention was to remain there only until that

---

1. Note that the Torah uses the word וַיֵּשֶׁב in reference to Jacob's stay in Canaan at a time when he hadn't yet been living there even ten years (*Genesis* 37:1).

2. As an example, he cites *Genesis* 47:9. *Rashi, Ritva* and *Abarbanel*, however, accept as given that *"vayagar"* means to reside temporarily.

'We have come to sojourn in this land because there is no pasture for the flocks of your servants, because the famine is severe in the land of Canaan. And now, please let your servants dwell in the land of Goshen.'"[1]

With few people — as it says: With seventy persons, your forefathers descended to Egypt, and now HASHEM, your God, has made you as numerous as the stars of heaven."[2]

There he became a nation — this teaches that the Israelites were distinctive there.

---

(1) *Genesis* 47:4. (2) *Deuteronomy* 10:22.

---

condition passed, and thus shows us that *"vayagar"* in this instance was to be a short stay.

106. In establishing that Jacob descended to Egypt *"with few people,"* why does the Haggadah not use the verse in *Genesis* (46:27) which describes the actual descent, rather than one from *Deuteronomy* which is retelling the story of Jacob's journey to Egypt?

Maasei Hashem explains that the Haggadah wishes to make clear that *"with few people"* is not an objective statement, for a family of seventy souls is not considered *"few people."* It is only that *relative to their future size* they were small in number when they traveled to Egypt, and through the beneficence of God, they increased and multiplied to the point where they could be referred to as being *"as the stars of heaven."* Thus, the Haggadah cites the verse in *Deuteronomy,* which communicates this relativity, rather than the verse in *Genesis,* which merely states that they went down to Egypt with seventy people.

107. How does the Haggadah deduce from *"There he became a nation"* that the Jews were distinctive during their stay in Egypt?

Ritva states that the key word in the verse is *"nation."* How is it, he asks, that a people could spend generations subjugated to a dominant, oppressive society, and still develop into a separate entity that could be referred to as *"a nation,"* even granting that they multiplied at an extraordinary rate? It must be that they stood out, remaining apart from their environment. *Netziv* and *Baruch She'amar* voice similar opinions, stressing that it was the choice of the term *goy,* "a nation," over *am,* a people, used to describe the Jews, which led the Haggadah to its

גָּדוֹל עָצוּם – כְּמָה שֶׁנֶּאֱמַר, וּבְנֵי יִשְׂרָאֵל פָּרוּ
וַיִּשְׁרְצוּ וַיִּרְבּוּ וַיַּעַצְמוּ בִּמְאֹד מְאֹד, וַתִּמָּלֵא הָאָרֶץ
אֹתָם.[1]

---

conclusion. *Goy, "a nation,"* generally depicts a people in glory and might,[1] sovereign inhabitants of a land, independent of others. Thus, the verse highlights that although the Jews were slaves, they nevertheless maintained a certain perceivably independent status. *Malbim* focuses on the word *"there."* This word, he says, is superfluous, for the verse just stated וַיָּגָר שָׁם, *"he sojourned there."* All that needed to be added was that he then developed into a great and mighty nation. The repetition of the word *"there"* indicates that the clause *"he became a nation"* is noteworthy in itself, because it tells us that the Jews retained a separate identity even as slaves. Furthermore, he notes that the word *"there"* emphasizes the role of the locale as it relates with regard to the matter being discussed. Thus, the message of the verse is that there *"he became a nation"* — *"there,"* in that alien environment, Jacob and his children were able to develop into a nation, because they steadfastly refused to blend in with their surroundings. *Malbim* adds that the Haggadah does not offer a supporting verse because this is the only place in the Torah where this feature of the exile is noted.

The *Gra* tells us that the word *goy, "nation,"* refers specifically to the aspects of a nation's identity which are reflected in its particular habits and customs. Thus, the verse is virtually unambiguous in its declaration that the Jews in Egypt carried themselves differently than the general populace. Indeed, our sages have indicated that they refused to submit to the lax moral standards of their host country or alter their manner of conducting themselves, particularly with regard to speech (see the next question).

108. In what way did the Jews stand out in Egypt?

Be'er Miriam writes at length to clarify this matter and its midrashic source, arriving at the conclusion that they were distinguishable in their dress, language and eating habits. These distinctions were a source of merit for which they were eventually redeemed by God. *Abarbanel* adds

---

1. See for example: *Genesis* 21:13, *Exodus* 19:6, *Deuteronomy* 4:6-8 and 28:50, *II Samuel* 7:23 and *Jeremiah* 5:15. Contrast with *Exodus* 32:9, *Deuteronomy* 32:6, *Isaiah* 1:4, 6:5 and 42:22 and *Jeremiah* 5:21.

Great, mighty — as it says: "And the Children of Israel were fruitful, increased greatly, multiplied, and became very very mighty; and the land was filled with them."[1]

---

(1) *Exodus* 1:7.

---

that they did not alter their names. *Kol Bo* and *Ritva* agree that the Jews stood apart in their manner of clothing, with the latter suggesting that the men even wore *tzitzis* (fringes) on their garments as the Torah would later require them to.

Avudraham, however, feels that the Jews stood out in terms of location. They all lived together in one area, the land of Goshen,[1] and not spread across many cities. This made them easily discernible as belonging to one nation.

Sh'lah HaKadosh interprets the Haggadah's characterization in terms of their singular pursuit of Godly knowledge. The poor downtrodden slaves never ceased studying what had been handed down to them from the Patriarchs, and thus succeeded in cultivating men of great stature and honor even under the wretched conditions of the exile. This was expressed by our sages in the statement: "Our forefathers lived without yeshivos" (*Yoma* 28b).

109. What do the words *"great, mighty"* refer to?

Most commentaries agree with *Abarbanel* that the word *"great"* refers here to the number of people; *"mighty,"* on the other hand, is a reference to great physical strength. He goes on to state that this latter point is one of several amazing characteristics of the exile which are highlighted by the verse *mikra bikkurim* which the Haggadah uses as the basis for our discussion. Our sages tell us that the Jewish women were regularly giving birth to six children at a time. Children of multiple births are generally underdeveloped and weak in nature, as they all have to share the nourishment provided by their mother's body. This was not the case during the Egyptian exile, however. The children of Israelites were well developed and of strong constitution.

Maharal, however, translates *"great"* as great in physical stature. In his view, the Haggadah places *"great"* and *"mighty"* together for they both describe the attribute of strength.

---

1. See *Genesis* 47:6,27, 50:8, *Exodus* 8:1, 9:26.

וָרֶב – כְּמָה שֶׁנֶּאֱמַר, רְבָבָה כְּצֶמַח הַשָּׂדֶה נְתַתִּיךְ,
וַתִּרְבִּי וַתִּגְדְּלִי וַתָּבֹאִי בַּעֲדִי עֲדָיִים, שָׁדַיִם נָכֹנוּ וּשְׂעָרֵךְ
צִמֵּחַ, וְאַתְּ עֵרֹם וְעֶרְיָה; וָאֶעֱבֹר עָלַיִךְ וָאֶרְאֵךְ
מִתְבּוֹסֶסֶת בְּדָמָיִךְ, וָאֹמַר לָךְ, בְּדָמַיִךְ חֲיִי, וָאֹמַר לָךְ,
בְּדָמַיִךְ חֲיִי.[1]

---

110. What is the implication of the word "numerous"? How does the accompanying verse from Ezekiel establish this point?

Shibbolei HaLeket and several others interpret the word as denoting quantitative greatness. What distinguishes this term from the previous description of the nation's size — "great" — is that it does not signify a static condition ("large") but a dynamic process ("increasing").

However, most commentaries take the position that "numerous" refers to the manner of the Jews' development. Abarbanel tells us that one extraordinary aspect of life in Egypt was that the Jewish children grew up by themselves, without the care and attention normally required to help children in their helpless and vulnerable infancy. Under the harsh conditions of slavery this level of attentiveness could not be maintained, yet, miraculously, the babies survived and flourished on their own. That is the point of the verse in Ezekiel — "I made you as numerous as the plants of the field." Just as they thrive by "nature's" hand, without constant human attention, so too did the children in Egypt thrive and grow. Furthermore, just as plants spring forth in a variety of colors and forms which no artisan can duplicate, so also did the Jews develop with an inimitable, inborn spiritual beauty, possessing qualities of character suitable to their future role as vessels for God's Torah.

Avudraham adds an additional parallel to plants. Just as the more a plant is pruned the more it grows, so too the Jews increased in population in proportion to the extent that they were oppressed (Exodus 1:12). Maharal and Malbim point to the fact that the "plants of the field" do not generally bloom in stages; instead, their stalks or leaves blossom at once. Likewise, the women in Egypt gave birth to many children at a time.[1]

Yalkut Shimoni focuses on the need for a seed to undergo decomposition before sprouting into a plant. The same is true, he says, of anything metamorphosing from one form of being to another; it must first achieve

---

1. Malbim says that the children also developed quickly, like the growths in the field.

Numerous — as it says: "I made you as numerous as the plants of the field; you grew and developed, and became charming, beautiful of figure; your hair grown long; but, you were naked and bare. And I passed over you and saw you downtrodden in your blood and I said to you, 'Through your blood shall you live!' And I said to you, 'Through your blood shall you live!' "[1]

---

(1) *Ezekiel* 16:7,6.

---

effacement of its earlier makeup before it can assume its new identity. Thus, the verse means to bring out that the Jews had to be suppressed into near non-existence before they could be rescued.

111. What does the verse mean by, *"but, you were naked and bare"*?

Rashi (in *Ezekiel* ch. 16) and *Avudraham* explain that the Jews were devoid — *"naked,"* as it were — of mitzvos in whose merit they would have been worthy of redemption. It was for this reason that they were given the mitzvos of Passover and circumcision. The double reference in the verse to blood as a source of life is an allusion to the fact that the blood associated with these two mitzvos was responsible for their freedom.

Malbim supports this interpretation by citing the story (Talmud, *Menachos* 43b) of how King David entered the bathhouse and bemoaned the fact that when he was unclothed he was standing without mitzvos. When he remembered the mitzvah of *milah,* however, he was comforted. *Malbim* explains that there are two types of mitzvos. One is external, meaning it requires contact or action with objects and factors outside of oneself — an article of clothing on which to place *tzitzis,* a doorpost on which to place a *mezuzah,* etc. The other is *milah,* which is a constant and is an integral part of the body itself. King David's original lament was that by being literally unclothed, he was also bare in a figurative sense, lacking the mitzvos of *tzitzis, tefillin*, etc. The mitzvah of *milah,* which was with him regardless of his current state of undress, served to "clothe" him once again. Thus, when bareness is a metaphor for being removed from mitzvos, there are two levels to speak of; one can indeed be physically naked, yet still "clothed" in mitzvos, and vice versa. The redundant language in the verse, *Malbim* says, is that not only were the Jews lacking all external mitzvos, they were even bare of the mitzvah of *milah.*

וַיָּרֵעוּ אֹתָנוּ הַמִּצְרִים, וַיְעַנּוּנוּ, וַיִּתְּנוּ עָלֵינוּ עֲבֹדָה קָשָׁה.[1]

וַיָּרֵעוּ אֹתָנוּ הַמִּצְרִים — כְּמָה שֶׁנֶּאֱמַר, הָבָה נִתְחַכְּמָה לוֹ, פֶּן יִרְבֶּה, וְהָיָה כִּי תִקְרֶאנָה מִלְחָמָה, וְנוֹסַף גַּם הוּא עַל שֹׂנְאֵינוּ, וְנִלְחַם בָּנוּ, וְעָלָה מִן הָאָרֶץ.[2]

◆§ וַיָּרֵעוּ אֹתָנוּ — *The Egyptians did evil to us.*

112. Why does the verse say *vayareiu osanu* — literally, "they made us evil" — instead of *vayareiu lanu* — "they did evil to us"?

Kol Bo, Abarbanel and *Netziv* translate these words as "they *made us out* to be evil." The Egyptians viewed the Jews as potential insurgents who were keenly aware of their weaknesses, and who would join forces with their enemies should a war arise (*Exodus* 1:10). *Baruch She'amar* adds that it means they made us out to be evil *in the eyes of the world*. In other words, the Egyptians told the nations that they were oppressing the Jews since they posed a risk to their security.

Yaavetz, on the other hand, understands that the verse implies that they made, or plotted to make, us wicked *in the eyes of God*. Their plan was to oppress and demoralize the Jews, for that might lead the Jews to rebel against their beliefs and the Creator for stalling or perhaps even revoking the Jews' promised redemption.

Chida interprets the words *vayareiu* as being rooted in the Hebrew word *rei'a*, friend. The verse thus means "they befriended us"; the servitude began by the Egyptians cajoling the Jews to join them, their hosts and friends, in building the country. This deceptive tactic was followed by, *"and they afflicted us; and imposed hard labor upon us."*

Malbim questions the need to search for alternate translations, showing that there are other verses that utilize the same, seemingly problematic form of grammar. He then offers a possible translation based on *vayareiv* being derived from *rei'a*, "thought" or "intent" (*Psalms* 139:2,17, *Ecclesiastes* 2:22). According to this approach the verse means "they thought about us." In other words, the Egyptians gave much consideration to the "Jewish problem," and busily plotted a "solution."

113. What point does the Haggadah seek to bear out when it recalls Pharaoh's advice to his people, *"Let us deal with them wisely . . ."*?

The Egyptians did evil to us and afflicted us; and imposed hard labor upon us.[1]

The Egyptians did evil to us — as it says: "Let us deal with them wisely lest they multiply and, if we happen to be at war, they may join our enemies and fight against us and then leave the country."[2]

---

(1) *Deuteronomy* 26:6. (2) *Exodus* 1:10.

Avudraham and *Malbim* explain that the Haggadah wants to underscore the connection between the incredible growth of the Jewish nation, discussed above, and its enslavement by the Egyptians. The fact that *"the Egyptians did evil to us and afflicted us; and imposed hard labor on us"* came *in reaction* to the preceding phrase, *"There he became a nation — great, mighty."*

Ritva's view is that the supporting verse, with its revelation of Pharaoh's premeditation and scheming, indicates that "the Egyptians doing evil to us" was only a first step of a larger program. It began with mild accusations and harassment and gradually progressed to full-scale oppression. He adds that this clever approach to the "problem" of the Jews was formulated partly out of embarrassment, so as not to appear inappropriate and uncivilized.

Maharal notes that no concrete evil act is described in the supporting verse, but only the contemplation of evil. Despite this, the Haggadah cites this verse in order to call attention to the fact that the Egyptians were *inherently* opposed to the Jews. This is borne out by the reality that only a true antagonist is consumed with plotting his enemy's destruction. In a similar vein, *Maasei Hashem* and *Bircas HaShir* suggest that the Haggadah wishes to prove that the Egyptians' intent in imposing labor upon the Jews was neither for the sake of heaven nor for their own practical benefit. Rather, their sole objective was oppression. This is plainly evident from Pharaoh's words: *"Let us deal with them wisely lest they multiply."*

114. What was the nature of Pharaoh's scheme for enslaving the Jews?

The Talmud (*Sotah* 11a) tells us that in order to entice the Jews to labor for him, Pharaoh had a mold for a brick hung around his neck, symbolizing his own participation in the menial tasks demanded of them. Thereafter, anyone who would refuse the call to work on the

וַיְעַנּוּנוּ — כְּמָה שֶׁנֶּאֱמַר, וַיָּשִׂימוּ עָלָיו שָׂרֵי מִסִּים,
לְמַעַן עַנֹּתוֹ בְּסִבְלֹתָם, וַיִּבֶן עָרֵי מִסְכְּנוֹת לְפַרְעֹה, אֶת
פִּתֹם וְאֶת רַעַמְסֵס.[1]
וַיִּתְּנוּ עָלֵינוּ עֲבֹדָה קָשָׁה — כְּמָה שֶׁנֶּאֱמַר, וַיַּעֲבִדוּ
מִצְרַיִם אֶת בְּנֵי יִשְׂרָאֵל בְּפָרֶךְ.[2]

---

grounds that he was too refined or delicate for such activity would be
reprimanded with the challenge: "Are you, perhaps, more refined and
delicate than Pharaoh himself"? In this manner, the Jews were coaxed
into assuming the role of slaves. The commentators elaborate on
Pharaoh's method. *Ohr HaChaim* (*Exodus* 1:11) describes how Pharaoh
first installed the Jews in the honorable position of overseers and
taskmasters of other laborers. In this capacity, they had to make up for
the deliberate underproduction of their charges. From there, it was a
short jump to actual slavery.

Ritva and *Avudraham* say that, initially, Pharaoh declared that the
work was urgent and would only last for one day, and, in a demonstration
of the matter's urgency, Pharaoh himself participated. Seeing how much
it meant to Pharaoh, the Jews took to the task vigorously and did even
more than was required, all in Pharaoh's honor. Thereafter, that
unusually heavy workload was continually requested of them, until they
were performing it on a regular basis.

In contrast to the other commentators, *Aruch HaShulchan* understands that the original intent of Pharaoh's scheme was to get the Jews
to *leave* the country, not to stay there in bondage forever.

**115. What is the meaning of the word "*parech,*" translated here as
"hard labor"?**

Rashi translates this term alternately as pressured, backbreaking work
(*Exodus* 1:13) and purposeless labor, meant to oppress and demoralize
the person performing it (*Leviticus* 25:43). *Rambam* (*Hilchos Avadim* 1:6)
rules that limitless work, which has no defined parameters in time or
volume, also falls into this category. The Talmud (*Sotah* 11b), in
describing how the term applies to the labor of the Jews, cites an opinion
that the word communicated the treachery and deception through which
that work was initially imposed upon the Jews. This is alluded to in the
words *peh rach* — "soft speech" — which are combined to form
"*parech.*" *Rashi* (ibid.) explains that Pharaoh cajoled and even paid the

And afflicted us — as it says: "They set taskmasters over them in order to oppress them with their burdens; and they built Pithom and Raamses as treasure cities for Pharaoh."[1]

They imposed hard labor upon us — as it is says: "The Egyptians subjugated the Children of Israel with hard labor."[2]

---

(1) *Exodus* 1:11. (2) 1:13.

Jews to work, until they grew accustomed to the labor. It was only then that he turned it into compulsory service.[1] In any event, the word *parech* certainly means cruel labor. The Talmud goes on to suggest that one of the oppressive habits of the Egyptians was to have the men do women's chores and the women perform functions usually reserved for men. The *Gra* cites this example when he interprets the word *parech* to include even a light form of labor if it is something one is unaccustomed to — and is offended by — doing.

116. Why was it necessary for the Haggadah to corroborate both elements of the verse (that they *"afflicted us"* and *"imposed hard labor upon us"*) separately? Are not the two notions virtually identical?

Quite clearly, they are not. The Haggadah associates a verse regarding taskmasters with *"and afflicted us."* This tells us that the "affliction" in question was something beyond the workload imposed on the Jews. *Malbim* explains that there were two distinct oppressions here. One was the overly difficult work that the Egyptians forced the Jews to do. The other was that the purpose of this work was solely to oppress them, not to serve some authentic need. The Haggadah supports this by citing the verse discussing taskmasters, which, according to *Malbim,* should be translated as "tax collectors." Traditionally, these were corrupt individuals who unjustly pressured people for money, and they forced the Jews to pay bribes in order to be left alone. This was even more troublesome and oppressive than labor.

Similarly, the *Gra* describes how Pharaoh tricked the Jews into working by engaging tax collectors to place heavy monetary demands on them. In order to meet their financial obligations, they submitted to labor. This was exactly what Pharaoh had in mind from the start.

Aruch HaShulchan also understands the sequence of verses in terms of finances. First, he says, Pharaoh sought to appropriate the Jews'

---

1. See the previous question.

וַנִּצְעַק אֶל יהוה אֱלֹהֵי אֲבֹתֵינוּ, וַיִּשְׁמַע יהוה אֶת קֹלֵנוּ, וַיַּרְא אֶת עָנְיֵנוּ, וְאֶת עֲמָלֵנוּ, וְאֶת לַחֲצֵנוּ.¹

וַנִּצְעַק אֶל יהוה אֱלֹהֵי אֲבֹתֵינוּ — כְּמָה שֶׁנֶּאֱמַר, וַיְהִי בַּיָּמִים הָרַבִּים הָהֵם, וַיָּמָת מֶלֶךְ מִצְרַיִם, וַיֵּאָנְחוּ בְנֵי יִשְׂרָאֵל מִן הָעֲבֹדָה, וַיִּזְעָקוּ, וַתַּעַל שַׁוְעָתָם אֶל הָאֱלֹהִים מִן הָעֲבֹדָה.²

resources monetarily, so he appointed tax collectors who were authorized to assess as high a levy as they desired. These people took so much money that they could afford to build the cities of Pithom and Rameses. That alone, however, was not enough to destroy the Jews. The verse tells us that as much as the Egyptians afflicted them, the Jews kept growing — in wealth. [52] And so, Pharaoh devised the idea of slave labor; not because he needed the labor, but because the Jews' oppression was the end unto itself. Indeed, *Malbim* and *Maasei Nissim* remind us that our sages (*Sotah* 11a) view the very names of the two cities, Pithom and Rameses, as alluding to the fact that the Egyptians never intended for these cities to remain standing; nor, for that matter, did they need them altogether.

Abarbanel, however, claims that in addition to the labor which Pharaoh placed upon the Jews (referred to as *"and afflicted us"*), each individual Egyptian made use of the Jews for his private needs, as personal slaves. That is what is indicated by the term *"hard labor."*

Maharal's opinion is that the *"affliction"* refers to the work itself, while the *"hard labor"* means to express that the load placed on the Jews was more than they could bear. That is why the Haggadah cites the verse of *"parech"* to support the latter point, for this word connotes work that is beyond one's capabilities.

___

וַנִּצְעַק אֶל ה' ‎ §⁓ — *And we cried out to* HASHEM.

117. What was the nature of the Jews' outcry to God?

Ohr HaChaim (*Exodus* 2:23) and *Maasei Nissim* assert that the Jews were not praying or crying out to God in repentance as it might appear

___

52. He cites *Genesis* 30:43 as proof that the words *vechein yifrotz* — "and so it would spread out" — in *Exodus* 1:12 refer to wealth.

We cried out to HASHEM, the God of our fathers; and HASHEM heard our cry and saw our affliction, our burden, and our oppression.[1]

We cried out to HASHEM, the God of our fathers — as it says: "It happened in the course of those many days that the king of Egypt died; and the Children of Israel groaned because of the servitude and cried; their cry because of the servitude rose up to God."[2]

---

(4) *Deuteronomy* 26:7. (2) *Exodus* 2:23.

---

from the primary verse here, which states, *"we cried out to HASHEM."* Rather, as the Haggadah illustrates through the supporting verse, they were simply groaning under the weight of crushing labor and bewailing their fate, *"and the Children of Israel groaned because of the servitude."* Mercifully, though, God listened to their cries of anguish and accepted them as prayer.

Most other commentators, however, view the Jews' cries as prayer *directed to God. Abarbanel* maintains that the verse in *Deuteronomy* (26:7) reveals what is not made clear in the verse in *Exodus.* In *Exodus,* it says only that they cried out *"because of the servitude"*; but in *Deuteronomy* it explains that they were actually calling out to *"the God of our fathers"* in supplication.

Yaavetz claims the verse *"We cried out to HASHEM, the God of our fathers"* is stressing that the Jews did not invoke the names of familiar Egyptian deities, but beseeched the God of their fathers. *Baruch She'amar, Be'er Miriam* and *Yalkut Shimoni* view this verse as indicating that the Jews prayed to be redeemed *in the merit* of their ancestors.

Netziv declares that the phrasing of the verse, *"min ha'avodah — because of the servitude,"* as opposed to *"al ha'avodah — concerning the servitude,"* tells us that the Jews were not skilled in the art and language of prayer. Thus, their cries were simply *"because of the servitude"*; they were an anguished cry caused by the situation, not a supplication in classic style which they offered concerning the labor. Nevertheless, God hearkened to their pleas.

118. How was the outcry of the slaves related to the death of the Egyptian king?

Malbim suggests that the death of Pharaoh offered the Jews a cover under which they could safely cry out to God regarding their terrible

וַיִּשְׁמַע יהוה אֶת קֹלֵנוּ – כְּמָה שֶׁנֶּאֱמַר, וַיִּשְׁמַע
אֱלֹהִים אֶת נַאֲקָתָם, וַיִּזְכֹּר אֱלֹהִים אֶת בְּרִיתוֹ אֶת
אַבְרָהָם, אֶת יִצְחָק, וְאֶת יַעֲקֹב.[1]

condition without fear of reprisal on the part of the Egyptians. This opportunity presented itself during the funeral and eulogies that accompanied Pharaoh's passing, when all the inhabitants of Egypt joined in mourning. To all appearances, the Jews were sharing in the grief over the loss of the country's leader. However, the verse tells us that they were really crying out *"because of the servitude."* Only God perceived the true meaning of their cry, as alluded to by the next part of the phrase, *"their cry because of the servitude rose up to God."* Others, however, did not understand that their cry was because of the servitude.

Maasei Hashem and *Netziv* claim that it was not until they had a chance to rest from their work that the Jews could take stock of their situation. Pharaoh's death afforded them such respite, either because the country was too preoccupied with the funeral to maintain the routine of labor, or because, as stated in the verse (*Exodus* 1:11), the building of the cities was undertaken *"for Pharaoh."* It would seem, then, that the work came to a halt when he died. *Maharal* suggests that only when the first king died they cried out, in fear that the new king would continue this program of oppression, whereas they had given up hope and were resigned to remaining silent while he was still alive. In a similar vein, *Daas Zekeinim* (ibid.) states that until Pharaoh's death, the Jews had reason to hope that his eventual passing would bring with it an end to the policy of oppression. But when he passed away and nothing changed, they finally gave vent to their distress.

Rashi quotes a *midrash* that Pharaoh had not actually died. Rather, he had become afflicted with *tzaraas,* and began, on orders from his physicians, to slaughter the children of his Jewish slaves so that he could bathe in their blood. It was this outrage which caused the Jews to cry out at this juncture.

HaShir VeHaShevach makes the point that the Jews had constantly appealed to God, except that their cries did not elicit response because the appointed time for the start of the process of redemption had not yet arrived. Now, though, it had. Therefore, the Torah gives us an account here of their prayer and its effect.

119. Why does the Torah use three different expressions to describe the Jewish outcry — ze'akah, shaavah, and naakeh?

HASHEM heard our cry — as it says: "God heard their groaning, and God recalled His covenant with Abraham, with Isaac, and with Jacob."[1]

---

(1) *Exodus* 2:24.

Maharal explains that there are three criteria for a prayer's acceptance by God:

(a) The person must be suffering in some way because of the circumstance he is praying for relief from.

(b) The subject of his prayer is something which truly merits entreating God, and is not a trivial matter.

(c) The person who is praying is not so distanced from God that his plea is deemed unworthy of consideration.

Therefore, *Maharal* goes on, we are first told that the Jews *"groaned,"* implying that they were truly suffering. It then says that their cries because of the servitude went up to heaven — it was a significant cause. Finally, we are told that God heard their pleas — they were not distanced from Him. Thus, the three terms found here represent the three underlying factors which insured the efficacy of the Jews' prayers. *Maharal* then presents another list of criteria:

(a) The person praying must concentrate and direct his words heavenward with all his heart.

(b) The opponents and prosecutors in heaven must not prevent the plea from reaching the throne of God, forcing it aside.

(c) It must be a "time of good will and acceptance" in the heavenly spheres.

Again, *Maharal* demonstrates that each of the three expressions used by the Torah is referring to one of these criteria. First, the verse describes how the Jews cried out, meaning their prayers were heartfelt and properly directed. Then it says that their appeals went up to God, and were not pushed aside. Finally, the Torah states that God did hear their pleas and accept them, indicating that the timing was auspicious.

120. The Torah only mentions a covenant made with Abraham (*Genesis* 15). Why, then, does the verse speak of a covenant with Isaac and Jacob as well?

Abarbanel explains that because God recalled His covenant with Abraham for Isaac and Jacob, and reaffirmed it for them, it is considered as if He had actually forged a covenant with them. He also suggests that the "three heifers" mentioned in the covenant with Abraham (*Genesis* 15:9)

וַיַּרְא אֶת עָנְיֵנוּ – זוֹ פְּרִישׁוּת דֶּרֶךְ אֶרֶץ, כְּמָה שֶׁנֶּאֱמַר, וַיַּרְא אֱלֹהִים אֶת בְּנֵי יִשְׂרָאֵל, וַיֵּדַע אֱלֹהִים.¹

represented the three Patriarchs, so that, in a sense, they were all "present" at that covenant.

121. Earlier the Haggadah interpreted the word וַיְעַנּוּנוּ [vaye'anunu] — "they afflicted us" (which is from the same root as the word עָנְיֵנוּ [anyeinu] — "our affliction"), as a reference to the physical oppression of the Jews when Pharaoh placed taskmasters over them *"in order to oppress them with their burdens."* Why, then, does it now explain this "affliction" in terms of the family separation that was imposed on the Jews — an act which is, in fact, not specifically mentioned in the Torah at all? Furthermore, how is *"the disruption of family life"* indicated by the supporting verse from *Exodus*?

Abarbanel explains that the Haggadah felt that the oppression indicated by the two terms וַיְעַנּוּנוּ and עָנְיֵנוּ could not be referring to the same phenomenon, because then the verse would be repetitive: *The Egyptians . . . afflicted us . . . and He saw our affliction.*" The Torah could have said more succinctly, ". . . and God saw what was done to us." Thus, the Haggadah concludes that there must be some difference between the oppression of וַיְעַנּוּנוּ and that of עָנְיֵנוּ — there must have been a second form of affliction involved in the Egyptians' treatment of their Jewish slaves. But what did this second type of maltreatment consist of? It was apparently a form of persecution that only God could see, as the verse says, *"He saw our affliction."* This is understood to refer to the abstinence practiced by the Jews. (*Abarbanel* understands that the separation was not forced, but voluntary. The people simply did not want to bring children into the world only to suffer such dire persecution.) After all, the word עִנּוּי (translated here as "oppression" or "affliction") is often used to indicate such abstinence (see *Yoma* 77b). The Haggadah then cites a verse from *Exodus* (2:25) which uses the same word as our verse — *"and God saw."* This cited verse, by virtue of its similarity in wording, is understood to be a reference to the affliction of our verse. The verse in *Exodus* adds an additional point that is not mentioned in our verse, however: God's *reaction* to the affliction that He saw. We are told that *"God knew."* The Haggadah relates this to the expression *"knew"* as it refers to marital intimacy. Thus, the meaning of the verse is that God inspired a change of attitude on the part of the Jews, by which they abandoned their pessimistic outlook and resumed "knowing" each other

And saw our affliction — that is the disruption of family life, as it says: "God saw the Children of Israel, and God knew."[1]

---

(1) *Exodus* 2:25.

---

through normal family life.

Maasei Nissim cites *Rashi's* comment on the verse in *Exodus*: "*And God knew* — He put His heart to the situation." That is, He realized that the time had come to act and to bring about the deliverance of His people. Thus, "God saw" has the connotation "God was stirred to action." What was it that caused God to become aroused in this way? As the previous verse (2:24, quoted by the Haggadah in the preceding paragraph) says, "*God heard their groaning, and God recalled His covenant with Abraham, with Isaac and with Jacob.*" But why would this prompt Him to take immediate, emergency action? Doesn't the covenant referred to in the verse specifically say that "*They will serve them and they will oppress them for four hundred years*" (*Genesis* 15:13)? The covenant did not call for redemption for another two centuries! Thus, we must conclude that God saw something in the manner of the Egyptians' persecution of the Jews that went beyond the "enslavement" and "oppression" that were allowed for in the covenant. The intimation of "*and He saw*" is thus — as it is in *Exodus* — "[God] was stirred to action by something extraordinary that He saw." The backbreaking labor imposed upon the Jews by the Egyptians was within the parameters of the persecution foreseen at the Covenant; that would not have been a cause to "stir God to immediate action." Rather, the Torah must be referring to an alternative meaning of the word עֲנֹ — namely, abstinence from marital relations — which went beyond the tolerated limits of oppression.

Baruch She'amar points out that whenever the word "to see" is used in the Torah it is always followed by a description of what it was that was seen. (For instance, "And God saw the light" — *Genesis* 1:4.) But in the verse cited from *Exodus* the object of the "seeing" is not adequately specified — "*God saw the Children of Israel, and God knew.*" What did He see in the Children of Israel that prompted Him to recall His covenant? It is for this reason that the Haggadah interprets the "seeing" as relating to a subject which, for reasons of modesty, the Torah preferred to leave vague. Thus, by citing this verse the Haggadah seeks to prove that there was such abstinence altogether, and that it was this abstinence that God "*saw.*"

וְאֶת עֲמָלֵנוּ – אֵלוּ הַבָּנִים, כְּמָה שֶׁנֶּאֱמַר, כָּל
הַבֵּן הַיִּלּוֹד הַיְאֹרָה תַּשְׁלִיכֻהוּ, וְכָל הַבַּת תְּחַיּוּן.[1]
וְאֶת לַחֲצֵנוּ – זוֹ הַדְּחַק, כְּמָה שֶׁנֶּאֱמַר, וְגַם

---

122. How do we establish that "our burden" is a reference to the infanticide practiced against the Jews?

Maasei Nissim maintains that the Haggadah intends only to show that the Egyptians killed the Jews' sons, not the fact that *"burden"* refers to one's children, for that is well known. Children are a parent's *"burden"* because of all the trouble one goes through in their upbringing, teaching them proper behavior and Torah, and through the toil that one undertakes in order to leave them some financial support (*Ritva*). *Shibbolei HaLeket* and *Abudraham* note that in *Ecclesiastes* 5:5 sons are referred to as "the work of one's hands," according to Talmudical interpretation. *Abarbanel* suggests that it is the children of that particular generation who are called *"burden,"* because of the many strenuous precautions their parents had to undertake in order to keep their birth and early upbringing hidden from Pharaoh's zealous secret police, who tried to enforce his brutal policy.

Malbim explains that the word *amal* — *"burden"* — generally refers to self-imposed labor which a person does without achieving the desired end. Oppression imposed by another person is never referred to by this word. Thus, the Haggadah knew that *"our burden"* could not refer to the forced labor imposed by the Egyptians. Rather, it must refer to something that the Jews toiled for, which the Egyptians subsequently deprived them of. The Haggadah points out that the bearing of children who the Egyptians subsequently killed fits this description perfectly.

In a more homiletic vein, *Bircas HaShir* recalls an interpretation that has been mentioned earlier. The Covenant Between the Parts called for a period of subjugation to last for four hundred years. If, however, four hundred years' worth of oppression would be experienced in a shorter period of time, God would redeem the people before the allotted time would elapse. So too, greater population growth would also effect an early deliverance. Thus, when the Egyptians began to practice infanticide they were indirectly causing an increase in the *"burden"* of work of the Jews, for through the ensuing population decrease, they would have to either work much harder or for a much longer period of time.

123. Why did Pharaoh spare the Jewish daughters? If it was because he pitied them, why do we find it appropriate to mention Pharaoh's gentler

Our burden — refers to the children, as it says: "Every son that is born you shall cast into the river, but every daughter you shall let live."[1]

Our oppression — refers to the pressure, as it says: "I have

---

(1) *Exodus* 1:22.

---

acts in the Haggadah?

Malbim explains that this last phrase of *"every daughter you shall let live"* is *not* fitting at this point, but it is mentioned anyway because we always try to avoid quoting a verse of the Torah without completing it, however irrelevant the rest of the verse may be to the topic at hand.

Others, however, explain that it was not out of kindness that Pharaoh spared the Jewish girls. The *Malbim* himself quotes an opinion of the sages that Pharaoh wanted to keep the girls alive for promiscuous purposes.

Bircas HaShir cites the well-known *midrash* that says that Amram (the father of Aaron, Moses and Miriam) divorced his wife when he heard about Pharaoh's decree. He did not want to bring children into the world only to meet a cruel death upon birth. The *midrash* continues to tell us that Amram's example was followed by many other Jews as well. Miriam, however, convinced her father (Amram) to remarry, because Pharaoh's decree was only applicable to half the unborn children (the males), while separation eliminated the possibility of having *any* children. Thus, *Bircas HaShir* explains, Pharaoh did not want to extend his decree to cover the girls as well as the boys, for then the Jews would all divorce their wives and there would be no babies at all for him to kill!

HaShir VeHaShevach explains that Pharaoh wished to dispose of the threat of insurrection while not losing his formidable slave work force. He accomplished both goals by killing the boys, who might one day form a rebellion, while sparing the girls, who were just as good workers as their brothers, but were less threatening militarily. Furthermore, he hoped that the extraordinary fertility exhibited by the Jewish women might be transplanted to his own people when these women would be forced to marry Egyptian men for lack of Jewish partners.

124. The Hebrew words *lachatz* (לַחַץ), translated here as *"oppression,"* and *dechak* (דְּחַק, "pressure") seem to be virtually synonymous. Why, then, does the Haggadah define one word in terms of the other? Furthermore, how does the supporting verse show that לַחַץ should be interpreted as "pressure" any more than our own verse?

According to *Abarbanel* the word *lachatz* can be understood in two ways:

רָאִיתִי אֶת הַלַּחַץ אֲשֶׁר מִצְרַיִם לֹחֲצִים אֹתָם.[1]

וַיּוֹצִאֵנוּ יהוה מִמִּצְרַיִם בְּיָד חֲזָקָה, וּבִזְרֹעַ נְטוּיָה, וּבְמֹרָא גָּדֹל, וּבְאֹתוֹת וּבְמֹפְתִים.[2]

It may refer either to physical manhandling, as in the verse "Balaam's leg was pressed (vatilacheitz —וַתִּלָחֵץ) against the wall," or it may denote a harsh, stressful attitude on the part of one's superior. The word dechak (דְּחַק), however, can only be used in the second sense. The Haggadah tells us that lachatz in our verse is to be understood as dechak. Not only did the Egyptians enslave the Jews with difficult labor, they also tormented them mentally by not allowing them any rest in their work. The reason the Haggadah opts for the second meaning of the word is that physical oppression was already mentioned in a previous verse (". . . they imposed hard labor upon us").

Another possibility suggested by Abarbanel (and also mentioned by Ritva) is that dechak refers to religious persecution. The Egyptians tried to persuade the Jews to abandon their beliefs and worship their own deities. According to this interpretation, we can understand why the Haggadah brings the supporting verse from Exodus. There it says, "I have also seen the oppression . . . and I recalled My covenant." What sort of persecution would prompt God to react by confirming His covenant with the Jews? Abarbanel explains that God means to say: "I have seen the perseverance of the Jews in their adherence to their ancestral religion and covenant with Me." Thus lachatz is shown to be a reference to religious coercion.

Maasei Hashem explains that lachatz can be understood as either a type of oppression which is enforced because of some benefit that the oppressor receives from it — such as enslavement — or as a kind of persecution that is motivated completely by deep hatred for the victim. Dechak, however, indicates only the second form of affliction. After the Torah tells us that "the Egyptians . . . afflicted us and imposed hard labor on us," which may be seen as acts of greed rather than hatred, it goes on to say that they also afflicted us with "affliction, burden and oppression." The Haggadah has already defined "affliction" as the disruption of family life and "burden" as the murder of Jewish infants, which are clearly acts of adversity motivated by hatred and not by personal greed. This is how the Haggadah concludes that the third element in this trio — namely, "oppression" (lachatz) — is also to be interpreted in the sense of dechak, or hate-motivated persecution.

Maasei Nissim understands dechak to be an added dimension to lachatz,

also seen the oppression with which the Egyptians are oppressing them."[1]

Hashem brought us out of Egypt with a mighty hand and with an outstretched arm, with great terror, with signs and with wonders.[2]

---

(1) *Exodus* 3:9. (2) *Deuteronomy* 26:8.

---

a very intense kind of oppression. Just prior to the Haggadah's supporting verse (*Exodus* 3:9) the Torah tells us, "I have seen the suffering (*ani*) of My people . . . *and I have also seen the oppression (lachatz) with which the Egyptians are oppressing them.* Now go, and I will send you to Pharaoh . . .." The implication is that the "suffering" of the Jews was not sufficient for God to redeem them, but that the additional factor of *"oppression"* was necessary. This is because "suffering" (*ani*) was foretold in the Covenant Between the Parts (*Genesis* 15:13). The *"oppression"* placed upon the people, however, was above and beyond what was allowed for in that covenant, and that is what prompted God to take immediate action. This is how the Haggadah knows that *"lachatz"* must be more than mere "suffering" in this case, but must refer to the more intense form of *"oppression"* which it indicates with the words *"dechak."*

---

§ וַיּוֹצִאֵנוּ ה׳ מִמִּצְרַיִם — *"Hashem brought us out of Egypt . . ."*
— not through an angel . . . nor through a messenger,
but the Holy One . . . Himself.

---

125. This statement seems to contradict the verse (*Numbers* 20:16): **"He sent a messenger (or "angel") and brought us out of Egypt." Furthermore, what is the identity of the messenger mentioned in that verse? Another seeming contradiction to the Haggadah's assertion is found in** *Exodus* **12:23: ". . . and He will not permit the destroyer to enter your houses to smite." Apparently there *was* an agent acting on God's behalf!**

The "angel" or messenger (the Hebrew word *malach* can mean either) referred to in *Numbers* 20:16 is either Moses (for prophets are sometimes called *malachim* — Rashi) or a heavenly angel (*Ibn Ezra*).

If the "angel" in that verse is Moses, we can resolve the contradiction to the Haggadah's statement by suggesting that Moses was God's messenger only to approach Pharaoh and speak to him, urging him to send out the Jews, which of course resulted, indirectly, in the Exodus. He was not

וַיּוֹצִאֵנוּ יהוה מִמִּצְרַיִם – לֹא עַל יְדֵי מַלְאָךְ, וְלֹא עַל יְדֵי שָׂרָף, וְלֹא עַל יְדֵי שָׁלִיחַ, אֶלָּא הַקָּדוֹשׁ בָּרוּךְ הוּא בִּכְבוֹדוֹ וּבְעַצְמוֹ. שֶׁנֶּאֱמַר, וְעָבַרְתִּי בְאֶרֶץ מִצְרַיִם בַּלַּיְלָה הַזֶּה, וְהִכֵּיתִי כָל בְּכוֹר בְּאֶרֶץ מִצְרַיִם מֵאָדָם וְעַד בְּהֵמָה,

---

directly involved, however, in the miraculous process of the Exodus itself, for that was the doing of God alone (*Shibbolei HaLeket,* quoting *Rabbeinu Yeshayah*).

Shibbolei HaLeket suggests another explanation, in the name of his brother *R' Binyamin.* When the Haggadah says that there were no agents involved when God took the Jews out of Egypt, it is referring only to the tenth plague (as the supporting verse clearly indicates), the smiting of the firstborn. Concerning the other nine plagues, however, the Torah always mentions the role that Moses or Aaron played in the onset of that particular punishment. It is this role that the verse in *Numbers* refers to when it mentions a "messenger."

As far as the verse concerning "the destroyer," *Maasei Nissim* explains that when someone acts on behalf of someone else out of his own free will, only then can he be called an "agent" for that person. However, if the "agent" is completely subservient to the one who sent him, and does not have the ability to contravene his sender's instructions, the "agent" is, in fact, no more than a "tool" in the hands of the sender, much like a club in the hand of a policeman. The destroyer was such a "tool," as the Torah testifies: "He will not permit the destroyer to enter" — the destroyer was completely subject to the directives of the One Who sent him.

Actually, according to several commentators, the word *hamashchis* should not be translated as "the destroyer," but as "the plague" (*Sforno, Shibbolei HaLeket, Abudraham*). According to one explanation of *Abar-banel,* it refers to the irate Egyptians, who wanted to stop the Jews' slaughter of lambs, which they considered sacrilegious. According to these interpretations, of course, the "contradiction" disappears entirely.

Abarbanel also cites the opinion of *Ran,* who explains that God was *accompanied* by angels during the plague of the firstborn. Thus, He attended to this duty personally, as the Haggadah says, but the destroyer was also present to do His bidding.

Maasei Hashem suggests that the destroyer brought a pestilence upon the Egyptians, but it was God Who actually killed the firstborn among them. He uses this approach to resolve several other difficulties in this

HASHEM brought us out of Egypt — not through an angel, not through a *seraph,* not through a messenger, but the Holy One, Blessed is He, in His glory, Himself, as it says: "I will pass through the land of Egypt on that night; I will slay all the firstborn in the land of Egypt from man to beast;

---

passage. Firstly, why did *all* Jewish houses have to smear their doorposts with blood as a sign, and not just those where there was a firstborn? Also, if the destroyer could not distinguish between Jew and Egyptian without the help of a sign, how could he differentiate between the firstborn and the non-firstborn? The answer is that the destroyer certainly could not distinguish between Jew and Egyptian, much less between firstborn and non-firstborn. Thus, he struck *all* of the Egyptians with pestilence, but he spared those houses where he saw the blood smeared. [This explains why, when God began to cause the deaths of the firstborn, the Egyptians, who had all been stricken with illness, said, "We are all dying" (*Exodus* 12:33), not yet realizing that the punishment of death was limited to the firstborn.] Thus, all the Jewish homes needed protection from him. [This also explains why the Torah says, "The plague of the destroyer will not be among you" (loc. cit., v. 13). Not only would there be no *death* among them, for God would not permit that, but even the *pestilence,* which was entrusted to the hands of the destroyer, would not affect them if they would smear their doorposts with the blood as a sign.]

Yalkut Shimoni brings the following explanation in the name of the *Gra.* Based on their numbers, the rules of probability would dictate that several Jews should have died of natural causes on that night. Therefore God promised the Jews that no Jews would die that night. He would not allow the destroyer — the angel of death — to enter their homes on that night. The plague of the firstborn was indeed administered directly and solely by God, and the destroyer mentioned in the verse is totally unrelated to this plague.

126. How does the Haggadah see in the verse that God acted alone, and not through an agent?

Kol Bo explains that since the word "HASHEM" was already mentioned in the preceding verse ("and HASHEM heard our cry, and He saw . . ."), the Torah could have simply continued using the pronoun "He" — "*He* brought us out of Egypt." Since the verse repeats HASHEM's name, the Haggadah understands that this is to indicate a special, direct intervention by God.

וּבְכָל אֱלֹהֵי מִצְרַיִם אֶעֱשֶׂה שְׁפָטִים, אֲנִי יְהוָה.¹

וְעָבַרְתִּי בְאֶרֶץ מִצְרַיִם בַּלַּיְלָה הַזֶּה — אֲנִי וְלֹא מַלְאָךְ.
וְהִכֵּיתִי כָל בְּכוֹר בְּאֶרֶץ מִצְרַיִם — אֲנִי וְלֹא שָׂרָף. וּבְכָל
אֱלֹהֵי מִצְרַיִם אֶעֱשֶׂה שְׁפָטִים — אֲנִי וְלֹא הַשָּׁלִיחַ. אֲנִי
יְהוָה — אֲנִי הוּא, וְלֹא אַחֵר.

בְּיָד חֲזָקָה — זוֹ הַדֶּבֶר, כְּמָה שֶׁנֶּאֱמַר, הִנֵּה יַד יְהוָה
הוֹיָה בְּמִקְנְךָ אֲשֶׁר בַּשָּׂדֶה, בַּסּוּסִים, בַּחֲמֹרִים בַּגְּמַלִּים

---

127. — Who are these *"gods of Egypt"* and why doesn't the Torah describe the judgments executed upon them?

Rashi explains, "The wooden [idols] rotted and the metal [idols] melted." *Ramban* comments, "The Torah does not specify what these judgments would be, because it does not want to bother dealing with these worthless pieces of wood. Similarly, during the actual plague of the firstborn, when these judgments were presumably carried out, the Torah makes no mention of them, and they are mentioned again only on the following day, when 'the Egyptians were burying those whom God had killed among them, all the firstborn, and He had executed judgments upon their gods.' This is because the Egyptians were so frightened by what was happening to their firstborn, they did not notice what had happened to their idols until the next day, when they went to visit their temples. My own opinion (as opposed to *Rashi*'s), however, is that the *'gods of Egypt'* mentioned here refer to the celestial beings who represent Egypt in Heaven, for, as mentioned in *Tanach,* every nation has a representative angel in Heaven. It was these Heavenly forces which God subdued when He vanquished Egypt."

128. Why was it necessary for *all* Jewish houses to have blood smeared on their doorposts, and not only those houses where firstborn were living?

Bircas HaShir has an interesting explanation for this. (A similar answer is also quoted by *Yalkut Shimoni* in the name of *Chesed L'Avraham.*) Let us begin by addressing another question. *Rashi* tells us, based on the words "there will not be *among you* any pestilence" (*Exodus* 12:13), that if an Egyptian firstborn would realize that the Jews were not being affected by the plague and would try to hide in a Jewish home, he would nevertheless be struck down. The question arises, then: How can the Torah say that God "passed over" the Jewish houses? He in fact did enter some of these

and upon all the gods of Egypt will I execute judgments. I, HASHEM."[1]

"I will pass through the land of Egypt on that night" — I and no angel. "I will slay all the firstborn in the land of Egypt" — I and no *seraph*. "And upon all the gods of Egypt will I execute judgments" — I and no messenger. "I, HASHEM" — it is I and no other.

With a mighty hand — refers to the pestilence, as it says: "Behold, the hand of HASHEM is against your livestock which are in the field, the horses, the donkeys, the camels,

---

(1) *Exodus* 12:12.

---

houses, to strike down any Egyptians who were hiding out there! Furthermore, if it was the destroyer who administered the plague of the firstborn (ibid., 12:23), and the destroyer, once set loose, was not capable of distinguishing between a person of one nationality and another, as *Rashi* says (and as the Torah implies by the necessity of smearing blood as a sign), once the destroyer entered the house to slay the Egyptian, the Jewish firstborn in that house should have been killed as well!

Bircas HaShir explains that the slaying of the known firstborn was delegated to the destroyer. But when it came to those firstborn who required a process of identification or selection because they were hiding among Jews, it was necessary for God Himself to deliver the plague, since the destroyer was incapable of making such distinctions. This is why the Torah says, "HASHEM will pass over (or, as Targum renders: "will have mercy on") that doorway and not permit the destroyer to enter your house." God had mercy on these houses in the sense that he did not allow the destroyer to enter them, but He Himself did enter them if necessary, to deal with any Egyptian seeking shelter there. (See question 125 for *Maasei Hashem's* answer to this question.)

According to this explanation, we can now understand how the Haggadah can say that God's deliverance of the Jews was carried out directly, and not through means of agents and messengers, although the Torah specifically speaks of the destroyer (see also question 125). Both statements are true — part of the plague was administered by God and part by the destroyer, as explained above.

129. Why is the plague of pestilence, more than the other nine plagues, referred to as "God's *mighty hand*"?

בַּבָּקָר וּבַצֹּאן, דֶּבֶר כָּבֵד מְאֹד.[1]

Several commentators suggest that since the pestilence was the fifth of the plagues, and each plague is called *"the finger of God"* (*Exodus* 8:15), it was this plague that showed the fifth finger — the complete hand — of God (*Baruch She'amar, Maasei Nissim, Gra*). The *Gra* adds that these five fingers of the *"hand"* of the pestilence may be said to stand for the five victims that were affected by it — horses, donkeys, camels, cattle and sheep (*Exodus* 9:3). He also points out that the *second* set of five plagues also ends off with a *"hand"* — the *"outstretched arm"* which the Haggadah associates (in the next paragraph) with the *"sword"* which the angel of death wielded against the firstborn in the tenth plague.

But why is the plague of pestilence referred to as God's *"mighty hand"*? *Baruch She'amar* cites a *midrash* which discusses an incident which is retold at the end of the Book of *Samuel*. King David was told to choose one of three punishments to be meted out to him and his nation (for having commissioned a census of the people) — a disastrous war, a famine, or a pestilence. David responded, "Let us fall into the hand of HASHEM, for His mercies are abundant; but let me not fall into man's hand" (*II Samuel* 24:14) — meaning that he chose pestilence over famine or war.[1] The *midrash* explains that had David chosen war or famine, the people would have accused him of selfish interests, as wealthy people are always the least affected in times of famine, and the king is always the most protected person in times of war. Pestilence was the only one of the three choices that would affect all segments of the population with relentless, absolute equality. It is this inescapability from the ravages of disease, says *Baruch She'amar*, that accords it the description of the *"mighty hand"* of God.

Another approach is taken by *Bircas HaShir*. He says that generally when a contagious disease strikes all kinds of animals, it affects humans as well. In this case the air which carried the disease throughout the fields of Egypt miraculously did not affect the populated towns that were in between them. This unnatural occurrence showed the *"mighty hand"* of God — that He manipulated the usual course of nature in order to

---

1. It is interesting to note that in this verse also pestilence is referred to as *"the hand of HASHEM."* *Rashi* (in *II Samuel*) explains that famine can be caused by man as well as by God, as when "shortage" is created by people hoarding food. And we can certainly understand why war is considered to be "the hand of man" rather than being a direct punishment from God. Pestilence, however, can be brought about only by God, and there is no human hand involved whatsoever.

הגדה של פסח — כי ישאלך בנך / 130

the cattle, and the sheep — a very severe pestilence."[1]

---

(1) *Exodus* 9:3.

---

ensure that this plague would affect only the livestock and not the humans.

130. — Now that the Haggadah has identified the *"mighty hand"* of God as the plague of pestilence, what is the meaning of the entire phrase, *"HASHEM brought us out of Egypt with a mighty hand"*? It was through the plague of the firstborn that the Egyptians ultimately sent the Jews out, not through the pestilence, which was only the fifth plague!

R' Shlomo Alkabetz cites the verse, "For now I could have sent My hand and stricken you and your people with the pestilence and you would have been obliterated from the earth. However, for this have I let you endure, in order to show you My strength, and so that My Name may be declared throughout the world" (*Exodus* 9:15-16). This teaches us that in fact the Jews by right should have left Egypt after the pestilence, and it was only so that God's Name could be glorified through the total ruination of Egypt that the Exodus did not take place then. It is interesting to note that it is, in fact, only after this plague that the Torah tells us that "HASHEM hardened Pharaoh's heart." The decree and framework for the release of the Jews and the punishment of the Egyptians had already been set; from this point on, Pharaoh only acted as an instrument in the hands of God.

131. Why is the pestilence, of all the ten plagues, singled out for special reference in this paragraph?

Shibbolei HaLeket and *Malbim* both quote the *midrash* that says that *each* of the ten plagues was accompanied by the additional element of pestilence. The verse thus speaks not about just one of the ten plagues, but about a facet that was present in all of the plagues.

Netziv and *Aruch HaShulchan* both suggest that the "pestilence" that the Haggadah associates with God's *"mighty hand"* is not the plague of pestilence that God brought upon the Egyptians, but rather the pestilence by which, according to the *midrash,* He eliminated many thousands of *Jews* who were not deemed worthy of leaving Egypt, during the three days of darkness. This explains the uniqueness of pestilence in this context, as well as why the Torah says, "HASHEM brought us out of Egypt with a mighty hand" — i.e., after removing those Jews deemed unworthy to participate in the Exodus (see question 130).

131 / THE HAGGADAH WITH ANSWERS

וּבִזְרֹעַ נְטוּיָה – זוֹ הַחֶרֶב, כְּמָה שֶׁנֶּאֱמַר, וְחַרְבּוֹ
שְׁלוּפָה בְּיָדוֹ, נְטוּיָה עַל יְרוּשָׁלָיִם.[1]
וּבְמֹרָא גָּדֹל – זוֹ גִּלּוּי שְׁכִינָה, כְּמָה שֶׁנֶּאֱמַר, אוֹ
הֲנִסָּה אֱלֹהִים לָבוֹא לָקַחַת לוֹ גוֹי מִקֶּרֶב גּוֹי, בְּמַסֹּת,

---

132. How can we say that *"an outstretched arm"* refers to the sword — there is no *"sword"* mentioned in connection with the Exodus from Egypt. To which sword, then, is the Haggadah referring?

There is a *midrash* on the verse "[Give thanks to] Him Who struck the Egyptians *by their firstborns"* (Psalms 136:10) that explains that when the firstborn among the Egyptians heard what the tenth plague was to be, they rose up against Pharaoh and his advisers and demanded that the Jews be released immediately. During this uprising they killed many of their countrymen, and it is concerning this rebellion that the verse in *Psalms* says that the Egyptians "were struck *by their firstborns."* *Avudra-ham,* as well as *Kol Bo* and *Shibbolei HaLeket,* suggest that it is this *"sword"* of uprising that the Haggadah refers to here.

Most commentators (*Abarbanel, Gra, Malbim,* etc.) explain that the sword referred to is the *"sword"* of the angel of death, which was wielded against the firstborn. *Bircas HaShir* adduces a statement in the Talmud that compares the angel of death's "handiwork" to the slitting of the throat. *Abarbanel* notes that the supporting verse also deals with the sword of the angel of death, similarly unsheathed in an act of mass death.

The *Netziv* cites the *midrash* that death reigned in Egypt between each of the plagues, to fill in the "gaps" between them, thus ensuring that the Egyptians would not be able to recover from any of the calamities inflicted on them sufficiently for them to retaliate against the Jews. It is the *"sword"* of the angel of death which was wielded on *these* occasions, suggests the *Netziv,* that the Haggadah is referring to here.

133. What is the difference between God's *"mighty hand"* and His *"outstretched arm"*?

Maasei Nissim explains that the ten plagues may be divided into two groups. After each of the first five plagues, Pharaoh "hardened his heart" and did not allow himself to be chastened by God's punishment. After each of the last five, however, it was God Who hardened Pharaoh's heart; he had already lost the privilege of repenting of his sins. The first five

With an outstretched arm — refers to the sword, as it says: "With his sword drawn in his hand, stretched out over Jerusalem."[1]

With great terror — alludes to the revelation of the *Shechinah,* as it says: "Or has God ever attempted to take unto Himself a nation from the midst of another nation

---

(1) *I Chronicles* 21:16.

---

plagues are represented by the last of that group — the pestilence — and the last five plagues are in turn represented by their last component — the *"sword"* of the plague of the firstborn. The *Zohar* explains that the term the angel with the outstretched sword (cited by the Haggadah here from *I Chronicles*) means that the angel had full authorization from Above to carry out immediate, summary justice. Thus, the last five plagues, when Pharaoh had already lost any chance of redeeming himself, are categorized as the *"outstretched arm."* The first five plagues, however, when Pharaoh was constantly offered the opportunity to change his ways, showed only the might of God's hand, but not the attribute of His arm being outstretched, poised for immediate retribution.

&§ וּבְמֹרָא גָּדֹל &§ — *With great terror*

---

134. — What is meant by *"the revelation of the Shechinah,"* and where in the story of the Exodus did this take place?

Ritva explains that God revealed Himself three times during the process of the Exodus from Egypt: once at the beginning of Nissan, when He told Moses and Aaron the laws of the Passover sacrifice — at which time, the *midrash* says, His voice was heard throughout the land of Egypt; a second time on the night of the Exodus itself (when He *Himself* passed through the land of Egypt, killing every firstborn in the land of Egypt — *Exodus* 12:12); and a third time at the Splitting of the Red Sea (when the people *"saw* His great hand" and sang out, "This is my God" — *Exodus* 14:31, 15:2).

Malbim explains that the constant manifestations of God's mastery over the forces of nature, as He performed miracles and wonders to punish the Egyptians and redeem the Israelites, is what the Haggadah calls *"the revelation of the Shechinah,"* for the might and omnipotence of God was truly revealed for all to see.

According to *Bircas HaShir* the "revelation of the *Shechinah* " refers to

בְּאֹתֹת, וּבְמוֹפְתִים, וּבְמִלְחָמָה, וּבְיָד חֲזָקָה, וּבִזְרוֹעַ
נְטוּיָה, וּבְמוֹרָאִים גְּדֹלִים, כְּכֹל אֲשֶׁר עָשָׂה לָכֶם יהוה
אֱלֹהֵיכֶם בְּמִצְרַיִם לְעֵינֶיךָ.[1]

---

the fact that it was God Himself Who personally inflicted the plague of the firstborn upon the Egyptians, rather than sending an angel or other agent to administer it, as was established above.

A novel interpretation of *"the revelation of the Shechinah"* is given by *Yalkut Shimoni,* who asserts that the Haggadah means the revelations *made by* God when He searched out and discovered all the known and unknown firstborn males in Egypt, as the *midrash* relates. According to this explanation we can readily understand why the Haggadah equates the revelation of the *Shechinah* to the *"great terror"* of our verse. Anyone who witnessed God's ability to recognize the deepest, most intimate secrets of man was immediately struck with a sense of profound fear and terror of God's omniscience and power.

135. Why did God deem it necessary to provide this uncustomary *"revelation of the Shechinah"*?

Malbim, who explained the *"revelation of the Shechinah"* as referring to the suspension of the laws of nature (see above), asserts that this display of miracles was necessary in order to wean the Israelites away from the state of impurity and idolatry to which they had gradually descended as a result of their prolonged contact with the Egyptians. This, in fact, is the main reason why God saw fit to draw out the ordeal of the Egyptians for several months, with plague after miraculous plague. Had He stricken the Egyptians with one sudden, horrible blow to induce them to free the Jews, it would not have been enough to purge the Jews of the moral impurities which they had so thoroughly absorbed over the years.

Bircas HaShir, who interprets the *"revelation of the Shechinah"* to be a reference to God's personal involvement in the plague of the firstborn (see above), cites the *Arizal,* who explained that this personal participation was necessary because the depravity and impurity of Egypt was so potent that even an angel might have been adversely affected by being exposed to it. He notes that the numerical value of the word *gilui* (גִּלּוּי) — revelation — is 49, representing the 49 levels of impurity to which the Jewish people had sunk at the time. To this the Haggadah adduces the supporting verse *"Or has God ever attempted to take. . .,"* which proves that there was a "personal" intervention on God's part in the redemption

by trials, signs, and wonders, by war and with a mighty hand and outstretched arm and by great terrors, as all that HASHEM, your God, did for you in Egypt, before your eyes?"[1]

---

(1) *Deuteronomy* 4:34.

---

of the people. (See question 137, which discusses more fully how the supporting verse proves the point of the main verse.)

136. Why does the Haggadah relate *"great terror"* to *"the revelation of the Shechinah"*? What is the connection between the two?

Rashi explains that the word *mora* (מוֹרָא) (translated here as *"terror"*) can also be understood as being derived from the root ראה, "to see," and the meaning of the word would then be "a sighting" or "witnessing." (This is indeed how Targum translates the word here.[1]) The relationship to *"revelation of the Shechinah"* thus becomes quite clear.

In a similar vein, *Baruch She'amar* suggests that the word *mora* is a transmutation of the word *ma'or* (מָאוֹר), "light" or "brilliance." Here, too, the connection to the *Shechinah's* revelation becomes apparent.

According to *Ritva* (and *Avudraham*), whenever the *Shechinah* is beheld by a person he becomes frightened and awed by its glory and he falls on his face. Thus a *"revelation of the Shechinah"* is equated here with *"great terror."* *Netziv* illustrates this phenomenon by pointing out that several times during the Jews' forty years of travel in the desert, when there was a spirit of dissension or rebellion among the people, there was a sudden appearance of God's glory, upon which the people immediately fell silent and ceased their contentiousness (see *Exodus* 16:10, *Numbers* 14:10, 16:19, 17:7, 20:6).

137. How does the Haggadah confirm the assertion that the *"great terror"* of the verse means a *"revelation of the Shechinah"*?

Malbim explains that this verse lends support to the thesis that he developed earlier — that *"the revelation of the Shechinah"* was necessary in order to make a sufficient impact upon the Jews to induce them to abandon their evil, idolatrous ways that they had adopted from the Egyptians. This supporting verse explains the way that God *"took us unto Himself . . . from the midst of another nation,"* i.e., how He formed a separation between the Egyptians and their equally corrupt Jewish neighbors — it was *"with trials, signs, etc.,"* which enabled the Jews to

---

1. Similarly, *Rashi* adduces from the end of the verse which the Haggadah cites — where it says that *mora'im* were *"before your eyes,"* that *mora* implies seeing.

וּבְאֹתוֹת — זֶה הַמַּטֶּה, כְּמָה שֶׁנֶּאֱמַר, וְאֶת הַמַּטֶּה
הַזֶּה תִּקַּח בְּיָדֶךָ, אֲשֶׁר תַּעֲשֶׂה בּוֹ אֶת הָאֹתֹת.[1]

gather the spiritual fortitude necessary to elevate themselves above the depravities of the environment to which they had become accustomed. Thus, the supporting verse establishes that there was indeed a *"revelation of the Shechinah,"* and that it took place through the wonders and miracles which God wrought in Egypt.

Rashbam (reflecting the interpretation given by *Bircas HaShir* in question 135) explains that the *"revelation of the Shechinah"* mentioned refers to the fact that God Himself delivered the fatal blow to the Egyptian firstborn during the tenth plague. This assertion is verified by the supporting verse, which indeed speaks of God Himself going among the Egyptians and separating the Jews from their midst.

Maasei Nissim explains this passage by quoting the Talmud (*Pesachim* 87b) which states that when Moses shattered the Tablets of the Ten Commandments (*Exodus* 32:19), the letters that had been engraved on them "ascended up to Heaven." To prove this assertion the Talmud cites the verse, ". . . and I smashed them before your eyes" (*Deuteronomy* 9:17). How does this verse prove that the letters of the Tablets ascended Heavenward? *Rashi* explains that since the Torah used *"before your eyes"* (*le'eineichem*) rather than the more common *"before you"* (*lifneichem*), it is implying that something beyond the physical smashing of the Tablets mentioned explicitly in the verse was seen by the people. We may thus conclude that whenever the Torah uses *"before your eyes"* it refers to some extraordinary, spiritual vision, as opposed to the simple witnessing of a physical act. The Haggadah is thus justified in bringing the supporting verse to prove that there was a revelation of the *Shechinah* during the Exodus, as it too uses the term *"before your eyes"* (*le'einecha*).

Netziv suggests that there is a possible alternative application of the *"great terror,"* namely the great terror of the Jews' forty-year trek in the barren desert. It is in order to reject this alternate meaning that the supportive verse is brought. In that verse the plural *moraim gedolim* (מוֹרָאִים גְּדוֹלִים) is used, which cannot apply to the terror of their desert journey which was a single protracted terror, not a number of ordeals. The term must therefore refer to the terrors experienced by the Egyptians, which were many and varied. By drawing an analogy between the two similar terms, the Haggadah seeks to show that the

With signs — refers to the staff, as it says: "And this staff you shall take in your hand, with which you shall perform the signs."[1]

_____

(1) *Exodus* 4:17.

_____

mora gadol of our verse must also refer to the terrors inflicted upon the Egyptians, as opposed to that experienced by the Jews in the desert.

138. — What does the Haggadah mean when it says that the term "*signs*" refers to the staff? The staff was the *instrument* through which the signs (plagues) were done, and is not *synonymous* with them.

Ramban, in his commentary to the Torah (*Genesis* 12:6), lays down an important principle which explains many passages throughout the Scriptures. That is, many times a prophecy about a future event is accompanied by a physical act, which somehow sets the foretold event "into action" (e.g., *Jeremiah* Chap. 13 and 51:63-64, and especially *II Kings* 13:14-19. False prophets also used the same method to try to bolster their fabrications; see, for example, *I Kings* 22:11, *Jeremiah* 28:11, etc.). In these instances, the physical deed brings the predicted occurrence from the realm of the theoretical into the world of the actual. *Maasei Nissim* suggests that Moses' staff played a similar role: Rather than the plague appearing "out of nowhere," the staff was used to perform the physical act that actualized the disaster which had been predicted. In this sense the staff was itself a "*sign*," for a sign is something that attests to the veracity of a particular statement or prophecy. This was precisely the role of the staff in the plagues — to take a "mere" prophecy and transfer it into concrete action.

Many commentators (*Ritva, Malbim, Yalkut Shimoni, Bircas HaShir*, among others) call attention to the *midrash* that says that the initial letter of each of the plagues was engraved on the staff. The word *osos* (אותות) — translated here as "*signs*" — can also mean "letters," so it is this that prompted the Haggadah to identify this term with the staff.

In connection with the engraving of the initial letters of the plagues (דצ"ך עד"ש באח"ב) on the staff, *Yalkut Shimoni* adds an interesting observation. The numerical value of these letters is 501, which is also the numerical value of the word *asher* (אֲשֶׁר), "*which.*" This fact is alluded to in the verse "all the maladies which (*asher*) I inflicted upon Egypt" (*Exodus* 15:26), for the word *asher* represents the ten plagues, as

וּבְמֹפְתִים — זֶה הַדָּם, כְּמָה שֶׁנֶּאֱמַר, וְנָתַתִּי מוֹפְתִים בַּשָּׁמַיִם וּבָאָרֶץ —

explained. It is further alluded to in the very verse cited here by the Haggadah — "this staff . . . with which (asher) you shall perform the signs," for these letters, which add up to 501, were inscribed on the staff. Further allusions may be seen in the verses "I am HASHEM . . . Who (asher) took you out of Egypt" (Exodus 20:2) — i.e., through the ten plagues, represented by the word asher, I took you out of Egypt — and "My wonders which (asher) I placed among them" (ibid. 10:2), which also refers to the plagues.

139. Why did the Haggadah not interpret the "signs" in its simple sense — namely, as referring to the miracles of the plagues — rather than seeing it as a reference to the staff?

Malbim explains that since our verse has already alluded to the plagues of pestilence and the death of the firstborn (by mentioning the words "mighty hand" and "outstretched arm"), as the Haggadah has explained earlier, it is no longer possible to say that "signs" and "wonders" refer to all the plagues, as that would make these words repetitious. For this reason the Haggadah interprets "signs" as a reference to the instrument through which the plagues were inflicted, rather than the plagues themselves.

Many commentators understand the "signs" of the supporting verse to refer to the miracle of the staff becoming a serpent and then reverting to being a staff, for at the time the command "And this staff you shall take in your hand" was given to Moses, this was the only thing he had been instructed to do with the staff.[1] (The command to use the staff to start the plagues did not come until much later.) If this is the case, this was a single miracle, so why does the verse use the plural osos — "signs"? The answer is that, as *Rashi* points out, not only did the staff turn into a serpent and then revert to being a stick, but after it already returned to its original state it swallowed up the staffs of Pharaoh's magicians (see Exodus 7:12). Thus there were indeed two signs associated with the staff at this time (Shibbolei HaLeket and Sh'lah).

---

1. If "signs" refers to the staff becoming a serpent we must understand how the verse can say "HASHEM brought us out of Egypt with a mighty hand and with . . . signs," What did this miracle have to do with the Exodus? Apparently, we must conclude that it was through this sign, by which Moses originally introduced himself and the power of God to Pharaoh, that the chain of events which eventually led to the Exodus was begun.

With wonders — alludes to the blood, as it says: "And I will show wonders in the heavens and on the earth:

---

140. Five of the ten plagues were generated through the staff — namely, the plagues of blood, frogs, lice, hail and locusts. In addition to these, the plagues of pestilence and death of the firstborn were also alluded to in this verse (by the words *"mighty hand"* and *"out-stretched arm,"* as explained previously). Assuming that the *"signs"* represented by the staff refers to the plagues which were inflicted through its action, this leaves several plagues without allusion in this verse. Why should this be so?

Abarbanel asserts that the three unmentioned plagues — wild beasts, boils and darkness — are indeed alluded to in the word *"u'vemofsim — and with wonders,"* which the Haggadah associates with *"the blood."* This *"blood,"* explains the *Abarbanel,* actually refers to these three missing plagues. See question 142 for the explanation of how this is so.

141. What is the difference in meaning between a *"sign"* (*os*) and a *"wonder"* (*mofeis*), and why is the staff classified as the former while the blood is classified as the latter?

Abarbanel contends that both terms — which refer to an affirmation of some event (such as a prophecy for the future) or principle (such as the omnipotence of God) — may refer to a natural, man-made event as well as to a supernatural, miraculous one. The difference between the two expressions is simply one of degree — a *"sign"* is less of a confirmation than a *"wonder,"* because it is less convincing. The changing of Moses' staff into a serpent, and his hand becoming leprous, are termed *"signs"* (*Exodus* 4:8-9). If Pharaoh would not be convinced by these two *"signs,"* God told Moses he was to take some water and change it into blood in front of Pharaoh (ibid.). This act, the Haggadah tells us here, is such an indisputably supernatural act that it is considered a *"wonder."*

To prove this point, the Haggadah cites the verse from *Joel* 3:3, where the prophet seeks to describe the potency of the portents which will take place in the end of days, and says, "I will display *wonders* in the heavens and on the earth . . . ." In effect, *Abarbanel* continues, each miracle which took place during the course of the Exodus was either a *"sign"* or *"wonder,"* depending on its respective degree of intensity. The *"staff"* represents the miracles which were of a lower order, such as the transformation of the staff into a serpent, while the *"blood"* represents those miracles which were on a higher level, as discussed earlier.

Maharal cites a passage in the *Sifri* which seems to present a difficulty when compared to the Haggadah's statement here. It says there (commenting on *Deuteronomy 13:2*) that a *"sign"* is something seen in the heavens, while a *"wonder"* is an event witnessed on earth. How, then, can the Haggadah classify the staff as a *"sign"*? The key to this issue, *Maharal* explains, is that when the *Sifri* talks about "heaven" and "earth" it intends only to give *examples* of *"signs"* and *"wonders,"* not to *define* them. The actual distinction between the two terms is that a *"sign"* is a change effected by the *causer* of an act, while a *"wonder"* is a change achieved in the *object* of an act. The *Sifri* refers to these two categories as "heaven" and "earth" because Heaven is the ultimate source of all actions, while the earthly realm — the physical world which we perceive with our senses — is the place where these actions take place.

Let us now see how the statements of the Haggadah may be understood according to this definition: Most of the plagues were not supernatural events per se, but were only miraculous by virtue of their scope and timing, so that, through their ferocity and precise targeting, they convinced the Egyptians that God was punishing them for their enslavement of the Jews. Devastating locust plagues do occur occasionally, as do attacks of wild beasts, pestilence, etc. What was unique in these plagues was that Moses' staff was able to bring these events about at the specified time, upon the specified locations, and in the specified intensity. The supernatural aspect of these plagues was not the lice or frogs that were brought about, but the staff which, unlike any normal staff, was able to initiate their arrival. The only one of ten plagues which featured an event which went totally beyond the scope of the laws of nature was the plague of blood, where the object of the plague itself — the waters of Egypt — underwent a miraculous physical change. This is why the Haggadah interprets the word *"signs"* to refer to those miracles wrought by the staff, where the miraculous aspect was evident through the *causer* of the action (the staff), while the term *"wonders"* is related to the plague of blood, where the miraculous aspect was evidenced in the *object* of the plague.

According to the *Gra,* a *"sign"* is a prediction that "if you do not do such-and-such, then such-and-such will happen to you." A *"wonder"* is any supernatural event which is intended to prove something. The staff is called a *"sign"* because it had the initials of the ten plagues engraved on it, as mentioned earlier, and thus, in effect, displayed a warning of what was to befall Pharaoh and his people if they did not heed God's demands. The blood certainly fits the definition of wonder — a supernatural event intended to prove something — as it served to show that God is the Master over all the forces of nature and can change them at will.

Yalkut Shimoni has an interesting explanation for why the plague of blood is referred to as a *mofeis,* which also means "a proof." The *midrash* tells us (and proves it from several Biblical verses) that when God punishes a nation He first strikes down its gods. Since the Egyptians deified the Nile, God chose it as the first target of His retribution, and that is why blood was the first of the plagues.

Similarly, concerning the verse in *Joel* which describes the terrors of the end of days (*"And I will show wonders in the heavens and on earth — blood, fire and columns of smoke;* the sun will turn to darkness and the moon to blood [red] before the coming of the great and awesome Day of HASHEM"), the *Midrash Tanchuma* comments that the point of dimming the sun and the moon before the cataclysmic events of the Messianic era is because these heavenly bodies are deified by many peoples, and God will first show the world that it is He Who rules over these heavenly bodies, bringing destruction to the people's deities before bringing it upon them themselves. This is why the Haggadah cites this supporting verse, says the *Yalkut Shimoni* — to show that God changes things to *"blood"* (be it water or the moon) as a proof (*mofeis*) of His mastery over all the forces of the world.

142. To which blood does *"With wonders"* refer?

Many commentators (*Shibbolei HaLeket,* etc.) explain that the *"blood"* mentioned here refers to the plague of blood, when all the water in Egypt was transformed into blood.

There are others (*Kol Bo,* etc.) who say that the reference is to the wonder that God commanded Moshe to perform before Pharaoh by taking a small amount of water from the Nile and spilling it onto the floor, where it would become blood (*Exodus* 4:9).

The *Gra* explains that since the plural *"wonders"* (*mofsim*) is used (see next question), the Haggadah must be referring to *both* of the aforementioned instances. (*Malbim* gives this explanation as well.)

According to *Aruch HaShulchan,* the *"blood"* here represents all the ten plagues, *"blood"* being representative since it was the first plague.

Abarbanel notes (see above, question 140) that this verse has made mention of seven of the plagues — the five initiated by the staff: blood, frogs, lice, hail and locusts (the *"signs,"* which refer to the staff); pestilence (the *"mighty hand,"* which refers to the pestilence); and the death of the firstborn (and the *"outstretched arm,"* which refers to the "sword"). The Haggadah now tells us, says *Abarbanel,* that the other

As each of the words דָּם, "blood," אֵשׁ, "fire," and עָשָׁן, "smoke," is said,
a bit of wine is removed from the cup, with the finger or by pouring.

דָּם וָאֵשׁ וְתִימְרוֹת עָשָׁן.[1]

three plagues are also alluded to in this verse, for when it says *"blood"* it refers to these plagues of wild beasts, boils and darkness, as follows. Wild beasts wreaked havoc by entering areas of population and mauling people — wounding them and causing them to bleed to death. The boils made the people ill, or perhaps even killed them, by poisoning their blood. The darkness falls under the category of *"blood"* because the darkness was brought about by the sun turning bloodlike in color, until it shed no light.

It is clear from the supporting verse that the Haggadah brings, *Abarbanel* adds, that the *"blood"* referred to here cannot be the plague of blood, for the verse in *Joel* refers only to *"wonders in the heavens and on the earth,"* but not in the *water.* He goes on to say that each of the three wonders mentioned in that verse — *"blood, fire and columns of smoke"* — represents one of the three plagues being discussed (wild beasts, boils and darkness). *"Blood"* corresponds to the plague of wild beasts, as shown above. *"Fire"* represents the plague of boils, as they cause a sensation of heat on the affected skin (note that in English as well as Hebrew the name for this skin disease is related to a word meaning "heat"). The *"columns of smoke"* correspond to the plague of darkness, for, as the verse in *Joel* (3:4) continues in describing these phenomena, the smoke will cause "the sun to turn to darkness and the moon to blood [red]."

143. — Why does the Torah use the plural word *"wonders"* to describe a single thing — *"the blood"*?

According to the interpretations of the word *"blood"* of the *Gra, Abarbanel* and *Aruch HaShulchan,* we understand very well why the plural is used, as the word *"blood"* represents several phenomena. According to the other commentators, who understand *"blood"* to refer to the plague of blood, an explanation of the plural word is in order. The *Ritva* explains that the plague of blood was in fact a compound miracle, for according to the *midrash* not only did all the water in Egypt turn to blood, but the very same *"blood"* would remain water for the Jews. If an Egyptian and a Jew would be drinking from the same cup, says the *midrash,* the Egyptian would taste blood and the Jew would taste water!

As each of the words דָּם, "blood," אֵשׁ, "fire," and עָשָׁן, "smoke," is said, a bit of wine is removed from the cup, with the finger or by pouring.

Blood, fire and columns of smoke."[1]

(1) *Joel* 3:3.

144. Why is it customary to pour out a bit of wine when mentioning the three words *"blood, fire and columns of smoke,"* as well as when mentioning each of the ten plagues and their abbreviations?

Be'er Miriam suggests that this is because we use our cup of wine to represent the "cup of Divine wrath" through which the Almighty dispenses judgment to the nations when the time for retribution arrives. This is a common metaphor throughout the Books of the *Prophets* (e.g., *Isaiah* 51:17, 51:22; *Jeremiah* 25:15ff, 49:12; *Ezekiel* 23:32). Thus, when mention is made of punishment meted out to the nations, we spill some wine to depict the vengeance of God being poured out from the "cup of wrath." In fact, *Talmud Yerushalmi* says that the reason four cups of wine were instituted for the Seder was to represent the four cups of punishment from which God will "give the nations to drink" in the future, alluded to in various verses in Scripture.

Maasei Nissim cites a *midrash* which says that God struck the Egyptians with the fourth finger of His hand (*"It is the finger of God!"* — *Exodus* 8:15), as it were (of course, this has deep symbolic meaning, and cannot be understood in any way literally). He therefore says that we should remove the wine from the cup with our fourth finger as well.

The *Gra* says that the removal of the wine from the cup symbolizes the fact that after each plague the Egyptians lost a little bit of their resistance and strength.

It is also possible to suggest another reason based on the *midrash* that says that God scolded the angels for singing praises to Him for the miracle of the Splitting of the Red Sea. "Creatures made by My hands are drowning in the sea," God said, "and you sing praises?!" On the other hand, we ourselves must praise God for the miraculous salvation that He performed for us. In order to reconcile both of these opposite emotions — the necessity to show gratitude to God, on the one hand, and the need to feel compassion for those who perished, on the other hand — we have a cup of wine before us during the recitation of the Haggadah, but we spill a bit of it out upon mentioning the suffering of the Egyptians.

דָּבָר אַחֵר — בְּיָד חֲזָקָה, שְׁתַּיִם. וּבִזְרֹעַ נְטוּיָה,
שְׁתַּיִם. וּבְמֹרָא גָּדֹל, שְׁתַּיִם. וּבְאֹתוֹת,
שְׁתַּיִם. וּבְמֹפְתִים, שְׁתַּיִם.

אֵלּוּ עֶשֶׂר מַכּוֹת שֶׁהֵבִיא הַקָּדוֹשׁ בָּרוּךְ הוּא עַל
הַמִּצְרִים בְּמִצְרַיִם, וְאֵלּוּ הֵן:

---

145. How does the Haggadah see an allusion to the ten plagues in this verse . . . "בְּיָד חֲזָקָה — with a mighty hand . . ."?

Most commentators explain the count as follows. The phrase *yad chazakah — "a mighty hand"* consists of two words — a noun and an adjective. Since the noun could have been written without any modifier, this phrase is seen as an allusion to two plagues. The same is true of *zero'ah netuyah — "an outstreched arm,"* and *mora gadol — "great awe."* The words *osos — "signs"* — and *mofsim — "wonders,"* being in the plural, are also seen as references to two plagues each.

As far as *which* two plagues are alluded to by each word or phrase, most commentators seem to echo *Abarbanel's* initial assessment, that there is no particular correspondence between any one word and any one of the plagues alluded to; it is rather only the *number* ten that the verse seeks to hint at. (Later in his commentary, however, *Abarbanel* does venture to conjecture that perhaps a particular reference may be assigned to each phrase or word in the verses.)

In connection with the grouping of the plagues into pairs of two each, it is interesting to note *Ibn Ezra's* comment that two plagues had their origin in the water, two in the air, two on the land, two from a distant place, and two from the heavenly bodies.

Maharal shows a different way that the ten plagues may be paired up two by two. He shows that each of the first five plagues parallels the corresponding plague in the last set of five, except that the first five took place in the "lower world," while the last five occurred in the "upper world." Thus blood (plague 1) parallels boils (plague 6), for the way boils affect their victims is through causing a poisoning of the blood. In the first plague, the blood appeared in the waters on the ground, which are part of the "lower realm," while the blood-related affliction produced by the boils affected the blood of man, who belongs to the upper, more spiritual realms of the world. The plague of frogs (plague 2) corresponds to hail (plague 7), for the frogs were emitted by

Another explanation of the preceding verse: [Each phrase represents two plagues,] hence: **mighty hand** — two; **outstretched arm** — two; **great terror** — two; **signs** — two; **wonders** — two.

These are the ten plagues which the Holy One, Blessed is He, brought upon the Egyptians in Egypt, namely:

---

the rivers and waters of Egypt (which belong to the lower realms), and the hail came from the "upper waters" (mentioned in *Genesis* 1:6-7), as does all rain, as explained in the Talmud (*Taanis* 9b). The plague of lice (plague 3) lines up with locusts (plague 8), for lice are insects from the lower realm, on the earth, and locusts are from the upper realm (the sky), being referred to as "flying teeming creatures" in *Leviticus* 11:20-22. The plague of wild beasts (plague 4) parallels the plague of darkness (plague 9), for wild beasts are active mostly in the dark of night (*Psalms* 104:20). (There is a further similarity between them in that the name for "wild beasts" is actually *arov* (עָרוֹב), which also means "mixture," and the word for "evening" is *erev* (עֶרֶב), related etymologically to "mixture" because it is the time of day when things become less visible and discernible.) The wild beasts roam on earth, in the lower realm, while darkness is caused by lack of sunlight, the sun being in the upper realms. And the plague of pestilence (plague 5) is related to the plague of the firstborn (plague 10), which was also a form of sudden death by disease, except that the former took the lives of animals, which belongs to the lower world, while the latter took away the souls of human beings, which originate from the "breath of God" (*Genesis* 2:7), from the upper realm. According to this analysis we can understand why the Haggadah sees the ten plagues as groups of two.

עֶשֶׂר מַכּוֹת — *The Ten Plagues*

---

146. Why does the Torah tell us after the first five plagues that "Pharaoh did not take it to heart" or "Pharaoh hardened his heart," while in reference to the last five plagues we are told that "HASHEM hardened Pharaoh's heart"?

Another question that must be addressed in connection with this topic touches on a very basic issue: How can God force a person to act in a certain way ("hardening his heart") and then punish him for his

As each of the plagues is mentioned, a bit of wine is removed from the cup.
The same is done at each word of Rabbi Yehudah's mnemonic.

דָּם. צְפַרְדֵּעַ. כִּנִּים. עָרוֹב. דֶּבֶר. שְׁחִין. בָּרָד. אַרְבֶּה. חֹשֶׁךְ. מַכַּת בְּכוֹרוֹת.

actions? *Rambam* (*Teshuvah* 6:3) explains this as follows: There are many verses throughout Scripture which indicate that sometimes a person or nation has sinned so badly that God seals their destiny for punishment and removes the option of repentance from them. This is what He did in the case of Pharaoh. After having sinned by flouting God's warnings and signs five times, Pharaoh had reached the point of no return, and God thereupon decreed that Pharaoh would no longer be permitted to achieve His grace by repenting before Him. He therefore saw to it (by "hardening his heart") that Pharaoh would not mend his ways.

Ramban (*Exodus* 7:3), while agreeing with *Rambam's* basic premise, suggests another explanation for this difficulty. He says that after five plagues Pharaoh was completely worn out by the anguish and deprivation brought on by these afflictions, and he was ready to yield to God's demand, if only in order to achieve some relief from his suffering. God knew that his "repentance" was motivated solely by opportunism and not by contrition. This being the case, He provided Pharaoh with the unnatural strength of heart and stubbornness that afforded him the opportunity to make a genuine choice as to whether or not to repent — a fair test, which he once again failed.

Maharal, in line with his system of dividing the plagues into two groups — the first five belonging to the lower realms, and the last five belonging to the upper realms (see question 145) — adds an additional element to *Ramban's* explanation. The first five plagues, being of a lower intensity, were on a level which Pharaoh could have withstood and come to grips with. God therefore left it up to Pharaoh whether he would take them to heart or not, and he failed the test. The last five plagues, however, belonging to a higher degree of punishment, were not bearable under normal circumstances, and God had to supply him with inordinate strength of heart in order to withstand them, as explained above.

147. What is the significance of God's inflicting exactly ten plagues upon the Egyptians?

Abarbanel contends that the number ten has a certain sanctity to it, as

As each of the plagues is mentioned, a bit of wine is removed from the cup. The same is done at each word of Rabbi Yehudah's mnemonic.

1. Blood 2. Frogs 3. Lice 4. Wild Beasts 5. Pestilence 6. Boils 7. Hail 8. Locusts 9. Darkness 10. Plague of the Firstborn.

the Heavenly echelons of the kabbalistic system consist of ten spheres. This, he asserts, is why the world was created with ten utterances, why there were ten items created just before the end of the six days of Creation, why Noah was the tenth generation from Creation, and why Abraham was in the tenth generation after Noah. (All these "tens" are enumerated in *Avos,* Chap. 5.)

Maasei Hashem elaborates on this theme and explains that the very existence of the world is dependent on the observance of the Torah, as the Sages often point out. Since the quintessence of the Torah is the Ten Commandments, the world was created with ten utterances, to stress the fact that Creation itself is rooted in the Torah. The wicked, who disregard the words of the Torah, and thus, in a sense, are voiding the purpose of Creation, deserve to be penalized with a ten-fold punishment.

Maharal quotes a *midrash* which says that it was because Abraham was put through — and passed — ten tests (*Avos* 5:3) that the Egyptians were punished with ten plagues. The reasoning for this connection, he explains, is that it takes ten times to reach the deepest essence of a person's being. Thus, in order to establish that Abraham was truly a righteous person — and not just outwardly so — God tested him with ten trials. God inflicted ten plagues in order that the punishment should reach the very essence of the nation.

See the following question, where *Maharal* gives a fascinating interpretation linking the ten utterances by which the world was created to the ten plagues.

148. Why did God see fit to inflict these particular plagues on the Egyptians rather than others?

Ritva explains the arrangement and progression of the ten plagues in the following manner: (*Aruch HaShulchan* gives a very similar explanation.) Pharaoh was a total non-believer (see *Exodus* 5:2). As such he denied the three basic principles of faith — the belief in the existence of a Creator, the belief that God observes the deeds of man and punishes or rewards each person according to his actions, and the belief that He communicates His word to certain holy individuals (prophets). The first three plagues were intended to demonstrate the first principle to him, for they showed God's absolute mastery over the forces of nature (*Aruch HaShulchan*). Thus, in reference to the plague of blood the Torah says that "through this you will realize that I am HASHEM!" The second set of plagues was designed to prove to Pharaoh the veracity of the second principle enumerated above — that God takes note of man's actions and deals with them accordingly. This is why this set (which begins with wild beasts) is introduced with the statement that it is "in order that you may know that I am HASHEM *in the midst of the land*" — i.e., my awareness and judgments are active in the midst of mankind, not only in the distant heavens. (*Aruch HaShulchan* notes that it is in this set that the Torah first tells us that the plagues affected only the Egyptians but not the Israelites. This underscores the idea that God specifically punishes the wicked and spares the righteous.) In the third set the point of the plagues was to show Pharaoh the third element of faith — the fact that God can and does communicate His will to mankind through prophets. This is why these plagues are accompanied with such comments as "Whoever among the servants of Pharaoh feared the word of Hashem chased his servants and his livestock into the houses" (*Exodus* 9:20), and Pharaoh's plea to Moses and Aaron to "entreat HASHEM your God," where there is a recognition of the unique prophetic status of these righteous men.

Both *Ritva* and *Aruch HaShulchan* note that in each set of three plagues, we find that Moses gave Pharaoh an advance warning before inflicting the first two upon him, while the third plague of the set (lice, boils, darkness) was not preceded by any such warning. This, they explain, corresponds to the customary way of punishing criminals — they are given warnings for the first two offenses but upon the third violation they are punished without any warning.

This division of the plagues into groups of three, as analyzed by *Ritva* and *Aruch HaShulchan,* also explains what R' Yehudah is trying to tell us by arranging the plagues into the mnemonic — דצ״ך עד״ש באח״ב (see also question 151).

There are several other explanations given as to why God chose these particular plagues. *Rashi,* quoting *Midrash Tanchuma,* shows that the plagues follow the strategy used by mortal kings when they lay siege. First the water supply of the besieged city is cut off, in order to starve the inhabitants into submission. (This corresponds to the plague of blood.) Then the army is instructed to blow horns and make loud, frightening noises in order to unnerve the inhabitants and destroy their resolve to fight (this corresponds to the croaking of the frogs); and so on, through all the ten plagues, culminating with the killing of the Egyptians' firstborn.

Abarbanel quotes the sages as giving a different analysis of this issue. The Nile's turning into blood, they explained, was a punishment for the Egyptians' not allowing the women of Israel to immerse themselves in water to cleanse themselves from their impurity, in accordance with Torah law. The loud croaking of the frogs was in retribution for their policy of infanticide, by which the women of Israel had to give birth clandestinely, and restrain themselves from crying out during childbirth. The plague of lice was intended to prevent them from working their fields, for they had stolen many fields from the Israelites, and so on.

Abarbanel also suggests the following reasons for the appropriateness of each plague:

- The River was turned to blood to avenge the blood of the newborn Jewish males who were thrown into the River years earlier.

- To recall the anguished cries of the Jewish mothers as their children were taken from them and tossed into the Nile, God caused the raucous croaking of the frogs which the Nile spawned.

- The land was stricken by having its dirt turn to lice (*Exodus* 8:12) in retaliation for the hard labor which the Jews were forced to do in cultivating the fields.

- Just as all the people of Egypt abused the Jews and indiscriminately forced them to do all kinds of work for them, the wild beasts came and invaded all the populated areas, indiscriminately attacking all the people.

- The Israelites, being totally preoccupied in their slave labor for the Egyptians, were forced to neglect caring for their own livestock, and in retribution the livestock of Egypt was killed by pestilence, while "of the livestock of Israel not even one had died" (*Exodus* 9:7).

- The boils that plagued the Egyptians were in order to prevent them from marital intimacy, as they had imposed upon the Israelites (as the Haggadah derived earlier).

- The Egyptians would throw stones at the Jews and shout at them. In retaliation, God unleashed the plague of hail, with its loud noises (*Exodus* 9:28).

- The Egyptians would often help themselves to produce grown by the Jews for self-subsistence, so God sent the plague of locusts to consume the Egyptians' produce.

- Because the Egyptians forced the Jews to be enveloped by the *"darkness"* and despair of exile and slavery, they were subjected to the plague of darkness.
- And lastly, because the Egyptians removed God's firstborn son (Israel — *Exodus* 4:22) from His presence (so to speak), God struck down the firstborn sons of the Egyptians.

Maharal follows a different approach in explaining the significance of these particular ten plagues. He shows how each one of the plagues parallels one of the ten utterances through which the world was created. These "ten utterances" consist of the nine times the phrase "and God said . . ." appears in the story of the Creation (*Genesis* Chap. 1), as well as the first verse of the Torah ("In the beginning God created the heavens . . .), for we know from elsewhere that also the heavens "were made by the word of HASHEM" (*Psalms* 33:6). The direct correspondence between the plagues and the "utterances" shows that God wished to punish the Egyptians totally and thoroughly, affecting every single facet of their existence, just as each aspect of the world's Creation was created by one of the ten utterances. The order of the ten plagues does not follow the order of the ten utterances, however. This is because the plagues had to come in order of ascending intensity; it would not have been logical to strike out at the Egyptians with a severe plague and afterwards afflict them with a lesser one. Creation, on the other hand, had to follow a specific order of its own, each item created being necessary for the emergence of the one following it.

This is how *Maharal* shows the parallels between the two sets of ten:
- The plague of blood, which deprived all of Egypt — man and beast — of all forms of nourishment and sustenance corresponds to the tenth utterance: "God said: Behold, I have given to you all herbage yielding seed that is on the surface of the entire earth . . . it shall be yours for food" (*Genesis* 1:29).
- The second plague, in which the River spawned the invidious frogs, parallels the utterance, "God said: Let the waters teem with teeming living creatures . . ." (loc. cit., v. 20).
- The next plague, in which the dirt of the ground was transformed into lice, corresponds to the utterance, "God said: Let the waters. . . be gathered together into one area, and let the dry land appear" (loc. cit., v. 9).
- The plague of wild beasts correlates with the utterance, "God said: Let the earth bring forth living creatures . . . cattle, creeping things and beasts of the land . . ." (loc. cit., v. 24).

- Pestilence corresponds to the utterance, "God said: Let there be luminaries in the firmament . . ." (loc. cit., v. 14), for there is a connection between the heavenly bodies and the state of health of the air which we breathe.
- The boils, which devastated the appearances and bodies of the Egyptians, paralleled the utterance of, "God said: Let us make man in Our image, after Our likeness" (loc. cit., v. 26).
- The hail represented the utterance, "God said: Let there be a firmament in the midst of the waters, and let it separate between [the upper] waters (where rain originates - ed.) and [the lower] waters" (loc. cit., v. 6).
- The plague of locusts countered the utterance, "God said: Let the earth sprout vegetation . . ." (loc. cit., v. 11), for the locusts decimated the vegetation and fruits that had been created by that utterance.
- The plague of darkness, of course, corresponds to the utterance of "God said: Let there be light" (loc. cit., 3).
- Lastly, the plague of the firstborn parallels the first utterance of the Torah, "In the beginning . . ." (loc. cit., v. 1), for just as this established the beginning of Creation, so does a firstborn constitute the beginning of a man's building of his family.

(*Maasei Nissim* also depicts a connection between each of the plagues and each of the ten utterances, although in a different manner from that of *Maharal.*)

149. Why did Moses tell Pharaoh, when he was introducing the plague of hail, that "This time I am sending all my plagues" (*Exodus* 9:14)?

Rashi comments on this verse, "From here we may learn that the plague of the firstborn was equal to all the other plagues combined." (For this reason it is called "all my plagues.") The obvious question here is that it is the plague of *hail* that was about to take place, and not the plague of the firstborn! *Sifsei Chachamim* suggests that we should understand *Rashi* as if the word *bechoros* (בְּכוֹרוֹת) — firstborn — refers to *bikkurim* (בְּכּוּרִים) — first fruits of the season — for it was these crops that were stricken by the hail, as opposed to the later-ripening crops, which were still tender enough to withstand the hail without being broken by it (*Exodus* 9:31-32). However, *Rashi* himself says (in his comment to *Exodus* 4:23) that the plague of the firstborn was the harshest of all the plagues. *Sifsei Chachamim* resolves this by suggesting that in the eyes of *Pharaoh* (for it is he who was being addressed in 4:23) the plague of the firstborn was the worst of them all, while to the

רַבִּי יְהוּדָה הָיָה נוֹתֵן בָּהֶם סִמָּנִים:
דְּצַ"ךְ • עֲדַ"שׁ • בְּאַחַ"ב.

populace at large (and it is to them that Moses was referring in 9:14) it was the hail that was harshest, for it was through that plague that they lost all their sources of food.

Zeroa Yamin records that there are those who favor an alternate reading in *Rashi*, found in some manuscripts, substituting the word *batzores* (בַּצּוֹרֶת) — famine — for the word *bechoros* (בְּכוֹרוֹת) — firstborn. This would be a reference to the plague of hail, which deprived the people of their source of food. He cites another suggestion that originally *Rashi* had written the abbreviation *mem-beis* (מ"ב), to stand for *makkas barad* (מַכַּת בָּרָד), the plague of hail, but a copyist mistakenly expanded this abbreviation into *makkas bechoros* (מַכַּת בְּכוֹרוֹת), the plague of the firstborn.

Regardless of which of these opinions we accept, we must still understand what it was about the plague of hail that made it "equal to all the other plagues combined." *Kol Eliyahu* explains that God has three legions at His disposal which He uses to inflict punishment on evildoers — fire, water and wind. Sodom was punished with fire (*Genesis* 19:24), the generation of the Flood was punished with water, and the generation of the Dispersal was punished with the "wind," which scattered them to all corners of the earth. All three legions were called into action against Egypt. Blood and frogs were brought about through water, locusts through the wind (*Exodus* 10:13), and boils through fire (loc. cit., 9:8). In the plague of hail, however, all three elements were involved at one time, as it says, "HASHEM sent loud noises (caused by the wind) and hail (water), while fire went forth towards the earth . . ." (*Exodus* 9:23). Thus, regarding hail the verse says, "This time I am sending *all* my plagues."

150. Why are all the plagues called by a single word (blood, frogs, etc., as opposed to "plague of blood," "plague of frogs," etc.), while the last plague is given the fuller title "plague of the firstborn"?

The simplest explanation for this (offered by *Malbim* and others) is that with each of the first nine plagues the kind of destruction wrought by the plague is made quite clear with a one-word description. If the last plague were called just "firstborn," however, it would not be descriptive of any kind of disaster or destruction at all.

Baruch She'amar suggests another reason, however. He cites the

Rabbi Yehudah abbreviated them thus:
D'tzach, Adash, B'achav.

---

midrash which describes how the firstborn stood up in revolt when they learned the anticipated nature of the tenth plague. They demanded of Pharaoh that the Jews be let go immediately, so that they might be spared, and when they met with resistance, they killed many of their countrymen. It is possible that this is what the Haggadah is referring to when it speaks of the *"plague* (or "smiting") *of the firstborn"* — the smiting that was carried out, *by* the firstborn on other Egyptians.

151. What is the significance of R' Yehudah's mnemonic? Anyone can see that the ten plagues can be abbreviated by representing them with their initial letters!

Rashi is quoted as explaining that if not for R' Yehudah's mnemonic, we might have thought that the plagues did not occur in the order in which they are described in the Torah, for it is quite common for events to be recorded out of chronological sequence in the Torah (אֵין מוּקְדָּם וּמְאוּחָר בַּתוֹרָה). Furthermore, the plagues are described in a completely different order in *Psalms* (Chap. 78). R' Yehudah, by arranging the initial letters of the plagues, is telling us that the plagues occurred in the order in which they are written in the *Torah*.

Many commentators assert that it is the division of plagues into three distinct groupings that R' Yehudah is emphasizing. *Ritva's* explanation for why the plagues are divided up in this manner was discussed at length in question 148.

Maasei Hashem points out that in each group of three plagues the first two were somewhat removed from the people physically, while the last one actually touched their bodies: In the first set of three plagues, the blood was in the water; the frogs came closer to the people, but did not actually affect their bodies; but the lice infected their very persons.

In the second group, the wild beasts were not attached to the Egyptians' bodies, though the lice had been, so Pharaoh began to think that the plagues were lessening in intensity. The next plague, pestilence, took place in the field, far away from centers of human population. But then came the boils, which affected the very bodies of the Egyptians, even more so than had the lice.

The hail fell in the fields, once again leading Pharaoh into a false sense of security. The locust swarms darkened the skies and thus affected the people a bit more directly, while the plague of darkness intensified this phenomenon even more. The plague of the firstborn, of course, went back to directly affecting the human body.

The point of this division into three sets of plagues, each set with varying degrees of personal danger, was a realization of God's desire to "make a mockery out of Egypt" (*Exodus* 10:2), for He thereby "played" with Pharaoh's feelings and convictions. Just as Pharaoh was led to believe that he was about to experience some reprieve, he was reminded of the outstretched arm that God wielded against him.

Shibbolei HaLeket suggests that it is the letters themselves that are significant. These ten letters add up to a numerical value of 501, which is the total of the number of plagues suffered by the Egyptians at the Red Sea according to R' Yose (50), R' Eliezer (200) and R' Akiva (250) combined.[1]

Baruch She'amar notes that it is R' Yehudah who says in *Sifrei* (*Parashas Haazinu*), "A person should always organize the words of the Torah into categories, for if he remembers them as individual facts he will be encumbered by them." Thus it is possible that R' Yehudah's statement here has no deeper significance other than serving as a mnemonic to facilitate easier memorization of the names of the ten plagues.

Yaavetz quotes *Riva* as saying that the third plagues of each of the three sets of three plagues (plague 3, plague 6, plague 9) all joined forces when each of them was meted out. That is, the third plague was lice, boils and darkness, all together, and so was the sixth, and the ninth as well. *Yaavetz* proves that these three plagues are in fact interrelated by showing that if the three plagues are written down one under the other, in a column, thus:

כ נ ם

ש ח ן

ח ש ך

the names of these plagues are spelled out both horizontally and vertically (in reverse). This, he says, is the reason that R' Yehudah divided the plagues up into this grouping.

Netziv explains the division of the plagues into these groupings as follows. In reference to the first set of plagues the Torah tells us that "Pharaoh's heart was hardened and he did not listen to them"; concerning the second set it says, "He did not send out the people" (for wild beasts and pestilence) or "He did not listen to them" (for boils); and in the third set we read "He did not send out the Children of Israel."

---

1. In *gematria* there is tolerance for a differential of 1.

These four expressions parallel the four expressions (in *Exodus* 6:6-7) of redemption (for which the four cups of wine of the Seder were instituted): "I shall take you out from the burdens of Egypt" (meaning an easing of the backbreaking labor enforced upon the Jews); "I shall save you from their labor" (indicating a total cessation of labor, but still being in a state of subservience); "I shall redeem you" (from being under Egyptian rule altogether, but not yet to be designated as God's chosen people); and "I shall take you to Me for a people." After the first three plagues Pharaoh "did not listen to them" to ease their burden in the slightest degree. The last seven plagues, however, saw a certain alleviation of the Jews' condition, for, as the Talmud tells us (*Rosh Hashanah* 11a), their servitude to the Egyptians came to an end at the beginning of Tishrei, and each of the plagues lasted one month (*Rashi* to *Exodus* 7:25). Thus, after the plague of wild beasts, Pharaoh began to "listen to them" and to realize that he was being punished for enslaving the Israelites, so he eased their burden of labor (in fulfillment of the first expression of redemption quoted above), although he did not formally emancipate them yet. This is why the fourth plague is followed by "He did not send out the people" rather than "He did not listen to them." Some further progress was made after the fifth plague as well, so again the Torah tells us, "He did not send out the people," indicating that there was an increased level of reprieve from work (a fulfillment of the second expression of redemption), while Pharaoh stopped short of actually "sending out the people." After the sixth plague Pharaoh went back to his previous attitude of not making any concession whatsoever, so the Torah says, "He did not listen to them." After the seventh plague (hail) Pharaoh recognized the unique importance of the Jewish people as a nation (in fulfillment of the third expression of redemption), and the Torah says that "he did not send out *the Children of Israel,*" for the only remaining obstacle was that Pharaoh did not want the Children of Israel to physically leave his territory en masse. After the eighth plague God asks Pharaoh, "How long will you refuse to humble yourself before Me?" That is, "You have humbled yourself before the Children of Israel and capitulated to all their demands, but you still have not humbled yourself to *Me,* by allowing them to leave Egypt and fulfill the final stage of their redemption by becoming My chosen people." R' Yehudah's division of the plagues into groups thus helps us to see the stages by which the four steps of redemption were implemented: in the first set not at all, in the second set the two levels of cessation of labor, and in the third set the ultimate realization of complete redemption.

The cups are refilled. The wine that was removed is not used.

רַבִּי יוֹסֵי הַגְּלִילִי אוֹמֵר: מִנַּיִן אַתָּה אוֹמֵר שֶׁלָּקוּ
הַמִּצְרִים בְּמִצְרַיִם עֶשֶׂר מַכּוֹת, וְעַל הַיָּם
לָקוּ חֲמִשִּׁים מַכּוֹת? בְּמִצְרַיִם מָה הוּא אוֹמֵר, וַיֹּאמְרוּ
הַחַרְטֻמִּם אֶל פַּרְעֹה, אֶצְבַּע אֱלֹהִים הוּא.¹ וְעַל הַיָּם

---

152. Why was it that there was no warning given for the third, sixth and ninth plagues?

One reason for this, given by several commentators (*Ritva, Tur* and others), is that this is the normal way in which lawbreakers are dealt with — for the first two infractions they are given warnings, and upon the third violation they are punished without prior notification.

Ramban (on *Exodus* 8:15) gives a different reason for this phenomenon. He suggests that warnings were only given for those plagues which had potentially fatal consequences. The devastation of Egypt's water supply was clearly such a case, as was the plague of frogs (for, as the sages tell us, the frogs actually maimed the people physically). Lice, however, are by no means life threatening. Wild beasts and pestilence are certainly potentially lethal plagues, so warning was necessary, but boils is not a deadly disease. Hail and locusts threatened the very lives of the Egyptians in that they ruined all the crops of the field. Darkness, once again, was not hazardous to anyone's health, so it did not require a warning.

Maharal notes an interesting pattern in regard to the warnings issued by Moses and Aaron. For the first plague of each set of three, they were told to meet Pharaoh early in the morning, as he left his house to go down to the waterfront. This was to show a certain amount of restraint in the level of confrontation with Pharaoh; they did not wish to intrude on him at home. For the second offense of each set the warning was given in a somewhat bolder fashion, by entering Pharaoh's home (for in plagues 2, 5, and 8 it says, "Go to Pharaoh"). The third plague came without any warning altogether, which demonstrated the greatest manifestation of domination and control over Pharaoh.

153. The Mishnah (*Pesachim*, Chap. 10) does not mention these passages about the numerous miracles at the Sea, but skips from the enumeration of the ten plagues to the passage *"Rabban Gamliel used to say . . . ."* What is the reason that the Mishnah does not see fit to mention the words of these sages, and why, in turn, do we say them today?

Rabbi Yose the Galilean said: "How does one derive that the Egyptians were struck with ten plagues in Egypt, but with fifty plagues at the Sea? Concerning the plagues in Egypt the Torah states: 'The sorcerers said to Pharaoh: "It is the finger of God." '[1] However, of those at the Sea,

---

(1) *Exodus* 8:15.

Abarbanel notes that *Rambam's* Haggadah also does not include these passages. A possible reason for this omission is that the sages of the Mishnah thought it was not relevant to the Seder night — when the miracles of the Exodus from Egypt are to be discussed — to speak of the miracles of the Splitting of the Red Sea, which took place seven days later. However, the sages of the *Mechilta,* upon whose words our text of the Haggadah is based, *did* see fit to include this discussion in the Seder, feeling that it is appropriate to discuss the great miracles that God performed for us at the Sea. This discussion is particularly pertinent because it bases itself upon the fact that there were ten plagues in Egypt, and this fact has just been elaborated upon in the Haggadah.

154. Doesn't this statement of R' Yose the Galilean contradict the mishnah in Avos 5:5 that says, "Ten miracles were done for our forefathers in Egypt and ten at the Sea"?

Abarbanel distinguishes between the *plagues* inflicted upon the Egyptians, which were ten in Egypt and fifty at the Sea, and the *miracles* wrought for Israel in Egypt and at the Sea. It is to the *miracles* that the Mishnah in *Avos* is referring, not the plagues, and there were exactly ten miracles in Egypt (namely, that each one of the ten plagues miraculously affected only the Egyptians, but not the Jews who lived among them) and ten at the Sea (as enumerated in *Avos D'Rabbi Nasan*).

In an alternate interpretation *Abarbanel* explains that the ten basic punishments that the Egyptians had experienced in Egypt were repeated at the Sea (e.g. the River turning to blood — much blood was spilled into the Sea when the Egyptians were killed there, etc.). However, the *intensity* and extent to which these basic punishments were meted out to them was five times as powerful at the Sea than it was in Egypt. Thus, when R' Yose the Galilean and R' Eliezer and R' Akiva speak of there being five or twenty or twenty-five times as many plagues at the Sea as there were in Egypt, they are speaking not in terms of actual numbers of plagues but of *degrees* of punishment.

מָה הוּא אוֹמֵר, וַיַּרְא יִשְׂרָאֵל אֶת הַיָּד הַגְּדֹלָה אֲשֶׁר
עָשָׂה יהוה בְּמִצְרַיִם, וַיִּירְאוּ הָעָם אֶת יהוה, וַיַּאֲמִינוּ
בַּיהוה וּבְמֹשֶׁה עַבְדּוֹ.¹ כַּמָּה לָקוּ בְּאֶצְבַּע? עֶשֶׂר מַכּוֹת.
אֱמוֹר מֵעַתָּה, בְּמִצְרַיִם לָקוּ עֶשֶׂר מַכּוֹת, וְעַל הַיָּם לָקוּ
חֲמִשִּׁים מַכּוֹת.

---

155. What is the meaning of the first half of Rabbi Yose the Galilean's question — namely: *"How does one derive that the Egyptians were struck with ten plagues in Egypt"?* Is this not explicitly stated in the Torah? Furthermore, he does not address this part of the question in his answer, but deals only with proving that there were fifty plagues at the Sea!

Abarbanel and *Malbim* both explain that what R' Yose meant to say was, "How do we know — now that we have shown that there were ten plagues in Egypt — that there were fifty at the Sea?" In other words the fact that there were ten plagues in Egypt was indeed not part of his question, but was an assumed fact.

Iyun Tefillah suggests a novel approach to this question. As mentioned several times before, the *midrash* speaks of an uprising of firstborn males in Egypt, who, when they learned what the tenth plague was going to be, demanded that the Jews be set free. When they met with resistance they killed their opponents, which resulted in a great massacre. Thus there were in fact two "plagues of the firstborn" — one inflicted *by* the firstborn upon their countrymen, and the other inflicted *upon* the firstborn, by God. What R' Yose was asking was, "How can we know if we should count this 'eleventh plague' in our calculations or not?" To this he answered, "Since we are multiplying the number of plagues in Egypt by five because of the use of the phrase 'the hand of HASHEM,' it stands to reason that we should only count those plagues which were inflicted by the *hand* (or finger, to be more exact) *of God.* The other 'plague' was not inflicted by humans, and thus should not be counted in this discussion."

156. How can the Haggadah bring a proof for so theological an issue as the nature of God's involvement in the plagues from Pharaoh's heretical sorcerers' statement, *"It is the finger of God"*?

Rashbam says that, in fact, sorcerers did *not* know any distinctions between God's *"finger"* and His *"hand."* He explains that when the Torah the Torah relates: 'And Israel saw the great "hand" which HASHEM laid upon Egypt, and the people feared HASHEM and they believed in HASHEM and in His servant Moses.'[1] How many plagues did they receive with the finger? Ten! Then conclude that if they suffered ten plagues in Egypt [where they were struck with a finger], they must have been made to suffer fifty plagues at the Sea [where they were struck with a whole hand]."

---

(1) *Exodus* 14:31.

"quotes" the sorcerers as saying *"It is the finger of God,"* it is not actually an exact quote, but Moses' own paraphrase of their words. Since the exact phrase was penned by Moses it may be used as a proof for our discussion.

157. While one plague may have been referred to as *"the finger of God,"* but Moses said, concerning the plague of pestilence, that it was brought on by *"the hand of God"* (*Exodus* 9:3)!

Maasei Hashem cites the verse in *Proverbs* (14:10), "The heart knows its own misery." The Talmud uses this verse to establish that a sick person often knows more about what he needs than a doctor does. In our case, when comparing Moses' description of the plagues to that of the Egyptian sorcerers, who experienced them firsthand, it is *their* testimony that should be taken to be more accurate.

158. Why was it that the punishment of the Egyptians at the Red Sea led the people to *"fear HASHEM,"* a reaction which was not recorded in connection with any of the ten plagues which they had witnessed in Egypt?

Netziv quotes a *midrash* which says that when the Egyptians drowned in the Sea, each Egyptian died in a different way, according to the way in which he had tortured the Jews when they were under his service. When the Jews saw this, they realized the awesome ability of God to inflict a punishment to exactly fit each man's crime, and this is what instilled the fear of God in them.

159. The phrase *"It is the finger of God"* was said only regarding the plague of lice. How does the Haggadah conclude that all ten plagues came about through one finger?

Abarbanel answers that after showing that the plagues of blood and

רַבִּי אֱלִיעֶזֶר אוֹמֵר. מִנַּיִן שֶׁכָּל מַכָּה וּמַכָּה שֶׁהֵבִיא הַקָּדוֹשׁ בָּרוּךְ הוּא עַל הַמִּצְרִים בְּמִצְרַיִם הָיְתָה שֶׁל אַרְבַּע מַכּוֹת? שֶׁנֶּאֱמַר, יְשַׁלַּח

---

frogs could be duplicated through witchcraft, the sorcerers realized, after admitting their inability to duplicate the plague of lice, that Moses' wonders were indeed being produced by a supernatural Power. That is, they concluded (retroactively) that *all* the plagues and signs Moses was producing were not to be attributed to witchcraft. Thus, the expression *"It is the finger of God"* may indeed be taken as a reference to all the ten plagues.

160. The word *"hand"* is used in connection with the plagues in Egypt as well: "Behold the hand of HASHEM . . ." (*Exodus* 9:3); **"The Egyptians will know that I am HASHEM when I stretch out My hand over Egypt"** (loc. cit., 7:5); **"I shall send out My hand"** (op. cit., 3:20). **So how can the Haggadah say that it was only the *"finger of God"* that was involved in punishing Egypt until the time of the Splitting of the Red Sea?**

Abarbanel points out that the word *yad* (יָד), translated here as *"hand,"* is often used to mean other things. Sometimes it can mean "place" (e.g., *Numbers* 13:29, *Deuteronomy* 23:13); and sometimes it means "plague," which is the intent in the three instances cited in this question. When the Torah says, however, describing the scene at the Red Sea, that Israel saw God's *great* (i.e. *large*) hand, the Haggadah takes this as an indication that it is, metaphorically, the "actual" hand of God that is meant.

Gevuros Hashem explains that when the Torah speaks of the "hand (*yad*) of God" in the three instances mentioned in the question, it was really the *"finger"* of God that was at work, but the Torah refers to the "hand," since the entire "hand" had to be "sent forth" (*Exodus* 3:20) or "stretched out" (*Exodus* 7:5) in order for the "finger" to be put to work. It is only in the verse about the Sea, where the Torah does not speak of the hand's being sent out, and could just as well have said that Israel "saw the 'finger' of God," that the Haggadah takes it to refer to the *entire* hand of God.

Malbim notes that since the Torah implies that what the Israelites saw at the Splitting of the Sea was something new — inspiring them to *"fear HASHEM and believe in His servant Moses"* — it must be that the other times *"yad"* was used it did not refer to the full "hand" of Hashem.

Rabbi Eliezer said: "How does one derive that every plague that the Holy One, Blessed is He, inflicted upon the Egyptians in Egypt was equal to four plagues? As it says: 'He sent

---

שֶׁבָּל מַכָּה וּמַכָּה . . . הָיְתָה שֶׁל אַרְבַּע מַכּוֹת ﬞ— רַבִּי אֱלִיעֶזֶר אוֹמֵר . . .

Rabbi Eliezer said: ". . . every plague . . . was equal to four plagues. . ."

---

161. How are we to understand the quadruple nature of the plagues?

Maharal compares the situation to a wound inflicted by one person on another. A single blow can cause broken skin, ruptured blood vessels, a contusion, and perhaps infection, with warming of the affected area and a discharge of pus. So too, each plague affected the Egyptians in several different ways.

Elsewhere, *Maharal* elaborates on what exactly the four aspects of the plagues were. Firstly, the plagues were wide in scope, affecting the entire body of the Egyptian, not just a limited area. The Haggadah calls this *"wrath,"* as a person who is wrathful strikes out more fiercely and broadly than someone who is not. The second aspect is that the plagues came with extraordinary force. This is called *"fury."* The third facet of the plagues was that they were not sudden, but were preceded by a warning, so that the people suffered an extraordinary amount of angst in anticipation of each plague. This the Haggadah calls *"trouble,"* for the people were actually troubled by the impending disasters they were doomed to face. The fourth aspect was that the plagues were lasting and relentless, not quickly dispensed. This is called *"a band of emissaries of evil."*

Aruch HaShulchan attempts to actually enumerate the four facets of each plague. The *midrash* tells us that in addition to the plague itself, a measure of pestilence accompanied each plague. This, *Aruch HaShulchan* explains, was an additional facet of each plague.

In addition, along with the plague of blood there was, of course, a lack of drinking water and a resultant famine. The same may be said for frogs, lice (for the lice infested their food and water supplies as well), wild beasts, pestilence (for an epidemic usually contaminates food and water supplies), hail and locusts.

During the plague of darkness, we are told that the people did not get up for three days, so again they suffered from lack of food and drink.

The boils themselves were a triple affliction, for there are three types of boils — moist lesions, dry ones, etc., as described in *Bechoros*. And

בָּם חֲרוֹן אַפּוֹ — עֶבְרָה, וָזַעַם, וְצָרָה, מִשְׁלַחַת מַלְאֲכֵי
רָעִים.¹ עֶבְרָה, אַחַת. וָזַעַם, שְׁתַּיִם. וְצָרָה, שָׁלֹשׁ.
מִשְׁלַחַת מַלְאֲכֵי רָעִים, אַרְבַּע. אֱמוֹר מֵעַתָּה, בְּמִצְרַיִם
לָקוּ אַרְבָּעִים מַכּוֹת, וְעַל הַיָּם לָקוּ מָאתַיִם מַכּוֹת.

רַבִּי עֲקִיבָא אוֹמֵר. מִנַּיִן שֶׁכָּל מַכָּה וּמַכָּה שֶׁהֵבִיא
הַקָּדוֹשׁ בָּרוּךְ הוּא עַל הַמִּצְרִים
בְּמִצְרַיִם הָיְתָה שֶׁל חָמֵשׁ מַכּוֹת? שֶׁנֶּאֱמַר, יְשַׁלַּח בָּם
חֲרוֹן אַפּוֹ, עֶבְרָה, וָזַעַם, וְצָרָה, מִשְׁלַחַת מַלְאֲכֵי רָעִים.¹
חֲרוֹן אַפּוֹ, אַחַת. עֶבְרָה, שְׁתַּיִם. וָזַעַם, שָׁלֹשׁ. וְצָרָה,
אַרְבַּע. מִשְׁלַחַת מַלְאֲכֵי רָעִים, חָמֵשׁ. אֱמוֹר מֵעַתָּה,
בְּמִצְרַיִם לָקוּ חֲמִשִּׁים מַכּוֹת, וְעַל הַיָּם לָקוּ חֲמִשִּׁים
וּמָאתַיִם מַכּוֹת.

---

the plague of the firstborn involved death, the sword and warfare (for, as
mentioned earlier, there was an uprising of firstborns which led to much
bloodshed).

Altogether, then, there were four afflictions involved in each plague.

**162. Why did R' Eliezer not count the phrase "His fierce anger" as
number one, thus ending up with five rather than four facets for each
plague, as R. Akiva did?**

The commentators agree (Abudraham, Abarbanel, etc.) that R' Eliezer
sees the phrase "His fierce anger" as a general description of God's wrath,
which is followed by four specific dimensions. How did he know that this
first phrase should be taken as a general statement, as distinct from the
following four descriptions?

Malbim offers two possible suggestions. Firstly, the first expression
has the possessive pronoun "His" attached to it, which sets it apart from
the other four expressions which do not have this pronoun. Secondly,
the conjunction "and" is only used after "wrath," and is used again
between each item in the list. The fact that there is no "and" joining "His
fierce anger" with "wrath" suggests that it is not to be joined to the other
expressions, but is to be taken as a distinct unit — a general statement
followed by specifications.

upon them His fierce anger: wrath, and fury, and trouble, a band of emissaries of evil.'[1] [Since each plague in Egypt consisted of] (1) wrath, (2) fury, (3) trouble, and (4) a band of emissaries of evil, therefore conclude that in Egypt they were struck by forty plagues and at the Sea by two hundred!"

Rabbi Akiva said: "How does one derive that each plague that the Holy One, Blessed is He, inflicted upon the Egyptians in Egypt was equal to five plagues? As it says: 'He sent upon them His fierce anger: wrath, fury, trouble, and a band of emissaries of evil.'[1] [Since each plague in Egypt consisted of] (1) fierce anger, (2) wrath, (3) fury, (4) trouble, and (5) a band of emissaries of evil, therefore conclude that in Egypt they were struck by fifty plagues and at the Sea by two hundred and fifty!"

---

(1) *Psalms* 78:49.

It is interesting to note that *Abarbanel* has an alternate version of R' Eliezer's exegesis: *"His fierce anger"* is one, *"wrath"* is two, *"fury"* is three, and *"trouble of a band of emissaries of evil"* is considered to be the fourth (unlike R' Akiva, who divides these into numbers four and five).

163. Why were R' Yose, R' Eliezer and R' Akiva so intent on magnifying the number of plagues suffered by the Egyptians?

The *Gra* cites the verse, "All the illnesses that I put on Egypt I will not put upon you" (*Exodus* 15:26). Thus, the more afflictions and misfortunes we can attribute to the Egyptians, the more catastrophes we are guaranteed not to suffer ourselves!

Maasei Hashem notes that there are 248 parts of the body according to the sages. Thus, accounting for 248 illnesses would be equivalent to saying "all the diseases that are possible." R' Eliezer counted 40 plagues in Egypt and another 200 at the Sea, for a total of 240, which closely approximates the sought number. R' Akiva preferred to find all 250 afflictions at the Sea, perhaps because it is shortly after the Splitting of the Sea that God told the people, "All the illnesses that I put on Egypt I will not put upon you."

Chinuch (mitzvah 21) states that an important facet in our retelling the story of the Exodus is to detail how God punished the Egyptians. Thus, it is crucial that we analyze all the plagues inflicted upon them.

כַּמָּה מַעֲלוֹת טוֹבוֹת לַמָּקוֹם עָלֵינוּ.

כַּמָּה מַעֲלוֹת טוֹבוֹת לַמָּקוֹם עָלֵינוּ — *The Omnipresent has bestowed so many levels of goodness upon us!*

---

164. What is the relevance of this paragraph at this particular point in the Haggadah?

Shibbolei HaLeket explains as follows. After these sages showed in successively greater number the magnitude of God's benevolence to us, the Haggadah now states that we can still enumerate more of the many acts of kindness that God performed for us.

Malbim, however, sees this paragraph as belonging to the paragraphs which follow it. In order to arouse our hearts and increase our awareness of our indebtedness to God, in preparation for the Hallel which is to be said shortly, this section is introduced here.

165. Why are God's acts of benevolence referred to here by the strange term *"levels"* (ma'alos)?

Abarbanel suggests that this is because these acts of kindness were above and beyond what was necessary to simply redeem the Jews from Egypt — the basic requirement for satisfying the covenant with Abraham. The word *ma'alos,* translated here as *"levels,"* can also mean "superior things" or "things that are above."

He continues to note that the commentators suggest that there is a connection between the fifteen elements of God's benevolence mentioned here and the fifteen psalms beginning with the words, "A Song of Ascents (*ma'alos*)," and the fifteen stairs (*ma'alos*) which led to the holy Inner Courtyard of the Temple. It is to allude to this connection that the Haggadah refers to them as *"ma'alos."*

Maharal explains that there is a progression in these fifteen items of God's kindnesses, each one being on a greater level than the one before it, until the ultimate benevolence — the building of the Temple — which is mentioned last. It is for this reason that the Haggadah refers to them as *"ma'alos,"* which also means "stairs."

Malbim suggests that the word *"ma'alos"* is used here as a derivative of the word *le'aleih* (לְעַלֵּה) — "to exalt with praises." This is not merely a list of acts of kindness done by God, he says, but a list of *obligations* that we have to exalt and praise Him.

The Omnipresent has bestowed so many levels of goodness upon us!

---

166. What is the significance of mentioning these fifteen acts of kindness? Surely we could mention many more examples of God's beneficence to us!

Firstly, the significance of the number fifteen was mentioned in the previous answer.

Furthermore, the *Gra* comments that the number fifteen corresponds to the total achieved when one adds the seven levels of Heaven, plus the earth, plus the seven spaces in between them. This is why the verse says, "Extol Him Who rides upon the highest heavens with YAH, His Name" (*Psalms* 68:5), for the Name YAH (יָ-הּ) has the numerical value of fifteen. In addition, the Talmud tells us (*Sukkah* 51a) that when the people used to leave the area of the Temple's Altar on Sukkos they would say, "We are for YAH, and our eyes look to YAH," corresponding to the fifteen steps that were at the entrance to the Courtyard mentioned earlier. He also notes that there were fifteen generations from Abraham to Solomon, who built the Temple, which correspond to the fifteen days that it takes for the new moon (which is often said to represent the Jewish people) to reach its fullest, most complete state.

Olelos Ephraim adds that the Exodus took place on the fifteenth of the month, and that the Torah further alludes to this idea by stating, "Today you are going out, in the month of Spring (*aviv* — אָבִיב)," the numerical value of *aviv* being fifteen. He also points out that "David (דָּוִד)," the name of the king who was the fourteenth generation after Abraham, has a numerical value of 14. He also notes symbolic importance in the fact that the mitzvah of ridding our houses of *chametz* (*biur chametz*) is on the fourteenth of the month, as a prelude to the Pesach holiday on the fifteenth. This represents the fact that David, the fourteenth "step" in Jewish history (counting from Abraham), was the one who eliminated the "*chametz*" (the metaphorical embodiment of evil) from Israel, for he abolished all idolatry from the land, paving the way for his son. Solomon was the fifteenth — culminating — stage in Jewish history, just as the moon reaches its fullness on the fifteenth of the month. After Solomon's rule the fortunes of the Jewish people began to decline, as the moon wanes after the fifteenth of the month.

Olelos Ephraim goes on to homiletically interpret the verse, "For the hand (*yad* — יָד) is on the throne of YAH (*yah* — יָ-הּ): HASHEM maintains a war against Amalek" (*Exodus* 17:16), according to these ideas. The

אִלּוּ הוֹצִיאָנוּ מִמִּצְרַיִם וְלֹא עָשָׂה בָהֶם שְׁפָטִים דַּיֵּנוּ.
אִלּוּ עָשָׂה בָהֶם שְׁפָטִים וְלֹא עָשָׂה בֵאלֹהֵיהֶם דַּיֵּנוּ.

numerical value of "yad — hand" is fourteen, and the numerical value of YAH is fifteen. Thus, the verse may be explained as follows: There will be a "hand" (representing David — corresponding to 14 — whose "hand," or dominion, ruled over all the Jews), whose son will sit on the throne of YAH (Solomon — corresponding to 15 — who sat on the "throne of God," *I Chronicles* 29:23). At that time there will be a war of God against Amalek, for in Solomon's days the Amalekites had finally been subdued.

167. Are there any subgroupings among the list of fifteen acts of benevolence mentioned here?

Yalkut Shimoni finds the following pattern in the fifteen items. The Talmud (*Berachos* 54b) tells us that there are four kinds of experiences for which a person is obligated to give thanks to God: (a) when he is released from captivity, (b) when he traverses the sea unharmed, (c) when he safely travels through a desert, and (d) when he recovers from illness. The first five stiches here describe the miracles that were done for us in the Exodus from Egypt itself, corresponding to the first category of people who are obligated to express their thanks to God. Next are three miracles involved in the Splitting of the Red Sea, when the Jews traversed the Sea unmolested (the next three "*Dayenus*"), corresponding to the second category. These are followed by three miracles done for us during our travels in the desert, the third category of those obligated to give praise. After this, we mention the giving of the Torah at Mount Sinai, where, the sages tell us, all the people who had physical blemishes or illnesses found themselves miraculously cured, the fourth category of those who must give praise. Thus, the Haggadah points out to us how much we are obligated to give praise to God, for we fall under all four of the categories of people who are duty bound to give thanks to Him!

168. There are several statements regarding which it seems absurd to say *"It would have sufficed us."* For instance, how can we say, *"Had He split the Sea for us, but not led us through it . . . it would have sufficed us"*? We would surely have died at the hands of the Egyptians in such a scenario!

Several commentators explain that *"it would have sufficed us"* does not mean that it would have been sufficient to have only the first miracle occur. Rather, it means "this miracle alone would have been sufficient

Had He brought us out of Egypt,
>   but not executed judgments against the Egyptians,
>>   it would have sufficed us.
Had He executed judgments against them,
>   but not upon their gods,   it would have sufficed us.

---

reason for us to be obligated to give thanks to Him" (*Malbim, Haggadas Sofrim*). Nevertheless, many commentaries do take the phrase in its more literal sense, and some of their explanations for the ensuing difficulties are cited in the next several questions.

Yalkut Shimoni cites another interesting explanation: The Haggadah has told us that the deliverance from Egypt was carried out by the direct intervention of God Himself, without any intermediary agents, angels, etc. Here the Haggadah is saying that if *He* (personally) had taken us out of Egypt, but *He* had not executed judgments against them (personally, but through an intermediary) — it would have been enough for us. This interpretation helps to provide the answer to another question asked about this paragraph: Why, though we mention the manna, is there no mention of the miraculous Well of Miriam, which supplied the people with water for their forty-year sojourn in the desert? The answer is that the sages tell us (*Bava Metzia* 86b) that the manna was given to the people directly from God, while the Well was provided through an intermediary. Thus, it has no place in this list of beneficent acts which God *Himself* did for us.

169. Why is the execution of *"judgments against the Egyptians"* included in the list of things for which we are thankful to God? We should be happy about our own salvation, not about the downfall of others.

Maasei Nissim explains that it was through the punishments brought upon the Egyptians that it became manifest to all that the Jews were God's chosen people. The fact that God took us out of Egypt through great miracles and plagues was used later by Moses to plead to God on Israel's behalf (*Exodus* 32:11-12, *Numbers* 14:13-16). Thus it certainly is a matter for us to be thankful for!

170. What is the nature of the *"judgments against the Egyptian gods"* (mentioned also in *Exodus* 12:12 and *Numbers* 33:4)?

As noted in the answer to question 127, *Rashi* explains that "the gods (idols) of wood rotted, those of metal melted, etc." *Ramban*, however,

אִלּוּ עָשָׂה בֵאלֹהֵיהֶם וְלֹא הָרַג אֶת בְּכוֹרֵיהֶם   דַּיֵּנוּ.

אִלּוּ הָרַג אֶת בְּכוֹרֵיהֶם וְלֹא נָתַן לָנוּ אֶת מָמוֹנָם   דַּיֵּנוּ.

אִלּוּ נָתַן לָנוּ אֶת מָמוֹנָם וְלֹא קָרַע לָנוּ אֶת הַיָּם   דַּיֵּנוּ.

אִלּוּ קָרַע לָנוּ אֶת הַיָּם

וְלֹא הֶעֱבִירָנוּ בְּתוֹכוֹ בֶּחָרָבָה   דַּיֵּנוּ.

---

interprets it to mean the vanquishing of Egypt's heavenly champion (for every nation has an angel which "represents" it before God in Heaven — see *Daniel* 10:13 and *Isaiah* 24:21).

171. The Torah's mention of the slaying of the firstborn precedes that of execution of judgments against the gods of Egypt (*Exodus* 12:12 and *Numbers* 33:4). Why is the order reversed here?

Bircas HaShir cites the familiar maxim that "Seeing is believing" (or, as the sages put it, "Hearing is not comparable to seeing" — *Rashi*). Although the Jews were *told* about the plague of the firstborn in advance, they did not fully appreciate this fact until they *saw* the Egyptians burying their firstborn later in the day, as they were leaving Egypt. They saw melted and rotted idols, however, immediately upon leaving their houses in the morning. Thus, although the slaying of the firstborn actually preceded the execution of judgments against the Egyptian idols, the Haggadah lists the miracles of the Exodus in the order that *we* came to appreciate them, which, in this case, was in reverse sequence.

Marbeh Lesapper understands the whole concept of *"executing judgments against their gods"* differently. He believes that the Haggadah is referring to the events of the Sabbath before the Exodus. The *midrash* tells us that the Jews tied lambs to their bedposts in preparation for the Pesach sacrifice. When the Egyptians asked them why these sheep were being set aside, they explained that it was in preparation for a sacrifice. The Egyptians, who worshiped sheep, miraculously did not lift a finger against them. This weakened their celestial representative, whose constellation is the sheep. This event, which, of course, preceded the plague of the firstborn, is what the Haggadah is referring to here when it mentions the *"execution of judgments against their (Egypt's) gods."*

Rav Sar-Shalom of Belz explains this line as follows. According to the complex laws which govern the eradication of idolatry, if an idol or deity is destroyed, its accouterments and articles of service need not be destroyed afterwards. The converse, however, is not true — even if one

Had He executed judgments against their gods,
 but not slain their firstborn,   it would have sufficed us.
Had He slain their firstborn, but not given us their wealth,
 it would have sufficed us.
Had He given us their wealth, but not split the Sea for us,
 it would have sufficed us.
Had He split the Sea for us,
 but not let us through it on dry land,
 it would have sufficed us.

---

destroys all the paraphernalia associated with a particular idol, the idol itself must also be obliterated (see Talmud, *Avodah Zarah*, 52b). The firstborn males were the priests in the Egyptian religion, *Rav Sar-Shalom* asserts, and their destruction in the tenth plague was a part of the process of the annihilation of Egypt's gods. God chose to eliminate the firstborn priestly class before eradicating Egypt's idols, for had He wiped out the deities first, there would no longer have been a need to root out the firstborn, who were only accouterments to the idolatry itself. Although the slaying of the firstborn took place first, we thank God here in reverse order, for He could have accomplished the goal of eradicating Egypt's idolatry by *"executing judgments against their gods"* without *"slaying their firstborns"* at all.

Yalkut Shimoni explains that a person has three things in life that are more precious to him than anything else in the world: his God, his children (of whom the firstborn is the most precious) and his possessions. Here we mention the fact that God punished the Egyptians with respect to all three of these items, and we specify them in order of their preciousness — *"He executed judgments against their gods, he had slain their firstborn and had given us their wealth."*

172. How can we say that if God had not split the Sea for us it would have sufficed us? Pharaoh and his army were poised to kill the entire nation and were thwarted only by the Splitting of the Sea!

Kol Bo and *Rashbam* explain that the intention here is that God could have saved us from Pharaoh's army in some other, more natural way. For instance, *Abarbanel* suggests that God could have inspired Pharaoh to turn back from pursuing the Israelites, for it was only because God had hardened Pharaoh's heart that he chased after them (*Exodus* 14:8). Or the Jews could have defeated Pharaoh militarily, just as they ultimately

אִלּוּ הֶעֱבִירָנוּ בְּתוֹכוֹ בֶּחָרָבָה
וְלֹא שִׁקַּע צָרֵינוּ בְּתוֹכוֹ דַּיֵּנוּ.

אִלּוּ שִׁקַּע צָרֵינוּ בְּתוֹכוֹ
וְלֹא סִפֵּק צָרְכֵּנוּ בַּמִּדְבָּר אַרְבָּעִים שָׁנָה דַּיֵּנוּ.

אִלּוּ סִפֵּק צָרְכֵּנוּ בַּמִּדְבָּר אַרְבָּעִים שָׁנָה
וְלֹא הֶאֱכִילָנוּ אֶת הַמָּן דַּיֵּנוּ.

אִלּוּ הֶאֱכִילָנוּ אֶת הַמָּן וְלֹא נָתַן לָנוּ אֶת הַשַּׁבָּת דַּיֵּנוּ.

אִלּוּ נָתַן לָנוּ אֶת הַשַּׁבָּת וְלֹא קֵרְבָנוּ לִפְנֵי הַר סִינַי דַּיֵּנוּ.

---

did to several other enemies. *Yaavetz* offers that He could have led us around the Sea to the other side, or He could have had them swim to the other side.

173. How would it have sufficed us to have the Sea split if we had not passed through it?

Yalkut Shimoni quotes the *midrash* which says that when the Jews passed through the Red Sea the waters formed a wall on their right and left and also a roof over their heads, producing a sort of tunnel through which they walked. The Haggadah means to say that it would have been enough if God had led us "over" the split Sea rather than *"through"* it. This miracle was truly beyond what was absolutely necessary for us to be saved from the hands of the Egyptians.

Rashbam explains that it would have been sufficient if God had led us through the split Sea over a wet, muddy floor; He did not have to make it more comfortable for us by letting us pass *"through it on dry land."*

174. How could we have survived forty years in the desert without having our needs supplied?

Rashbam and others point out that the people had a great deal of money with which they could have purchased supplies from the surrounding nations. They also had much livestock which they could have used for food.

Abarbanel explains that God could have led the Jews on the direct route — the way of the Philistines (*Exodus* 13:17) — which was a populated, developed area, and then it would not have been necessary to supply food through supernatural means.

Had He let us through it on dry land,
  but not drowned our oppressors in it,
                                    it would have sufficed us.
Had He drowned our oppressors in it,
  but not provided for our needs in the desert for forty
  years,   it would have sufficed us.
Had He provided for our needs in the desert for forty years,
  but not fed us the manna,   it would have sufficed us.
Had He fed us the manna, but not given us the Sabbath,
                                    it would have sufficed us.
Had He given us the Sabbath,
  but not brought us before Mount Sinai,
                                    it would have sufficed us.

---

175. How could the Jews' needs have been met if not through the manna?

Shibbolei HaLeket suggests that when the Haggadah speaks of *"providing for our needs"* it refers to necessities other than food, such as the availability and maintenance of clothing. If God had done this for us and not supplied us with food as well, it would have been enough.

Abarbanel explains that God could have arranged for regular food to be miraculously available to us. He did not have to supply us with the manna, which was a special, ethereal food, as described by the Torah and the *midrashim*.

Aruch HaShulchan suggests that God could have commanded the people to cultivate their own crops in the desert. While growing food in the infertile soil of the desert would have also involved God's miraculous intervention, it would at least have called for some human involvement. God chose, however, to supply the manna, which involved no effort whatsoever on the part of the people.

Yalkut Shimoni explains this line as follows. The Talmud (*Bava Metzia* 86b) notes that the manna was supplied to the Jews by God "personally" (*Exodus* 16:4) while water was given to them through the agency of Moses (*Exodus* 17:6). The reason that this was so, says the Talmud, is because Abraham said to the angels, 'Let some water be brought [by someone else]' (*Genesis* 18:4), so his descendants were repaid by receiving water through the agency of someone else; he said, 'I [myself] will get a bit of bread' (ibid. 18:5), so his descendants were repaid by receiving

אִלּוּ קֵרְבָנוּ לִפְנֵי הַר סִינַי
וְלֹא נָתַן לָנוּ אֶת הַתּוֹרָה
אִלּוּ נָתַן לָנוּ אֶת הַתּוֹרָה
וְלֹא הִכְנִיסָנוּ לְאֶרֶץ יִשְׂרָאֵל

דַּיֵּנוּ.

דַּיֵּנוּ.

---

bread from God Himself." What the Haggadah means here is: Had God provided for our needs in the desert using intermediaries, and not "personally" given us the manna, it would have been enough.

176. What would have been the point of bringing us before Mount Sinai without giving us the Torah? How can we say that this would have sufficed?

Rashbam, *Kol Bo*, *Avudraham* and *Alshich* cite the Talmud (*Shabbos* 146a) which says that when the Jews arrived at Mount Sinai they were freed of the spiritual impurity which affected all of mankind since Adam and Eve's sin. This spiritual purification in and of itself would have been enough for us, even if God had not given us the Torah.

Shibbolei HaLeket explains that included in the phrase *"He brought us before Mount Sinai"* is the giving of the Ten Commandments. What the Haggadah means, then, is that if God had given us the Ten Commandments and not the other 603 mitzvos, we would still be grateful to Him.

Abarbanel interprets the Haggadah's statement similarly, and suggests an alternate interpretation as well. The meaning may be, he says, that if God had given the Ten Commandments through an intermediary, as He did the rest of the Torah, it would have been enough. The fact that He communicated [the first two of] these commandments *directly* to us was an extra act of benevolence.

Yet another approach is given by *Bircas HaShir*. The Talmud (*Makkos* 23b) tells us that there are 613 mitzvos in the Torah, deriving this fact from the verse that says, "The Torah that Moses commanded us . . ." (*Deuteronomy* 33:4). "Torah" (תורה) has the numerical value of 611; this, added to the first two of the Ten Commandments, which were communicated to us directly by God and not through Moses, makes 613. *Maharsha* (ad loc.) explains that the reason these two commandments are counted separately from all the others is that they form the basic foundation from which all the others emanate. (It is for this reason that the Talmud continues to say that the prophet Habakkuk (2:4) summed up all the Torah in one statement: "A righteous man lives by his faith.") Accordingly, *Bircas HaShir* suggests that the Haggadah means to say that if

Had He brought us before Mount Sinai,

but not given us the Torah,   it would have sufficed us.

Had He given us the Torah,

but not brought us into the Land of Israel,

it would have sufficed us.

God had only given us the basic two commandments of the Torah, without explicitly disclosing the other 611 commandments which are predicated by them, it would have been sufficient reason for us to be grateful.

Aruch HaShulchan offers the following explanation. In *Bava Metzia* (59b) the Talmud tells us that after the giving of the Torah at Mount Sinai, heavenly intervention — such as visions, prophetic revelations, oracles, and the like — do not affect the normative halachic process: "[The Torah] is not in the heavens" (*Deuteronomy* 30:12).[1] This, says *Aruch HaShulchan*, it what the Haggadah is saying. Had God brought us before Mount Sinai and told us the laws of the Torah, but not given it as a gift to us, without the ongoing "involvement," as it were, of Heaven, it would have been enough for us.

Yalkut Shimoni presents yet another possibility. We are taught (*Shabbos* 88a) that God "coerced" the Jews into accepting the Torah at Mount Sinai alluded to by the verse, "and [the people] stood *at the bottom* of the mountain," which implies that the mountain was being threateningly held over their heads. On the other hand, the Torah emphasizes the enthusiasm with which the Torah was voluntarily accepted by the Jews, by recording their famous words "we will do and we will hear" (*Exodus* 24:7), which conveyed a total, unconditional desire to comply. The *Midrash Tanchuma* resolves this contradiction by explaining that while the Written Torah was anxiously accepted by the people, the Oral Law had to be forced upon them. The Haggadah's statement can thus be interpreted as follows: *Had He brought us before* (but not "*under*") *Mount Sinai,* and thus given us only the Written Law, it would have been enough for us, but He went beyond that and *"gave us the* [entire] *Torah,"* including the Oral Law.

177. Why does the Haggadah refer to God's having *"brought us into the Land of Israel"* rather than that He "gave us" the Land, the term used concerning the other gifts God gave us — the Torah and the Sabbath?

Rav Michael Horowitz explained that unlike the Torah and the Sabbath

---

1. This does not apply to a direct prophecy applying to a specific, temporary situation.

אִלּוּ הִכְנִיסָנוּ לְאֶרֶץ יִשְׂרָאֵל
וְלֹא בָנָה לָנוּ אֶת בֵּית הַבְּחִירָה דַּיֵּנוּ.

עַל אַחַת כַּמָּה, וְכַמָּה טוֹבָה כְפוּלָה וּמְכֻפֶּלֶת לַמָּקוֹם
עָלֵינוּ. שֶׁהוֹצִיאָנוּ מִמִּצְרַיִם, וְעָשָׂה בָהֶם שְׁפָטִים,
וְעָשָׂה בֵאלֹהֵיהֶם, וְהָרַג אֶת בְּכוֹרֵיהֶם, וְנָתַן לָנוּ אֶת
מָמוֹנָם, וְקָרַע לָנוּ אֶת הַיָּם, וְהֶעֱבִירָנוּ בְתוֹכוֹ בֶּחָרָבָה,
וְשִׁקַּע צָרֵינוּ בְּתוֹכוֹ, וְסִפֵּק צָרְכֵּנוּ בַּמִּדְבָּר אַרְבָּעִים
שָׁנָה, וְהֶאֱכִילָנוּ אֶת הַמָּן, וְנָתַן לָנוּ אֶת הַשַּׁבָּת, וְקֵרְבָנוּ
לִפְנֵי הַר סִינַי, וְנָתַן לָנוּ אֶת הַתּוֹרָה, וְהִכְנִיסָנוּ לְאֶרֶץ
יִשְׂרָאֵל, וּבָנָה לָנוּ אֶת בֵּית הַבְּחִירָה, לְכַפֵּר עַל כָּל
עֲוֹנוֹתֵינוּ.

רַבָּן גַּמְלִיאֵל הָיָה אוֹמֵר. כָּל שֶׁלֹּא אָמַר שְׁלֹשָׁה
דְבָרִים אֵלּוּ בַּפֶּסַח, לֹא יָצָא יְדֵי חוֹבָתוֹ, וְאֵלּוּ הֵן,
פֶּסַח. מַצָּה. וּמָרוֹר.

---

which were unconditional gifts, our receiving the Land of Israel was
made contingent upon our observance of God's commandments. It is for
this reason that it is more appropriate to thank God for *"bringing us into
the Land"* . . . than for "giving" it to us.

Baruch She'amar, Kehillos Moshe and others note that our survival as
a nation is guaranteed through Torah, not by the fact that we have a
land. Indeed, we remained a unique and distinct nation through centuries of
exile, when we did not live in the Land of Israel. The Land of Israel did
not achieve its full distinction until the Jews conquered and settled it
after receiving the Torah. It was at this point that they became obligated
to observe the commandments connected to the land.

◄§ רַבָּן גַּמְלִיאֵל — *Rabban Gamliel* §►

---

178. Why is this paragraph inserted between our listing God's
kindnesses to us and our recitation of Hallel?

Had he brought us into the Land of Israel,
   but not built the Temple for us,
                                          it would have sufficed us.

Thus, how much more so should we be grateful to the
Omnipresent for all the numerous favors He showered
upon us: He brought us out of Egypt; executed judgments
upon them and against their gods; slew their firstborn; gave
us their wealth; split the Sea for us; led us through it on dry
land; drowned our oppressors in it; provided for our needs
in the desert for forty years; fed us the manna; gave us the
Sabbath; brought us before Mount Sinai; gave us the Torah;
brought us to the Land of Israel; and built us the Temple to
atone for all our sins.

Rabban Gamliel used to say: Whoever has not explained
the following three things on Passover has not fulfilled
his duty, namely:
   Pesach — the Passover offeirng;
   Matzah — the Unleavened Bread;
   Maror — the Bitter Herbs.

Maasei Hashem explains that the Haggadah is telling us that despite
our recounting how numerous the plagues in Egypt were and the
countless acts of benevolence for which we are indebted to God, we have
not fulfilled our obligation of discussing the Exodus until we explain the
significance of the Pesach, matzah and *maror*.

Malbim offers another explanation. Although we have discussed the
multitude of miracles that were done for our *ancestors*, one might still
have the attitude that this is good reason for *them* to have been grateful
to God, but what does it mean for *us*? Therefore, just before we recite
Hallel we show that the Torah requires each and every Jew in every
generation to reflect upon the fact that the Exodus was a meaningful
event for him personally: *"In every generation it is one's duty to regard
himself as though he personally had gone out from Egypt, as it says
(Exodus 13:8): 'And you shall tell your son on that day, saying, "It is
because of this that HASHEM did so for me when I went out of Egypt . . . ."'"*
Since the Haggadah will quote this verse to deduce a lesson from the

פֶּסַח שֶׁהָיוּ אֲבוֹתֵינוּ אוֹכְלִים בִּזְמַן שֶׁבֵּית הַמִּקְדָּשׁ הָיָה
קַיָּם, עַל שׁוּם מָה? עַל שׁוּם שֶׁפָּסַח הַקָּדוֹשׁ בָּרוּךְ
הוּא עַל בָּתֵּי אֲבוֹתֵינוּ בְּמִצְרָיִם. שֶׁנֶּאֱמַר, וַאֲמַרְתֶּם,

word "me," it also mentions the law that Rabban Gamliel derived from
this same verse, as explained in the following question.

Shibbolei HaLeket and *Maharal* explain that now that the basic story of
the Exodus from Egypt has been told in full, it is time for us to come
back and answer the questions asked by the child at the very beginning
of the Seder: Why do we eat matzah? Why do we eat *maror*?

179. How did Rabban Gamliel derive his ruling that there is an obligation to discuss these things?

Malbim asserts that he sees this in the words *"It is because of this that
HASHEM did so for me when I went out of Egypt"* (*Exodus* 13:8). *"Because
of this,"* it will be recalled, refers to the matzah and *maror*, as the
Haggadah pointed out earlier. It is this phrase that teaches us that the
mitzvah of retelling the story of the Exodus is specifically on Pesach
night, when these items are in front of us, and we can literally say,
"Because of this." Based on this, Rabban Gamliel understood that the
mitzvah of discussing the Exodus must therefore be done *through* these
objects, by explaining their significance. This, Malbim explains, is the
reason for Rabban Gamliel's stating: *"This matzah," "This maror."*

Tosafos note that in connection with the *Korban Pesach*, the Torah
says, *"You shall say, 'It is a Passover offering for HASHEM, Who passed
over the houses of the Children of Israel. . .'"* (*Exodus* 12:27). This clearly suggests that there is a requirement to actually *say* the reason for the
Pesach offering. Since the *mitzvos* of matzah and *maror* are analogous to
that of the *Korban Pesach*, the rule is extended to these as well.

Maharsha suggests a possible reason why the *Korban Pesach,* of all the
248 positive mitzvos in the Torah, should have a Biblically required
declaration of purpose as it is fulfilled. The rule is that if any sacrifice is
performed with the wrong intention (for example, a burnt-offering) the
sacrifice is nevertheless valid. The two exceptions to this rule are the
sin-offering and the Pesach sacrifice. After detailing the reason for these
exceptions, he notes that it is for this reason that the sacrificing and
eating of the Pesach sacrifice require a special level of concentration.

180. If one did not make the necessary declarations, which obligation is it that is not fulfilled — that of matzah and *maror*, or that of

Pesach — Why did our fathers eat a Passover offering during the period when the Temple still stood? Because the Holy One, Blessed is He, passed over the houses of our fathers in Egypt, as it says: "You shall say:

---

recounting the Exodus?

Most commentators understand that Rabban Gamliel refers to the mitzvah of recounting the Exodus. This seems to be the opinion of *Rambam* as well, based on his placement of Rabban Gamliel's ruling among the other *halachos* pertaining to this mitzvah. *Aruch HaShulchan*, however, understands *Tosafos* and *Ran* to mean that the *mitzvos* of matzah and *maror* were not fulfilled.

Ran asserts that Rabban Gamliel does not mean that one would not fulfill the mitzvah at all, but only that he would not discharge his obligation *in its most proper way*. It would appear that *Tosafos*, however, disagree with this lenient interpretation.

◄§ פֶּסַח — *Pesach*

---

181. Why does Rabban Gamliel mention the Pesach offering first, considering that it was the last of those three foods to be eaten?

Abarbanel explains that this is because of the greatness of the miracle that is associated with the Pesach offering. He also suggests that the Haggadah follows the order of the verse which describes how these foods should be eaten (*Numbers* 9:11), which states the three mitzvos in this order.

Ksav Sofer cites the obligation to praise God when misfortune befalls a person, just as one must when experiencing good fortune (*Berachos* 54a). The Pesach sacrifice, he says, is like a thanksgiving-offering. The reason Rabban Gamliel mentions it first is to illustrate that the thanksgiving expressed by offering the Pesach sacrifice is for *both* the hardships of the bondage and the beneficence of the deliverance.

182. We can understand how eating matzah recalls the great haste of the Israelites when leaving Egypt and how eating *maror* represents the bitterness of slavery, but how does eating lamb represent God's passing over the houses of the Israelites in any way?

Maasei Nissim explains that God's passing over the Jewish houses was, in a sense, a result of the original Pesach offering, the blood of which was

זֶבַח פֶּסַח הוּא לַיהוה, אֲשֶׁר פָּסַח עַל בָּתֵּי בְנֵי יִשְׂרָאֵל בְּמִצְרַיִם בְּנָגְפּוֹ אֶת מִצְרַיִם, וְאֶת בָּתֵּינוּ הִצִּיל, וַיִּקֹּד הָעָם וַיִּשְׁתַּחֲווּ.[1]

---

smeared on the Jewish doorposts so that the destroyer would not enter there. Eating the Pesach lamb recalls *that* original Pesach sacrifice, and does not directly represent the passing over of the Jews' houses in Egypt.

183. Why was it necessary for the Jews to "fend off" the plague of the firstborn by smearing the blood of the paschal lamb on their doorposts? All the other plagues affected the Egyptians alone and not the Jews, without the need for any protective measures.

184. Why did the Jews have to protect themselves from the plague of the firstborn at all? It was not they who were the guilty parties, but the Egyptians. Surely God had no reason to afflict the Jews with this punishment.

Maasei Nissim explains the difference between the plague of the firstborn and the other plagues by noting that this plague was administered by God directly, without any intermediary whatsoever, as noted. The forces of nature defer to the needs or demands of the righteous, as seen through many episodes in the Bible and the Talmud. Therefore, Moses was able to limit whom the plague should affect. However, when God Himself administers punishment, He does not recognize the wishes or decrees of prophets, only strict justice. Since the Jews at the time were not deserving of preferential treatment, this plague threatened to destroy them as well as the Egyptians. It is for this reason that they were commanded to show their devotion to God and slaughter the paschal lamb, at great personal risk to themselves (for the Egyptians worshiped these animals). Through this righteous deed they earned the right to be saved from the raging plague.

In a similar vein, *Maharal* explains that the other plagues, which were administered by intermediaries, affected only people of lower spiritual status; the intermediaries never had the spiritual strength to lord over the spiritually superior Jews. The plague of the firstborn, however, was effected by God Himself, Who had the ability to affect the Jews as well. Thus the precaution of the Pesach blood was necessary.

Maasei Hashem, however, takes a different approach. He first asserts

It is a Passover offering for HASHEM, Who passed over the houses of the Children of Israel in Egypt when He struck the Egyptians, and saved our houses. And [upon hearing this] the people bowed down and prostrated themselves."[1]

---

(1) *Exodus* 12:27.

---

that in addition to the plague of death which affected only the firstborn, there was a simultaneous plague of disease, which affected *all* people. He infers this from the wording of the verse which says *"when He struck (benagfo) the Egyptians"* (*Exodus* 12:27), a term which is generally used for striking with disease, rather than "when he smote (*behakoso*)," which is the word for smiting with death. Furthermore, he points out, the Torah says *"when He . . . saved our houses,"* and not "when He saved *our firstborns.*" This implies that *all* the houses were in danger of being affected. (This would also explain why the Egyptians thought, "We are *all* dying" — *Exodus* 12:33.) This extra plague of disease was not administered directly by God like the plague of the firstborn, but by the destroyer (*Exodus* 12:23). Thus, while the plague of the firstborn — administered by God Himself — was never a threat to the Jews, as God was capable of targeting His punishment, the disease — spread by the destroyer — was a threat since he was incapable of discerning between guilty and evil parties. The blood was smeared to prevent the destroyer from entering our homes. This analysis is further borne out, says *Maasei Hashem,* by the fact that all Jews must celebrate Passover. Had the smearing of the blood on the doorposts been necessary to fend off specifically the plague of the firstborn, the entire mitzvah of the Pesach would be appropriate for firstborn Jews alone, for the salvation affected only them.

185. What exactly is the meaning of the word *Pesach*, which is generally translated as "passed over"?

Ibn Ezra translates the word as "pitied." This is because God pitied the firstborn Jews because of the blood of the sacrifice. He also quotes "the Gaon" as relating it to the word *pi'seiach* — lame. Just as a lame person limps by putting his weight on one foot while he sweeps the other one along, so too the destroyer set his destructive force on the Egyptians while skipping over the Jewish houses.

The middle matzah is lifted and displayed while the following paragraph is recited.

מַצָּה זוֹ שֶׁאָנוּ אוֹכְלִים, עַל שׁוּם מָה? עַל שׁוּם שֶׁלֹּא הִסְפִּיק בְּצֵקָם שֶׁל אֲבוֹתֵינוּ לְהַחֲמִיץ, עַד שֶׁנִּגְלָה עֲלֵיהֶם מֶלֶךְ מַלְכֵי הַמְּלָכִים הַקָּדוֹשׁ בָּרוּךְ הוּא וּגְאָלָם. שֶׁנֶּאֱמַר, וַיֹּאפוּ אֶת הַבָּצֵק אֲשֶׁר הוֹצִיאוּ מִמִּצְרַיִם עֻגֹת מַצּוֹת כִּי לֹא חָמֵץ, כִּי גֹרְשׁוּ מִמִּצְרַיִם, וְלֹא יָכְלוּ לְהִתְמַהְמֵהַּ, וְגַם צֵדָה לֹא עָשׂוּ לָהֶם.¹

---

§ מַצָּה — *Matzah*

---

186. Here we note that we eat matzah to commemorate our Exodus, while earlier we refer to it as *"bread of affliction."* What purpose does matzah serve?

Abarbanel notes that there are two motives associated with the eating of matzah in the Torah. We are commanded to eat the meat of the Pesach together with matzah and *maror* (*Numbers* 9:11), indicating that the matzah is to remind us of our enslavement to the Egyptians. This, he suggests, is why the order of the three foods eaten this night is matzah, *maror* and then Pesach — because it was after the bitter enslavement to the Egyptians that the deliverance came. On the other hand, the Torah (*Deuteronomy* 16:3) also says the matzah is eaten "because you left Egypt in a hurry; so that you remember the day of your leaving Egypt . . .," which suggests that the symbolism of matzah is not to recall slavery but deliverance. These seeming contradictory concepts may be explained as follows. The matzah that the Jews were commanded to eat at the very first Passover (*Exodus* 12:8) — which took place even before they left Egypt — was to symbolize the affliction of slavery, while the matzah that was eaten with the subsequent Pesach sacrifices symbolized the hasty liberation from bondage.

187. On Sukkos, our commemoration of the Exodus lasts throughout the entire holiday. Why, then, does the Torah command us to commemorate the Exodus by refraining from eating *chametz* for seven days, but to observe the same event by eating matzah, *maror* and Pesach only the first night? Also, why is our celebration of the giving of the Torah — Shavuos — only one day (two outside Eretz Yisrael),

Matzah — Why do we eat this unleavened bread? Because the dough of our fathers did not have time to become leavened before the King of kings, the Holy One, Blessed is He, revealed Himself to them and redeemed them, as it says: "They baked the dough which they had brought out of Egypt into unleavened bread, for it had not fermented, because they were driven out of Egypt and could not delay; nor had they prepared any provisions for themselves."[1]

(1) *Exodus* 12:39.

---

while the holiday of commemorating the Exodus is observed for seven days (eight outside Eretz Yisrael)?

Maasei Hashem explains that the celebration of the Exodus lasts for seven days because it was not until the seventh day after the Jews left Egypt that they were *completely* liberated from their Egyptian oppressors — when the Egyptians were drowned in the Sea. Refraining from chametz, matzah reminds us of the hardships of our servitude to the Egyptians. Slaves do not eat enriched, leavened bread; if they eat bread at all it is of the unleavened kind. This is why chametz is forbidden for all seven days — until we were completely free from the Egyptians. The eating of matzah on the first night, however, is related to the first concept discussed above, to recall the hastiness of our escape from Egypt. This commemorates a single, sudden event, and is thus appropriately observed for only the first night of Pesach, when this escape took place.

188 — The verse states: "*They baked the dough . . . because they were driven out of Egypt and could not delay.*" This seems to imply that it was only because of lack of time that the Jews did not leaven their dough. In fact, however, they had been commanded before leaving Egypt that "for seven days, leaven may not be found in your houses" (*Exodus* 12:19);[58] hence they could not have leavened their bread even if they had had the time to do so!

Several approaches have been suggested by the commentators to deal with this difficulty. *Ramban,* in his commentary on the Torah, explains

---

58. Although this verse does not deal with the first Passover, but with subsequent Passovers (see v. 14), as the first Passover was celebrated for only one day (*Pesachim* 96b), *Ramban* nevertheless feels that at least for that one day the prohibition of owning chametz still applied.

The *maror* is lifted and displayed while the following paragraph is recited.

מָרוֹר זֶה שֶׁאָנוּ אוֹכְלִים, עַל שׁוּם מָה? עַל שׁוּם שֶׁמֵּרְרוּ הַמִּצְרִים אֶת חַיֵּי אֲבוֹתֵינוּ בְּמִצְרָיִם. שֶׁנֶּאֱמַר, וַיְמָרְרוּ אֶת חַיֵּיהֶם, בַּעֲבֹדָה קָשָׁה, בְּחֹמֶר וּבִלְבֵנִים, וּבְכָל עֲבֹדָה בַּשָּׂדֶה, אֵת כָּל עֲבֹדָתָם אֲשֶׁר עָבְדוּ בָהֶם בְּפָרֶךְ.[1]

---

the verse as follows: They baked the dough (that they had already kneaded in Egypt) into unleavened bread (which they were commanded to do) *on the way,* for they were driven out from Egypt and were thus not able to do so in Egypt itself. In other words, *"because they were driven out"* is the reason they baked matzah *on the road* rather than before they left; it is not the reason for their having baked matzah as opposed to bread.

Ran believes that the prohibition to *own chametz,* though mentioned in the Torah before the Exodus, did not apply that first year. He understands it as a commandment to be observed for future Passovers, and the Jews were enjoined only not to *eat chametz* on that first, one-day Passover. Thus they would have baked leavened bread to eat later, but were prevented from doing so because they were driven from Egypt.

Malbim asserts that when the Talmud tells us that the laws of Passover applied for one day and one night that first year, it means the day of the *fourteenth* of Nissan and the night which followed it. Thus, there was certainly no prohibition against having *chametz* in one's possession on the day of the fifteenth of Nissan, which is after the Jews left Egypt. According to this, the Jews could have baked and eaten leavened bread, but they did not do so *"because they were driven out."*

⇜§ מָרוֹר — *Maror*

---

189. *Maror* represents slavery; and matzah, as explained, our liberation. This being the case, why is *maror* eaten — and its significance explained — *after* matzah?

Maasei Hashem refers us to the verse (*Ecclesiastes* 7:14): *Beyom tovah he'yei betov, u'veyom ra'ah re'eh.* This verse is usually translated as "Be pleased on the day when things go well, but on a day of misfortune reflect." *Maasei Hashem,* however, interprets it as follows: "Be happy on a day that things go well, reflecting upon the bad days." That is, when a

The *maror* is lifted and displayed while the following paragraph is recited.

Maror — Why do we eat this bitter herb? Because the Egyptians embittered the lives of our fathers in Egypt, as it says: "They embittered their lives with hard labor, with mortar and bricks, and with all manner of labor in the field: Whatever service they made them perform was with hard labor."[1]

---

(1) *Exodus* 1:14.

---

person is happy over some stroke of good fortune, he can increase his happiness by reflecting about just how bad things were before this good fortune came his way. If one reflects upon the evils of his unfortunate times *before* experiencing his good fortune, however, he is likely to only increase his depression and disappointment. Bearing this in mind we can understand why the *maror* is eaten after the matzah. It is after we recall our deliverance from the hands of Egypt that we seek to intensify our joy by remembering just how bitter the enslavement that preceded it was.

Bircas HaShir explains that the bitterness of the Israelites' subjugation to the Egyptians was really for their own good, for the "iron crucible" of Egypt (*Deuteronomy* 4:20) prepared them to become the true servants of God. Of course, the Jews did not realize this while they were enslaved in Egypt, but only after the giving of the Torah. This is the facet of our subjugation that the *maror* commemorates; the Torah would not have made a mitzvah out of recalling the bitterness of slavery if not for this positive, spiritual aspect of our suffering. Thus the *maror* is eaten after the matzah — to show that it is only after our deliverance that the true purpose of our suffering became apparent.

190. Does the *maror* have any other symbolism besides recalling the embittered lives of our forefathers?

The sages (*Pesachim* 39a) note that one of the vegetables which can be used for *maror* (which means "bitterness") is *chassa*, meaning "pity," symbolizing the fact that God had pity on us and redeemed us from slavery. *Abarbanel* points out that all three of the Pesach foods represent two contrasting ideals. Matzah represents, on the one hand, the bread of affliction eaten by slaves, and, on the other, the fact that the redemption came so swiftly that there was no time for the Jews to allow their dough to rise. The *maror*, as just shown, shows both the bitterness of slavery

183 / THE HAGGADAH WITH ANSWERS

בְּכָל דוֹר וָדוֹר חַיָּב אָדָם לִרְאוֹת אֶת עַצְמוֹ כְּאִלּוּ הוּא יָצָא מִמִּצְרַיִם. שֶׁנֶּאֱמַר, וְהִגַּדְתָּ לְבִנְךָ בַּיּוֹם הַהוּא לֵאמֹר, בַּעֲבוּר זֶה עָשָׂה יהוה לִי, בְּצֵאתִי מִמִּצְרָיִם.¹ לֹא אֶת אֲבוֹתֵינוּ בִּלְבָד גָּאַל הַקָּדוֹשׁ בָּרוּךְ הוּא, אֶלָּא אַף אֹתָנוּ גָּאַל עִמָּהֶם. שֶׁנֶּאֱמַר, וְאוֹתָנוּ הוֹצִיא מִשָּׁם, לְמַעַן הָבִיא אֹתָנוּ לָתֶת לָנוּ אֶת הָאָרֶץ אֲשֶׁר נִשְׁבַּע לַאֲבוֹתֵינוּ.²

and the mercy shown to us by God. The Pesach sacrifice reminds us of the attribute of Divine Justice — His striking down the Egyptian firstborn — and also of His mercy in passing over and sparing our own houses.

The Talmud (ibid.) also describes the deeper significance of comparing the *maror* to the Egyptian slavery: Just as the Egyptians were originally decent and hospitable towards the Jews (when Jacob and his sons first settled there — *Yerushalmi*), and later changed their attitude to one of enmity and hostility, so too *maror* is soft when it begins to grow and only hardens later. The import of this fact, says *Ksav Sofer*, is that the hatred of one nation toward another is even more hurtful if it was preceded by mutual respect and harmony. The fact that the Egyptians originally treated the Israelites well made the subsequent affliction of the Israelites more difficult to bear.

◆§ בְּכָל דּוֹר וָדוֹר — *In every generation it is one's duty to regard himself as though he personally had gone out from Egypt.*

---

191. Why is this personal participation in the miracles performed for our ancestors required specifically on Pesach? On Purim too, for instance, we could make a point of saying that had God not thwarted Haman's evil plan we would all not be here today.

Maasei Nissim explains this as follows. The redemption for which we are giving thanks to God is not the physical deliverance from servitude to the Egyptians. Rather, we express our gratitude at our being chosen by God to be His people. While God made this choice at the time of the Exodus, we are direct beneficiaries as our forefathers were. All generations are equally indebted to God for having given us the privilege of

In every generation it is one's duty to regard himself as though he personally had gone out from Egypt, as it says: "And you shall tell your son on that day, saying, 'It is because of this that HASHEM did for "me" when I went out of Egypt.' "[1] It was not only our fathers whom the Holy One, Blessed is He, redeemed from slavery; we, too, were redeemed with them, as it says: "He brought us out from there so that He might take us to the land which He had promised to our fathers."[2]

---

(1) *Exodus* 13:8. (2) *Deuteronomy* 6:23.

---

being His nation. Thus the Haggadah here does not refer to God "having taken us out of Egypt" but rather His having *"redeemed"* our ancestors and us. The word *"ga'al"* — *"redeemed"* — can also mean "acquired." It is not the physical Exodus from Egypt that is being stressed here, but the *acquisition* of the Jewish people by God to be His chosen nation.

Netziv cites the *mishnah* (*Sanhedrin* 37a) which tells us, "Every person should say, 'The world was created for my sake.' " By adopting this attitude, one comes to recognize the importance of each of his actions and will strive to channel his behavior to conform to the will of his Creator, Who created the entire world on the person's behalf. In this case as well, by considering ourselves among those directly involved in the Exodus and the birth of the chosen nation, we can inculcate within ourselves the importance of our following the Torah of God, which God directly gave to each of us.

192. Why does the Haggadah cite the verse *"He brought us out from there"* to establish that it is as if we, ourselves, left Egypt. Is this not clear from the verse *"it is because of this that Hashem did for me . . .,"* which we just mentioned?

Malbim explains that the first verse might have been construed to be addressed only to the generation of Moses. When they grew up and had children, they were told, they were to tell their children about the events that they had experienced. The second verse, however, appears in a paragraph that begins, "If your son asks you *tomorrow,*" where *tomorrow* carries the implication of speaking about the distant future (*Deuteronomy* 6:20). This is why the first verse alone was insufficient. The second verse, on the other hand, has a weakness as well, in that it does not tell us that we must *verbalize* our feeling that we were personally

The matzos are covered and the cup is lifted and held until it is to be drunk. According to some customs, however, the cup is put down after the following paragraph, in which case the matzos should once more be uncovered. If this custom is followed, the matzos are to be covered and the cup raised again upon reaching the blessing אֲשֶׁר גְּאָלָנוּ, *Who has redeemed us* (p. 192). Some declare their intent to fulfill their obligation to drink the second of the four cups of wine.

לְפִיכָךְ אֲנַחְנוּ חַיָּבִים לְהוֹדוֹת, לְהַלֵּל, לְשַׁבֵּחַ, לְפָאֵר, לְרוֹמֵם, לְהַדֵּר, לְבָרֵךְ, לְעַלֵּה, וּלְקַלֵּס, לְמִי

---

involved in the Exodus. The first verse, however, begins with, "And *you shall tell . . . God did for me . . ."* This makes it clear that our personal connection to the Exodus must be expressed in words. Thus both verses are necessary, for each one teaches something which the other does not.

193. If the whole proof that each individual must relate to the Exodus on a personal level is derived from the verse cited, then it should only apply to the generations of Jews who lived in the Land of Israel, since the verse says that we were redeemed "so that He might take us to the land . . ." Why does this obligation pertain to us as well, who were born and raised in exile?

Abarbanel answers this question as follows. The Exodus from Egypt involved much more than just a physical redemption from slavery. The Exodus was the event which established that God chose us as His people and that He could and would protect and redeem us — even to the point of completely suspending the laws of nature. The giving of the Torah at Sinai, the miracles that accompanied us in the desert, the conquest of the Land of Israel, the building of the Temple, the centuries-long institution of prophecy — all these were direct results of the Exodus from Egypt. This, he notes, is the reason why the Torah connects so many mitzvos with perpetuating the memory of the Exodus. And this is also why it is so important for us to consider ourselves as having personally experienced the Exodus. While the Torah uses the phrase *"so that He might take us to the land . . .,"* the subsequent verses use the word *"we"* and *"us"* concerning more general subjects: "HASHEM commanded us to perform all these decrees, to fear HASHEM our God for our good *all the days*, to give us life . . . and it will be a merit for us if we are careful to perform this entire commandment before Hashem . . ." (*Deuteronomy* 6:24-25). Thus, we see that the Torah uses the word *"us"* (though it is discussing future generations) not only in regard to the Land of Israel, but also in regard to fearing God, our receiving goodness from Him all

The matzos are covered and the cup is lifted and held until it is to be drunk. According to some customs, however, the cup is put down after the following paragraph, in which case the matzos should once more be uncovered. If this custom is followed, the matzos are to be covered and the cup raised again upon reaching the blessing אֲשֶׁר גְּאָלָנוּ, *Who has redeemed us* (p. 192). Some declare their intent to fulfill their obligation to drink the second of the four cups of wine.

Therefore it is our duty to thank, praise, pay tribute, glorify, exalt, honor, bless, extol, and acclaim Him

---

the days, eternal life and other concepts. All of the aforementioned, which ultimately emanate from the events of the Exodus and reach far beyond our inhabiting the Land of Israel, are things from which we ourselves benefit and they obligate us to feel a personal connection with the Exodus.

Maharal makes another point concerning this issue. Throughout their long, precarious existence in their bitter exiles, the very survival of the Jews is nothing short of miraculous, in light of all the repeated assaults and persecutions that they experience. As *Ramban* states: "The entire manner in which God deals with us in our exile involves constant subtle miracles." Since God constantly supplies us with these minideliverances from our troubles, we each experience our own "Exodus from Egypt" from time to time. Thus, even in exile we can apply to ourselves the words *"and He brought us out from there."*

---

§ לְפִיכָךְ אֲנַחְנוּ חַיָּבִים — *Therefore it is our duty to thank, praise, pay tribute ...*

---

194. What is the significance of having so many synonyms of praise?

There are nine synonyms for "praise" in this prayer (although there are other versions which have only five). *Maharal* explains the significance of this number as follows. The Talmud (*Pesachim* 117a) tells us that there are ten different expressions for "praise" which the Book of *Psalms* uses to introduce various psalms. The tenth and greatest expression of all, the Talmud says, is *Halleluyah*. This is why the Haggadah has nine expressions of praise, followed by the phrase *"Let us recite ... Halleluyah"* — the tenth and ultimate kind of praise.

195. Why is this paragraph recited at this point in the Seder?

Rashbam considers this paragraph to be a transitional step. Having just declared our recognition of the fact that we consider it as if we ourselves have experienced the Exodus, we proclaim that it is our duty

שֶׁעָשָׂה לַאֲבוֹתֵינוּ וְלָנוּ אֶת כָּל הַנִּסִּים הָאֵלּוּ, הוֹצִיאָנוּ
מֵעַבְדוּת לְחֵרוּת, מִיָּגוֹן לְשִׂמְחָה, וּמֵאֵבֶל לְיוֹם טוֹב,
וּמֵאֲפֵלָה לְאוֹר גָּדוֹל, וּמִשִּׁעְבּוּד לִגְאֻלָּה, וְנֹאמַר לְפָנָיו
שִׁירָה חֲדָשָׁה, הַלְלוּיָהּ.

---

to sing praises to God just as our ancestors did — and we proceed to recite Hallel.

Kol Bo quotes an opinion that considers this paragraph as being in place of the blessing which is usually said upon the recitation of Hallel. He rejects this idea, however, because we find no other blessing which resembles this prayer. In order to be considered a "blessing," a prayer must actually state the praises of God, not merely say, *"It is our duty to ... praise ... Him."*

196. What is the significance of the five seemingly repetitive expressions of our advancing from adversity to good fortune?

Maasei Hashem sees these expressions as serving as a sort of introduction to Hallel, for Hallel contains invocations of thanksgiving for these five types of deliverance: *From slavery to freedom* corresponds to *"When Israel went forth from Egypt ..."* (Psalms 114:1); *from grief to joy* parallels *"trouble and sorrow have I found."* Then I called upon the Name of HASHEM ..." (loc. cit. 116:3-4); *from mourning to festivity* refers to *"You delivered ... my eyes from tears ..."* (loc. cit. 116:8) and *"This is the day Hashem has made..."* (loc. cit. 118:24); *from darkness to great light* corresponds to *"Hashem is God and He illuminated for us"* (loc cit., v. 27); and *from servitude to redemption* is a reference to the final severing of all ties of subservience to Egypt at the Splitting of the Red Sea, at which time *"The Sea saw and fled"* (loc. cit. 114:3).

Malbim, quoting the *Gra*, sees these five expressions as reflecting five major stages in the Jews' redemption and their achieving independence. *From slavery to freedom* refers to the Exodus from Egypt, when their slavery ended; *from grief to joy* represents the salvation at the Red Sea, when the people found themselves in a very precarious position and ended in expressing their joy through song; *from mourning to festivity* corresponds to the mourning which the Jews observed at Mount Sinai after the sin of the Golden Calf (*Exodus* 33:4), which was followed by the forgiveness of God for that sin on Yom Kippur (which is called a festival — *Taanis* 26b); *from darkness to great light* refers to the passing from the dark, bleak desert to *Eretz Yisrael*; and *from servitude to redemption*

Who performed all these miracles for our fathers and for us. He brought us forth from slavery to freedom, from grief to joy, from mourning to festivity, from darkness to great light, and from servitude to redemption. Let us, therefore, recite a new song before Him! Halleluyah!

---

parallels the period of the Judges, when the Jews faced constant harassment and subjugation at the hands of the neighboring nations, until their final deliverance in the days of David and Solomon. For these five stages leading to our ultimate redemption we must give thanks and recite Hallel.

197. To what "new song" do we refer?

The *Graz* asserts that the proper vowelization of the word ונאמר is וְנֶאֱמַר (*vene'emar*), and not וְנֹאמַר (*venomar*), so that the phrase is translated "*. . . and a new song was recited before Him.*" According to this, the reference is to the song sung at the Red Sea by Moses and the Israelites after the miraculous drowning of the Egyptians there, or, perhaps, Hallel (see *Pesachim* 117a). Had the Haggadah wanted to refer to the song that *we* will sing upon our future redemption in the times of the Messiah, he reasons, it would use the masculine form for *"new song"* (שִׁיר חָדָשׁ). The reason for this is that, as the *Tosafos* (*Pesachim* 116b) tell us, all songs described in the Bible are referred to by the feminine form of the word (שִׁירָה). This indicates that the events which they celebrate are like childbirth, where the joy of the birth is somewhat diminished by the realization that the difficult ordeal of labor might be undergone again in the future. The exception is the song for the End of Days, which is referred to in the masculine, for it will mark the end of all pain and suffering. By using the feminine form, the Haggadah must be referring to the Song at the Sea, and the passive וְנֶאֱמַר must be used.

But why do we call the Song at the Sea *"new,"* both here and in the morning prayers (*shirah chadashah shibchu ge'ulim* — "*a new song* the redeemed ones praised")? *Aruch HaShulchan* explains that until the Exodus the peoples of the world believed that God is too lofty to care about the mundane affairs of the world and He does not interest Himself in punishing or rewarding man for his deeds. After witnessing the miracles of the Exodus and the Red Sea, however, they came to the realization that this was not the case. They recognized that the glory of God actually expresses itself in the very fact that He *does* involve himself in the affairs of the world despite His exaltedness. At that time

הַלְלוּיָהּ הַלְלוּ עַבְדֵי יהוה, הַלְלוּ אֶת שֵׁם יהוה. יְהִי שֵׁם יהוה מְבֹרָךְ, מֵעַתָּה וְעַד עוֹלָם. מִמִּזְרַח שֶׁמֶשׁ עַד מְבוֹאוֹ, מְהֻלָּל שֵׁם יהוה. רָם עַל כָּל גּוֹיִם יהוה, עַל הַשָּׁמַיִם כְּבוֹדוֹ. מִי כַּיהוה אֱלֹהֵינוּ, הַמַּגְבִּיהִי לָשָׁבֶת. הַמַּשְׁפִּילִי לִרְאוֹת, בַּשָּׁמַיִם וּבָאָרֶץ. מְקִימִי מֵעָפָר דָּל, מֵאַשְׁפֹּת יָרִים אֶבְיוֹן. לְהוֹשִׁיבִי עִם נְדִיבִים, עִם נְדִיבֵי עַמּוֹ. מוֹשִׁיבִי עֲקֶרֶת הַבַּיִת, אֵם הַבָּנִים שְׂמֵחָה, הַלְלוּיָהּ.[1]

---

the Jews sang out, "Who is like You among the mighty forces" which exhibit their power on earth? "Who is like You, mighty in holiness" — Who concerns Yourself with these matters despite Your holiness and might? You are "awesome in praise" — exalted and feared, yet "the Doer of wonders" — You perform miracles for mortal men. This was a *new* concept that was introduced into the world at that time.

◆§ הַלְלוּיָהּ — *Halleluyah*

---

198. Why is no blessing recited over the recitation of Hallel at the Seder, unlike the other occasions of the year when Hallel is said?

Several commentators suggest that the reason for this is that Hallel tonight is split up into two parts, with a lengthy interruption in between (see next question). Thus Hallel is not being "sung" as it usually is, but merely "recited" (*Machzor Vitri*, *Or Zarua*).

Aruch HaShulchan suggests that the blessing *"Asher Ge'alanu"* — *"Who redeemed us"* (אֲשֶׁר גְּאָלָנוּ) serves as the blessing for at least the first part of Hallel. He also notes that there are many communities where Hallel is recited in the synagogue, before the Seder, with the usual blessing, and in these places the omission of the blessing at the Seder is more understandable.

Maharal explains in the name of *Rav Hai Gaon* that this Hallel is different from all other Hallels of the year, in that it is recited in celebration of a miracle which, as we stressed, has occurred to us personally. A blessing is not said before this type of Hallel, as it is a spontaneous expression of personal gratitude.

Halleluyah! Give praise, you servants of HASHEM; praise the Name of HASHEM! Blessed be the Name of HASHEM, from this time and forever. From the rising of the sun to its setting, HASHEM's Name is praised. High above all nations is HASHEM, above the heavens is His glory. Who is like HASHEM, our God, Who is enthroned on high — yet deigns to look upon the heaven and the earth? He raises the needy from the dust, from the trash heaps He lifts the destitute — to seat them with nobles, with the nobles of His people. He transforms the barren wife into a glad mother of children. Halleluyah![1]

_____

(1) *Psalms* 113.

_____

199. Why is Hallel split into two parts tonight?

Avudraham says the reason a part of Hallel is said before the meal is to "embellish" the second cup of wine with some words of praise. The rest of the recitation of the Maggid section would be merely "story-telling" if not for the inclusion of at least part of Hallel.

Maharal suggests that division of Hallel was originally intended to both precede and follow the eating of the meat of the Pesach sacrifice with Hallel, to make it clear that Hallel was being recited in honor of this offering (for the recitation of Hallel is required for the eating of the Pesach sacrifice — *Pesachim* 95a). If all of Hallel were said either before or after the meal, this point would not have been sufficiently highlighted. Today this practice is continued, because the matzah we eat takes the place of the paschal meat.

Maasei Nissim explains that the first two cups of the Seder correspond to the expressions of God's "taking out" and "saving" us from Egypt (*Exodus* 6:6). These references reflect the theme of the Exodus from Egypt exclusively. The last two cups, corresponding to the expressions of "redemption" and God's "taking them to Me as a people," convey a more general theme of redemption, which includes the ultimate, Messianic salvation which is yet to come. For this reason, the first two paragraphs of Hallel, which speak of the Exodus, are recited over the second cup of wine, while the rest of Hallel, which speaks of redemption in general, alluding to the future salvation, are said over the fourth cup.

בְּצֵאת יִשְׂרָאֵל מִמִּצְרָיִם, בֵּית יַעֲקֹב מֵעַם לֹעֵז. הָיְתָה יְהוּדָה לְקָדְשׁוֹ, יִשְׂרָאֵל מַמְשְׁלוֹתָיו. הַיָּם רָאָה וַיָּנֹס, הַיַּרְדֵּן יִסֹּב לְאָחוֹר. הֶהָרִים רָקְדוּ כְאֵילִים, גְּבָעוֹת כִּבְנֵי צֹאן. מַה לְּךָ הַיָּם כִּי תָנוּס, הַיַּרְדֵּן תִּסֹּב לְאָחוֹר. הֶהָרִים תִּרְקְדוּ כְאֵילִים, גְּבָעוֹת כִּבְנֵי צֹאן. מִלִּפְנֵי אָדוֹן חוּלִי אָרֶץ, מִלִּפְנֵי אֱלוֹהַ יַעֲקֹב. הַהֹפְכִי הַצּוּר אֲגַם מָיִם, חַלָּמִישׁ לְמַעְיְנוֹ מָיִם.[1]

According to all customs the cup is lifted and the matzos covered during the recitation of this blessing. [On Saturday night substitute the bracketed phrase for the preceding phrase.]

בָּרוּךְ אַתָּה יהוה אֱלֹהֵינוּ מֶלֶךְ הָעוֹלָם, אֲשֶׁר גְּאָלָנוּ וְגָאַל אֶת אֲבוֹתֵינוּ מִמִּצְרָיִם, וְהִגִּיעָנוּ הַלַּיְלָה הַזֶּה לֶאֱכָל בּוֹ מַצָּה וּמָרוֹר. כֵּן יהוה אֱלֹהֵינוּ וֵאלֹהֵי אֲבוֹתֵינוּ, יַגִּיעֵנוּ לְמוֹעֲדִים וְלִרְגָלִים אֲחֵרִים הַבָּאִים לִקְרָאתֵנוּ לְשָׁלוֹם, שְׂמֵחִים בְּבִנְיַן עִירֶךָ וְשָׂשִׂים בַּעֲבוֹדָתֶךָ, וְנֹאכַל שָׁם מִן הַזְּבָחִים וּמִן הַפְּסָחִים [מִן הַפְּסָחִים וּמִן הַזְּבָחִים] אֲשֶׁר יַגִּיעַ דָּמָם עַל קִיר מִזְבַּחֲךָ לְרָצוֹן.

‏אֲשֶׁר גְּאָלָנוּ . . . בָּרוּךְ אַתָּה — *Blessed are You . . . Who redeemed us*

---

200. When we say *"offerings and Passover sacrifices,"* **which** *"offerings"* **are meant, and why are they mentioned before** *"Passover sacrifices"*?

The *"offerings"* referred to are the additional *Chagigah* offerings which were brought for the festival. *Tosafos* says that since this offering is consumed before the Pesach sacrifice — as the Pesach sacrifice must be eaten when one is full — it is mentioned first in this prayer. *Avudraham*, however, says that the proper order of eating these foods was to begin with a bit of the Pesach meat, then to eat the *Chagigah* to satiety, and this was followed by more meat from the Pesach sacrifice.

When Passover began on Saturday night, and the Pesach was thus slaughtered on the Sabbath, no *Chagigah* was offered, as this offering,

When Israel went out of Egypt, Jacob's household from a people of alien tongue — Judah became His sanctuary, Israel His dominions. The Sea saw and fled; the Jordan turned backward. The mountains skipped like rams, the hills like young lambs. What ails you, O Sea, that you flee? O Jordan, that you turn backward? O mountains, that you skip like rams? O hills, like young lambs? Before the Lord's presence — did I, the earth tremble — before the presence of the God of Jacob, Who turns the rock into a pond of water, the flint into a flowing fountain.[1]

According to all customs the cup is lifted and the matzos covered during the recitation of this blessing. [On Saturday night substitute the bracketed phrase for the preceding phrase.]

Blessed are You, HASHEM our God, King of the universe, Who redeemed us and redeemed our ancestors from Egypt, and enabled us to reach this night that we may eat on it matzah and *maror*. So, HASHEM our God and God of our fathers, bring us also to future festivals and holidays in peace, gladdened in the rebuilding of Your city and joyful at Your service. There we shall eat of the offerings and Passover sacrifices (of the Passover sacrifices and offerings) whose blood will gain the sides of Your Altar for gracious acceptance.

---

(1) *Psalms* 114.

---

unlike the Pesach, does not override the Sabbath. Nowadays when Pesach begins on a Saturday night, the word *"offerings"* in this prayer takes on a new meaning: the other festive offerings that may be brought during the course of the Passover holiday, beginning Sunday morning. It is for this reason that some authorities are of the opinion that the order of the words *"offerings"* and *"Passover sacrifices"* should be reversed on Saturday night. Others maintain that such a change is unnecessary, since we are praying that we may be granted the opportunity to experience *future* Passovers at the Temple in Jerusalem, and these future Passovers will not all occur on Saturday night.

201. What is the meaning of the expression *"whose blood will gain the sides of Your Altar for gracious acceptance"*?

Chasam Sofer explains that even in exile we offer *"sacrifices"* to God

וְנוֹדֶה לְּךָ שִׁיר חָדָשׁ עַל גְּאֻלָּתֵנוּ וְעַל פְּדוּת נַפְשֵׁנוּ. בָּרוּךְ אַתָּה יהוה, גָּאַל יִשְׂרָאֵל.

בָּרוּךְ אַתָּה יהוה אֱלֹהֵינוּ מֶלֶךְ הָעוֹלָם, בּוֹרֵא פְּרִי הַגָּפֶן.

The second cup is drunk while leaning on the left side —
preferably the entire cup, but at least most of it.

רחצה

The hands are washed for matzah and the following blessing is recited. It is preferable to bring water and a basin to the head of the household at the Seder table.
Before washing, it is vital that one insure that there is adequate *matzah shemurah* for each of the participants. Some declare their intent to perform the commandment to eat matzah according to the laws of the Torah as codified by the Sages.

בָּרוּךְ אַתָּה יהוה אֱלֹהֵינוּ מֶלֶךְ הָעוֹלָם, אֲשֶׁר קִדְּשָׁנוּ בְּמִצְוֹתָיו, וְצִוָּנוּ עַל נְטִילַת יָדָיִם.

— Jews who give their lives in martyrdom, sanctification of God's Name. These sacrifices, however, are not *"for gracious acceptance,"* for God mourns the misfortunes of His people (see *Sanhedrin* 46a). We therefore pray that in the future we may be able to offer the kind of sacrifices that will be pleasing and acceptable to God — the sacrifices prescribed in the Torah — in the Temple.

Aruch HaShulchan offers an alternate interpretation. Sacrifices are often offered to atone for a sin which has been committed. The Pesach sacrifice, however, since it is not brought in the wake of any wrongdoing, is considered a truly *"graciously acceptable"* offering to God. In contrast to other Pesach sacrifices, the very first Pesach sacrifice, offered by the Jews in Egypt on the eve of the Exodus, was, in fact, a sort of atonement for past sins. As the Sages tell us, the Jews of that time had sunk to such a low spiritual state that God had to give them the mitzvah of the Pesach sacrifice in order that they attain some merit through which to be redeemed. Thus, in this prayer we beseech God that we may be able to bring the Pesach sacrifice *"whose blood will gain the sides of Your Altar."* We wish to bring a perfectly pleasing

We shall then sing a new song of praise to You for our redemption and the liberation of our souls. Blessed are You, HASHEM, Who has redeemed Israel.

Blessed are You, HASHEM our God, King of the universe, Who creates the fruit of the vine.

The second cup is drunk while leaning on the left side — preferably the entire cup, but at least most of it.

RACHTZAH

The hands are washed for matzah and the following blessing is recited. It is preferable to bring water and a basin to the head of the household at the Seder table.
Before washing, it is vital that one insure that there is adequate *matzah shemurah* for each of the participants. Some declare their intent to perform the commandment to eat matzah according to the laws of the Torah as codified by the Sages.

Blessed are You, HASHEM our God, King of the universe, Who has sanctified us with His commandments, and has commanded us concerning the washing of the hands.

---

sacrifice, as opposed to the original Pesach sacrifice whose blood was sprinkled on the doorposts and lintels of the Jewish houses. That was not a totally pleasing sacrifice to God, since it came in the wake of sinful behavior.

202. In the paragraph beginning *"Leficach, Therefore,"* the word used for *"song"* was *"shirah,"* the feminine form. Here the masculine form of the word, *"shir,"* is used. Why is this so?

Shibbolei HaLeket cites an explanation, based on a *midrashic* source. The halachah states that if a man dies, his unmarried daughters are given 10 percent of the estate before it is divided up among the heirs. This is in order to help with the daughters' future marriage expenses. In the days of the Exodus the Jews were granted the land of the seven Canaanite nations (*Deuteronomy* 7:1), $^{1}/_{10}$ of the total number of seventy nations who comprised the world (*Genesis,* Chap. 10). It is for this reason that the song sung at that time is referred to in the feminine. With the future redemption, the Jews will be granted a full share of the earth, like a male heir, so the song of the Messianic era is referred to in the masculine. (Also see question 197, where another reason is cited.)

מוֹצִיא

The following two blessings are recited over matzah; the first is recited over matzah as food, and the second for the special mitzvah of eating matzah on the night of Pesach. [The latter blessing is to be made with the intention that it also apply to the "sandwich," and the afikoman.]

The head of the household raises all the matzos on the Seder plate and recites the following blessings:

בָּרוּךְ אַתָּה יהוה אֱלֹהֵינוּ מֶלֶךְ הָעוֹלָם, הַמּוֹצִיא לֶחֶם מִן הָאָרֶץ.

Those who use three matzos put down the bottom matzah at this point.

מַצָּה

בָּרוּךְ אַתָּה יהוה אֱלֹהֵינוּ מֶלֶךְ הָעוֹלָם, אֲשֶׁר קִדְּשָׁנוּ בְּמִצְוֹתָיו, וְצִוָּנוּ עַל אֲכִילַת מַצָּה.

Each participant is required to eat an amount of matzah equal in volume to an egg. Since it is usually impossible to provide a sufficient amount of matzah from the two matzos for all members of the household, other matzos should be available at the head of the table from which to complete the required amounts. However, each participant should receive a piece from each of the top two matzos.

The matzos are to be eaten while reclining on the left side and without delay; they should not be dipped in salt.

מָרוֹר

The head of the household takes a half-egg volume of the maror, dips it into charoses, and gives each participant a like amount.

The following blessing is recited with the intention that it also apply to the maror of the "sandwich." The maror is eaten without reclining, and without delay.

בָּרוּךְ אַתָּה יהוה אֱלֹהֵינוּ מֶלֶךְ הָעוֹלָם, אֲשֶׁר קִדְּשָׁנוּ בְּמִצְוֹתָיו, וְצִוָּנוּ עַל אֲכִילַת מָרוֹר.

MOTZI

The following two blessings are recited over matzah; the first is recited over matzah as food, and the second for the special mitzvah of eating matzah on the night of Passover. [The latter blessing is to be made with the intention that it also apply to the "sandwich," and the *afikoman*.]

The head of the household raises all the matzos on the Seder plate
and recites the following blessing:

Blessed are You, HASHEM our God, King of the universe, Who brings forth bread from the earth.

Those who use three matzos put down the bottom matzah at this point.

MATZAH

Blessed are You, HASHEM our God, King of the universe, Who has sanctified us with His commandments, and has commanded us concerning the eating of the matzah.

Each participant is required to eat an amount of matzah equal in volume to an egg. Since it is usually impossible to provide a sufficient amount of matzah from the two matzos for all members of the household, other matzos should be available at the head of the table from which to complete the required amounts. However, each participant should receive a piece from each of the top two matzos.

The matzos are to be eaten while reclining on the left side and without delay;
they should not be dipped in salt.

MAROR

The head of the household takes a half-egg volume of the *maror*,
dips it into *charoses*, and gives each participant a like amount.

The following blessing is recited with the intention that it also apply to the *maror* of the "sandwich." The *maror* is eaten without reclining, and without delay.

Blessed are You, HASHEM our God, King of the universe, Who has sanctified us with His commandments, and has commanded us concerning the eating of *maror*.

כּוֹרֵךְ

The bottom (thus far unbroken) matzah is now taken. From it, with the addition of other matzos, each participant receives a half-egg volume of matzah with an equal volume portion of *maror* (dipped into *charoses* which is shaken off). The following paragraph is recited and the ''sandwich'' is eaten while reclining.

זֵכֶר לְמִקְדָּשׁ כְּהִלֵּל. כֵּן עָשָׂה הִלֵּל בִּזְמַן שֶׁבֵּית הַמִּקְדָּשׁ הָיָה קַיָּם. הָיָה כּוֹרֵךְ (פֶּסַח) מַצָּה וּמָרוֹר וְאוֹכֵל בְּיַחַד. לְקַיֵּם מַה שֶּׁנֶּאֱמַר, עַל מַצּוֹת וּמְרֹרִים יֹאכְלֻהוּ.[1]

שֻׁלְחָן עוֹרֵךְ

The meal should be eaten in a combination of joy and solemnity, for the meal, too, is a part of the Seder service. While it is desirable that *zemiros* and discussion of the laws and events of Passover be part of the meal, extraneous conversation should be avoided. It should be remembered that the *afikoman* must be eaten while there is still some appetite for it. In fact, if one is so sated that he must literally force himself to eat it, he is not credited with the performance of the mitzvah of *afikoman*. Therefore, it is unwise to eat more than a moderate amount during the meal.

צָפוּן

From the *afikoman* matzah (and from additional matzos to make up the required amount), a half-egg volume portion — according to some, a full egg's volume portion — is given to each participant. It should be eaten before midnight, while reclining, without delay, and uninterruptedly. Nothing may be eaten or drunk after the *afikoman* (with the exception of water and the like) except for the last two Seder cups of wine.

בָּרֵךְ

The third cup is poured and *Bircas HaMazon* (Grace After Meals) is recited.
According to some customs, the Cup of Elijah is poured at this point.

שִׁיר הַמַּעֲלוֹת, בְּשׁוּב יהוה אֶת שִׁיבַת צִיּוֹן, הָיִינוּ כְּחֹלְמִים. אָז יִמָּלֵא שְׂחוֹק פִּינוּ וּלְשׁוֹנֵנוּ רִנָּה,

KORECH

The bottom (thus far unbroken) matzah is now taken. From it, with the addition of other matzos, each participant receives a half-egg volume of matzah with an equal volume portion of *maror* (dipped into *charoses* which is shaken off). The following paragraph is recited and the "sandwich" is eaten while reclining.

In remembrance of the Temple we do as Hillel did in Temple times: He would combine Passover offering, matzah and *maror* in a sandwich and eat them together, to fulfill that which is written: "With matzos and *maror* they shall eat it."[1]

SHULCHAN ORECH

The meal should be eaten in a combination of joy and solemnity, for the meal, too, is a part of the Seder service. While it is desirable that *zemiros* and discussion of the laws and events of Passover be part of the meal, extraneous conversation should be avoided. It should be remembered that the *afikoman* must be eaten while there is still some appetite for it. In fact, if one is so sated that he must literally force himself to eat it, he is not credited with the performance of the mitzvah of *afikoman*. Therefore, it is unwise to eat more than a moderate amount during the meal.

TZAFUN

From the *afikoman* matzah (and from additional matzos to make up the required amount), a half-egg volume portion — according to some, a full egg's volume portion — is given to each participant. It should be eaten before midnight, while reclining, without delay, and uninterruptedly. Nothing may be eaten or drunk after the *afikoman* (with the exception of water and the like) except for the last two Seder cups of wine.

BARECH

The third cup is poured and *Bircas HaMazon* (Grace After Meals) is recited. According to some customs, the Cup of Elijah is poured at this point.

A Song of ascents. When HASHEM will return the captivity of Zion, we will be like dreamers. Then our mouth will be filled with laughter, and our tongue with glad song.

---

(1) *Numbers* 9:11.

אָז יֹאמְרוּ בַגּוֹיִם, הִגְדִּיל יהוה לַעֲשׂוֹת עִם אֵלֶּה. הִגְדִּיל יהוה לַעֲשׂוֹת עִמָּנוּ, הָיִינוּ שְׂמֵחִים. שׁוּבָה יהוה אֶת שְׁבִיתֵנוּ, כַּאֲפִיקִים בַּנֶּגֶב. הַזֹּרְעִים בְּדִמְעָה בְּרִנָּה יִקְצֹרוּ. הָלוֹךְ יֵלֵךְ וּבָכֹה נֹשֵׂא מֶשֶׁךְ הַזָּרַע, בֹּא יָבֹא בְרִנָּה, נֹשֵׂא אֲלֻמֹּתָיו.[1]

תְּהִלַּת יהוה יְדַבֶּר פִּי, וִיבָרֵךְ כָּל בָּשָׂר שֵׁם קָדְשׁוֹ לְעוֹלָם וָעֶד.[2] וַאֲנַחְנוּ נְבָרֵךְ יָהּ, מֵעַתָּה וְעַד עוֹלָם, הַלְלוּיָהּ.[3] הוֹדוּ לַיהוה כִּי טוֹב, כִּי לְעוֹלָם חַסְדּוֹ.[4] מִי יְמַלֵּל גְּבוּרוֹת יהוה, יַשְׁמִיעַ כָּל תְּהִלָּתוֹ.[5]

If three or more males, aged thirteen or older, participated in the meal, the leader is required to formally invite the others to join him in the recitation of Grace After Meals. Following is the "zimun," or formal invitation.

The leader begins:

רַבּוֹתַי נְבָרֵךְ.

The group responds:

יְהִי שֵׁם יהוה מְבֹרָךְ מֵעַתָּה וְעַד עוֹלָם.[6]

The leader continues [if ten men join the zimun, the words in parentheses are included]:

יְהִי שֵׁם יהוה מְבֹרָךְ מֵעַתָּה וְעַד עוֹלָם.[6]

בִּרְשׁוּת מָרָנָן וְרַבָּנָן וְרַבּוֹתַי,

נְבָרֵךְ (אֱלֹהֵינוּ) שֶׁאָכַלְנוּ מִשֶּׁלּוֹ.

The group responds:

בָּרוּךְ (אֱלֹהֵינוּ) שֶׁאָכַלְנוּ מִשֶּׁלּוֹ וּבְטוּבוֹ חָיִינוּ.

The leader continues:

בָּרוּךְ (אֱלֹהֵינוּ) שֶׁאָכַלְנוּ מִשֶּׁלּוֹ וּבְטוּבוֹ חָיִינוּ.

The following line is recited if ten men join the zimun.

בָּרוּךְ הוּא וּבָרוּךְ שְׁמוֹ.

Then they will declare among the nations: HASHEM has done greatly with these. HASHEM has done greatly with us, we were gladdened. O HASHEM, return our captivity like springs in the desert. Those who tearfully sow will reap in glad song. He who bears the measure of seeds walks along weeping, but will return in exultation, a bearer of his sheaves.[1]

May my mouth declare the praise of HASHEM and may all flesh bless His Holy Name forever.[2] We will bless HASHEM from this time and forever, Halleluyah![3] Give thanks to HASHEM for He is good, His kindness endures forever.[4] Who can express the mighty acts of HASHEM? Who can declare all His praise?[5]

If three or more males, aged thirteen or older, participated in the meal, the leader is required to formally invite the others to join him in the recitation of Grace After Meals. Following is the "zimun," or formal invitation.

The leader begins:

Gentlemen, let us bless.

The group responds:

Blessed be the Name of HASHEM from this time and forever![6]

The leader continues [if ten men join the zimun, the words in parentheses are included]:

Blessed be the Name of HASHEM from this time and forever![6]

With the permission of the distinguished people present, let us bless [our God], He of Whose we have eaten.

The group responds:

Blessed is [our God,] He of Whose we have eaten and through Whose goodness we live.

The leader continues:

Blessed is [our God,] He of Whose we have eaten and through Whose goodness we live.

The following line is recited if ten men join the zimun.

Blessed is He and blessed is His Name.

---

(1) *Psalms* 126. (2) 145:21. (3) 115:18. (4) 118:1. (5) 106:2. (6) 113:2.

בָּרוּךְ אַתָּה יהוה אֱלֹהֵינוּ מֶלֶךְ הָעוֹלָם, הַזָּן אֶת הָעוֹלָם כֻּלּוֹ, בְּטוּבוֹ, בְּחֵן בְּחֶסֶד וּבְרַחֲמִים, הוּא נָתַן לֶחֶם לְכָל בָּשָׂר, כִּי לְעוֹלָם חַסְדּוֹ.[1] וּבְטוּבוֹ הַגָּדוֹל, תָּמִיד לֹא חָסַר לָנוּ, וְאַל יֶחְסַר לָנוּ מָזוֹן לְעוֹלָם וָעֶד. בַּעֲבוּר שְׁמוֹ הַגָּדוֹל, כִּי הוּא אֵל זָן וּמְפַרְנֵס לַכֹּל, וּמֵטִיב לַכֹּל, וּמֵכִין מָזוֹן לְכָל בְּרִיּוֹתָיו אֲשֶׁר בָּרָא. בָּרוּךְ אַתָּה יהוה, הַזָּן אֶת הַכֹּל.

נוֹדֶה לְךָ יהוה אֱלֹהֵינוּ, עַל שֶׁהִנְחַלְתָּ לַאֲבוֹתֵינוּ אֶרֶץ חֶמְדָּה טוֹבָה וּרְחָבָה. וְעַל שֶׁהוֹצֵאתָנוּ יהוה אֱלֹהֵינוּ מֵאֶרֶץ מִצְרַיִם, וּפְדִיתָנוּ מִבֵּית עֲבָדִים, וְעַל בְּרִיתְךָ שֶׁחָתַמְתָּ בִּבְשָׂרֵנוּ, וְעַל תּוֹרָתְךָ שֶׁלִּמַּדְתָּנוּ, וְעַל חֻקֶּיךָ שֶׁהוֹדַעְתָּנוּ, וְעַל חַיִּים חֵן וָחֶסֶד שֶׁחוֹנַנְתָּנוּ, וְעַל אֲכִילַת מָזוֹן שָׁאַתָּה זָן וּמְפַרְנֵס אוֹתָנוּ תָּמִיד, בְּכָל יוֹם וּבְכָל עֵת וּבְכָל שָׁעָה.

וְעַל הַכֹּל יהוה אֱלֹהֵינוּ אֲנַחְנוּ מוֹדִים לָךְ, וּמְבָרְכִים אוֹתָךְ, יִתְבָּרַךְ שִׁמְךָ בְּפִי כָּל חַי תָּמִיד לְעוֹלָם וָעֶד. כַּכָּתוּב, וְאָכַלְתָּ וְשָׂבָעְתָּ, וּבֵרַכְתָּ אֶת יהוה אֱלֹהֶיךָ, עַל הָאָרֶץ הַטֹּבָה אֲשֶׁר נָתַן לָךְ.[2] בָּרוּךְ אַתָּה יהוה, עַל הָאָרֶץ וְעַל הַמָּזוֹן.

רַחֵם (נָא) יהוה אֱלֹהֵינוּ עַל יִשְׂרָאֵל עַמֶּךָ, וְעַל יְרוּשָׁלַיִם עִירֶךָ, וְעַל צִיּוֹן מִשְׁכַּן כְּבוֹדֶךָ, וְעַל מַלְכוּת בֵּית דָּוִד מְשִׁיחֶךָ, וְעַל הַבַּיִת הַגָּדוֹל וְהַקָּדוֹשׁ שֶׁנִּקְרָא שִׁמְךָ עָלָיו. אֱלֹהֵינוּ אָבִינוּ רְעֵנוּ זוּנֵנוּ פַּרְנְסֵנוּ וְכַלְכְּלֵנוּ וְהַרְוִיחֵנוּ, וְהַרְוַח לָנוּ יהוה אֱלֹהֵינוּ

Blessed are You, HASHEM, our God, King of the universe, Who nourishes the entire world, in His goodness — with grace, with kindness and with mercy. He gives nourishment to all flesh, for His kindness is eternal.[1] And through His great goodness, we have never lacked, and may we never lack nourishment, for all eternity. For the sake of His great Name, because He is God Who nourishes and sustains all, and benefits all, and He prepares food for all of His creatures which He has created. Blessed are You, HASHEM, Who nourishes all.

We thank You, HASHEM, our God, because You have given to our forefathers as a heritage a desirable, good and spacious land; because You removed us, HASHEM, our God, from the land of Egypt, and You redeemed us from the house of bondage; for Your covenant which You sealed in our flesh; for Your Torah which You taught us and for Your statutes which You made known to us; for life, grace and kindness which You granted us; and for the provision of food with which You nourish and sustain us constantly, in every day, in every season and in every hour.

For all, HASHEM, our God, we thank You and bless You. May Your name be blessed by the mouth of all the living, continuously for all eternity. As it is written: "And you shall eat and you shall be satisfied, and you shall bless HASHEM, your God, for the good land which He gave you."[2] Blessed are You, HASHEM, for the land and for the nourishment.

Have mercy, (we beg you) HASHEM, our God, on Israel Your people, on Jerusalem Your city, on Zion the resting place of Your Glory, on the monarchy of the house of David, Your anointed, and on the great and holy House upon which Your name is called. Our God, our Father — tend us, nourish us, sustain us, support us, relieve us; HASHEM, our God,

---

(1) *Psalms* 136:25. (2) *Deuteronomy* 8:10.

מְהֵרָה מִכָּל צָרוֹתֵינוּ. וְנָא אַל תַּצְרִיכֵנוּ יהוה אֱלֹהֵינוּ, לֹא לִידֵי מַתְּנַת בָּשָׂר וָדָם, וְלֹא לִידֵי הַלְוָאָתָם, כִּי אִם לְיָדְךָ הַמְּלֵאָה הַפְּתוּחָה הַקְּדוֹשָׁה וְהָרְחָבָה, שֶׁלֹּא נֵבוֹשׁ וְלֹא נִכָּלֵם לְעוֹלָם וָעֶד.

On the Sabbath add the following paragraph.

רְצֵה וְהַחֲלִיצֵנוּ יהוה אֱלֹהֵינוּ בְּמִצְוֹתֶיךָ, וּבְמִצְוַת יוֹם הַשְּׁבִיעִי הַשַּׁבָּת הַגָּדוֹל וְהַקָּדוֹשׁ הַזֶּה, כִּי יוֹם זֶה גָּדוֹל וְקָדוֹשׁ הוּא לְפָנֶיךָ, לִשְׁבָּת בּוֹ וְלָנוּחַ בּוֹ בְּאַהֲבָה כְּמִצְוַת רְצוֹנֶךָ, וּבִרְצוֹנְךָ הָנִיחַ לָנוּ יהוה אֱלֹהֵינוּ, שֶׁלֹּא תְהֵא צָרָה וְיָגוֹן וַאֲנָחָה בְּיוֹם מְנוּחָתֵנוּ, וְהַרְאֵנוּ יהוה אֱלֹהֵינוּ בְּנֶחָמַת צִיּוֹן עִירֶךָ, וּבְבִנְיַן יְרוּשָׁלַיִם עִיר קָדְשֶׁךָ, כִּי אַתָּה הוּא בַּעַל הַיְשׁוּעוֹת וּבַעַל הַנֶּחָמוֹת.

אֱלֹהֵינוּ וֵאלֹהֵי אֲבוֹתֵינוּ, יַעֲלֶה, וְיָבֹא, וְיַגִּיעַ, וְיֵרָאֶה, וְיֵרָצֶה, וְיִשָּׁמַע, וְיִפָּקֵד, וְיִזָּכֵר זִכְרוֹנֵנוּ וּפִקְדוֹנֵנוּ, וְזִכְרוֹן אֲבוֹתֵינוּ, וְזִכְרוֹן מָשִׁיחַ בֶּן דָּוִד עַבְדֶּךָ, וְזִכְרוֹן יְרוּשָׁלַיִם עִיר קָדְשֶׁךָ, וְזִכְרוֹן כָּל עַמְּךָ בֵּית יִשְׂרָאֵל לְפָנֶיךָ, לִפְלֵיטָה לְטוֹבָה לְחֵן וּלְחֶסֶד וּלְרַחֲמִים, לְחַיִּים וּלְשָׁלוֹם בְּיוֹם חַג הַמַּצּוֹת הַזֶּה. זָכְרֵנוּ יהוה אֱלֹהֵינוּ בּוֹ לְטוֹבָה, וּפָקְדֵנוּ בּוֹ לִבְרָכָה, וְהוֹשִׁיעֵנוּ בּוֹ לְחַיִּים. וּבִדְבַר יְשׁוּעָה וְרַחֲמִים, חוּס וְחָנֵּנוּ וְרַחֵם עָלֵינוּ וְהוֹשִׁיעֵנוּ, כִּי אֵלֶיךָ עֵינֵינוּ, כִּי אֵל (מֶלֶךְ) חַנּוּן וְרַחוּם אָתָּה.[1]

וּבְנֵה יְרוּשָׁלַיִם עִיר הַקֹּדֶשׁ בִּמְהֵרָה בְיָמֵינוּ. בָּרוּךְ אַתָּה יהוה, בּוֹנֵה (בְּרַחֲמָיו) יְרוּשָׁלָיִם. אָמֵן.

grant us speedy relief from all our troubles. Please, make us not needful, HASHEM, our God, of the gifts of human hands nor of their loans, but only of Your Hand that is full, open, holy, and generous, that we not feel inner shame nor be humiliated for ever and ever.

On the Sabbath add the following paragraph.

May it please You, HASHEM, our God — give us rest through Your commandments and through the commandment of the seventh day, this great and holy Sabbath. For this day is great and holy before You to rest on it and be content on it in love, as ordained by Your will. May it be Your will, HASHEM, our God, that there be no distress, grief, or lament on this day of our contentment. And show us, HASHEM, our God, the consolation of Zion, Your city, and the rebuilding of Jerusalem, city of Your holiness, for You are the Master of salvations and Master of consolations.

Our God and God of our forefathers, may there rise, come, reach, be noted, be favored, be heard, be considered, and be remembered — the remembrance and consideration of ourselves; the remembrance of our forefathers; the remembrance of Messiah, son of David, Your servant; the remembrance of Jerusalem, the city of Your Holiness; and the remembrance of Your entire people, the Family of Israel — before you for deliverance, for goodness, for grace, for kindness and for compassion, for life and for peace on this day of the Festival of Matzos. Remember us on it, HASHEM, our God, for goodness; consider us on it for blessing; and help us on it for life. In the matter of salvation and compassion, pity, be gracious and compassionate with us and help us, for our eyes are turned to You, because You are God the gracious and compassionate (King).[1]

Rebuild Jerusalem, the Holy City, soon in our days. Blessed are You, HASHEM, Who rebuilds Jerusalem (in His mercy). Amen.

---

(1) Cf. *Nehemiah* 9:31.

בָּרוּךְ אַתָּה יהוה אֱלֹהֵינוּ מֶלֶךְ הָעוֹלָם, הָאֵל אָבִינוּ מַלְכֵּנוּ אַדִּירֵנוּ בּוֹרְאֵנוּ גּוֹאֲלֵנוּ יוֹצְרֵנוּ קְדוֹשֵׁנוּ קְדוֹשׁ יַעֲקֹב, רוֹעֵנוּ רוֹעֵה יִשְׂרָאֵל, הַמֶּלֶךְ הַטּוֹב וְהַמֵּטִיב לַכֹּל, שֶׁבְּכָל יוֹם וָיוֹם הוּא הֵטִיב, הוּא מֵטִיב, הוּא יֵיטִיב לָנוּ. הוּא גְמָלָנוּ הוּא גוֹמְלֵנוּ הוּא יִגְמְלֵנוּ לָעַד, לְחֵן וּלְחֶסֶד וּלְרַחֲמִים וּלְרֶוַח הַצָּלָה וְהַצְלָחָה, בְּרָכָה וִישׁוּעָה נֶחָמָה פַּרְנָסָה וְכַלְכָּלָה וְרַחֲמִים וְחַיִּים וְשָׁלוֹם וְכָל טוֹב, וּמִכָּל טוּב לְעוֹלָם אַל יְחַסְּרֵנוּ.

הָרַחֲמָן הוּא יִמְלוֹךְ עָלֵינוּ לְעוֹלָם וָעֶד. הָרַחֲמָן הוּא יִתְבָּרַךְ בַּשָּׁמַיִם וּבָאָרֶץ. הָרַחֲמָן הוּא יִשְׁתַּבַּח לְדוֹר דּוֹרִים, וְיִתְפָּאַר בָּנוּ לָעַד וּלְנֵצַח נְצָחִים, וְיִתְהַדַּר בָּנוּ לָעַד וּלְעוֹלְמֵי עוֹלָמִים. הָרַחֲמָן הוּא יְפַרְנְסֵנוּ בְּכָבוֹד. הָרַחֲמָן הוּא יִשְׁבּוֹר עֻלֵּנוּ מֵעַל צַוָּארֵנוּ, וְהוּא יוֹלִיכֵנוּ קוֹמְמִיּוּת לְאַרְצֵנוּ. הָרַחֲמָן הוּא יִשְׁלַח לָנוּ בְּרָכָה מְרֻבָּה בַּבַּיִת הַזֶּה, וְעַל שֻׁלְחָן זֶה שֶׁאָכַלְנוּ עָלָיו. הָרַחֲמָן הוּא יִשְׁלַח לָנוּ אֶת אֵלִיָּהוּ הַנָּבִיא זָכוּר לַטּוֹב, וִיבַשֶּׂר לָנוּ בְּשׂוֹרוֹת טוֹבוֹת יְשׁוּעוֹת וְנֶחָמוֹת.

The following text — for a guest to recite at his host's table — appears in *Shulchan Aruch, Orach Chaim* 201.

יְהִי רָצוֹן שֶׁלֹּא יֵבוֹשׁ וְלֹא יִכָּלֵם בַּעַל הַבַּיִת הַזֶּה, לֹא בָּעוֹלָם הַזֶּה וְלֹא בָּעוֹלָם הַבָּא, וְיַצְלִיחַ בְּכָל נְכָסָיו, וְיִהְיוּ נְכָסָיו מוּצְלָחִים וּקְרוֹבִים לָעִיר, וְאַל יִשְׁלוֹט שָׂטָן בְּמַעֲשֵׂה יָדָיו, וְאַל יִזְדַּקֵּק לְפָנָיו שׁוּם דְּבַר חֵטְא וְהִרְהוּר עָוֹן, מֵעַתָּה וְעַד עוֹלָם.

Blessed are You, HASHEM, our God, King of the universe, the Almighty, our Father, our King, our Sovereign, our Creator, our Redeemer, our Maker, our Holy One, Holy One of Jacob, our Shepherd, the Shepherd of Israel, the King Who is good and Who does good for all. For every single day He did good, He does good, and will do good to us. He was bountiful with us, He is bountiful with us, and He will forever be bountiful with us — with grace and with kindness, and with mercy, with relief, salvation, success, blessing, help, consolation, sustenance, support, mercy, life, peace, and all good; and of all good things may He never deprive us.

The compassionate One! May He reign over us forever. The compassionate One! May He be blessed in heaven and on earth. The compassionate One! May He be praised throughout all generations, may He be glorified through us forever to the ultimate ends, and be honored through us forever and for all eternity. The compassionate One! May He sustain us in honor. The compassionate One! May He break the yoke of oppression from our necks and guide us erect to our land. The compassionate One! May He send us abundant blessing to this house, and upon this table at which we have eaten. The compassionate One! May He send us Elijah, the prophet — he is remembered for good — to proclaim to us good tidings, salvations and consolations.

The following text — for a guest to recite at his host's table — appears in *Shulchan Aruch, Orach Chaim* 201.

May it be God's will that this host not be shamed nor humiliated in This World or in the World to Come. May he be successful in all his dealings. May his dealings be successful and conveniently close at hand. May no evil impediment reign over his handiwork, and may no semblance of sin or iniquitous thought attach itself to him from this time and forever.

Those eating at their own table recite the following,
adding the appropriate parenthesized phrases:

הָרַחֲמָן הוּא יְבָרֵךְ

אוֹתִי (וְאֶת אִשְׁתִּי /בַּעֲלִי וְאֶת זַרְעִי) וְאֶת כָּל אֲשֶׁר לִי.

Guests recite the following.
Children at their parents' table add the words in parentheses.

הָרַחֲמָן הוּא יְבָרֵךְ

אֶת (אָבִי מוֹרִי) בַּעַל הַבַּיִת הַזֶּה,

וְאֶת (אִמִּי מוֹרָתִי) בַּעֲלַת הַבַּיִת הַזֶּה,

All guests recite the following:

אוֹתָם וְאֶת בֵּיתָם וְאֶת זַרְעָם וְאֶת כָּל אֲשֶׁר לָהֶם.

All continue here:

אוֹתָנוּ וְאֶת כָּל אֲשֶׁר לָנוּ, כְּמוֹ שֶׁנִּתְבָּרְכוּ אֲבוֹתֵינוּ
אַבְרָהָם יִצְחָק וְיַעֲקֹב בַּכֹּל מִכֹּל כֹּל,[1] כֵּן יְבָרֵךְ אוֹתָנוּ
כֻּלָּנוּ יַחַד בִּבְרָכָה שְׁלֵמָה, וְנֹאמַר, אָמֵן.

בַּמָּרוֹם יְלַמְּדוּ עֲלֵיהֶם וְעָלֵינוּ זְכוּת, שֶׁתְּהֵא לְמִשְׁמֶרֶת
שָׁלוֹם. וְנִשָּׂא בְרָכָה מֵאֵת יהוה, וּצְדָקָה מֵאֱלֹהֵי
יִשְׁעֵנוּ, וְנִמְצָא חֵן וְשֵׂכֶל טוֹב בְּעֵינֵי אֱלֹהִים וְאָדָם.[2]

On the Sabbath add the following sentence:

הָרַחֲמָן הוּא יַנְחִילֵנוּ יוֹם שֶׁכֻּלוֹ שַׁבָּת וּמְנוּחָה לְחַיֵּי הָעוֹלָמִים.

The words in parentheses are added on the two Seder nights in some communities.

הָרַחֲמָן הוּא יַנְחִילֵנוּ יוֹם שֶׁכֻּלוֹ טוֹב (יוֹם שֶׁכֻּלוֹ אָרוּךְ,
יוֹם שֶׁצַּדִּיקִים יוֹשְׁבִים וְעַטְרוֹתֵיהֶם
בְּרָאשֵׁיהֶם וְנֶהֱנִים מִזִּיו הַשְּׁכִינָה, וִיהִי חֶלְקֵנוּ עִמָּהֶם).

הָרַחֲמָן הוּא יְזַכֵּנוּ לִימוֹת הַמָּשִׁיחַ וּלְחַיֵּי הָעוֹלָם
הַבָּא. מִגְדּוֹל יְשׁוּעוֹת מַלְכּוֹ וְעֹשֶׂה חֶסֶד

The compassionate One! May He bless me,
(my wife/husband and my children) and all that is mine.

Guests recite the following.
Children at their parents' table add the words in parentheses.

The compassionate One! May He bless
[(my father, my teacher) the master of this house, and
(my mother, my teacher) lady of this house)]

All guests recite the following:

them, their house, their family and all that is theirs,

All continue here:

ours and all that is ours — just as our forefathers Abraham,
Isaac and Jacob were blessed in everything from everything,
with everything.[1] So may He bless us all together with a
perfect blessing. And let us say: Amen!

On high, may merit be pleaded upon them and upon us,
for a safeguard of peace. May we receive a blessing from
HASHEM, and just kindness from the God of our salvation,
and find favor and good understanding in the eyes of God
and man.[2]

On the Sabbath add the following sentence:
The Compassionate One ! May He cause us to inherit the day which
will be completely a Sabbath and rest day for eternal life.

The words in parentheses are added on the two Seder nights in some communities.

The compassionate One! May He cause us to inherit that
day which is altogether good, (that everlasting day, the
day when the just sit with crowns on their heads, enjoying
the reflection of God's majesty — and may our portion be
with them)!

The compassionate One! May He make us worthy of the
days of Messiah and the life of the World to Come. He
Who is a tower of salvations to His king and does kindness

---

(1) Cf. *Genesis* 24:1; 27:33; 33:11. (2) Cf. *Proverbs* 3:4.

לִמְשִׁיחוֹ לְדָוִד וּלְזַרְעוֹ עַד עוֹלָם.¹ עֹשֶׂה שָׁלוֹם בִּמְרוֹמָיו,
הוּא יַעֲשֶׂה שָׁלוֹם עָלֵינוּ וְעַל כָּל יִשְׂרָאֵל. וְאִמְרוּ, אָמֵן.

יְראוּ אֶת יהוה קְדֹשָׁיו, כִּי אֵין מַחְסוֹר לִירֵאָיו.
כְּפִירִים רָשׁוּ וְרָעֵבוּ, וְדֹרְשֵׁי יהוה לֹא יַחְסְרוּ כָל
טוֹב.² הוֹדוּ לַיהוה כִּי טוֹב, כִּי לְעוֹלָם חַסְדּוֹ.³ פּוֹתֵחַ אֶת
יָדֶךָ, וּמַשְׂבִּיעַ לְכָל חַי רָצוֹן.⁴ בָּרוּךְ הַגֶּבֶר אֲשֶׁר יִבְטַח
בַּיהוה, וְהָיָה יהוה מִבְטַחוֹ.⁵ נַעַר הָיִיתִי גַּם זָקַנְתִּי, וְלֹא
רָאִיתִי צַדִּיק נֶעֱזָב, וְזַרְעוֹ מְבַקֶּשׁ לָחֶם.⁶ יהוה עֹז לְעַמּוֹ
יִתֵּן, יהוה יְבָרֵךְ אֶת עַמּוֹ בַשָּׁלוֹם.⁷

Upon completion of *Bircas HaMazon* the blessing over wine is recited and the third cup is drunk while reclining on the left side. It is preferable to drink the entire cup, but at the very least, most of the cup should be drained.

בָּרוּךְ אַתָּה יהוה אֱלֹהֵינוּ מֶלֶךְ הָעוֹלָם, בּוֹרֵא פְּרִי
הַגָּפֶן.

The fourth cup is poured. According to most customs, the Cup of Elijah is poured at this point, after which the door is opened in accordance with the verse, "It is a guarded night." Then the following paragraph is recited.

שְׁפֹךְ חֲמָתְךָ אֶל הַגּוֹיִם אֲשֶׁר לֹא יְדָעוּךָ וְעַל מַמְלָכוֹת
אֲשֶׁר בְּשִׁמְךָ לֹא קָרָאוּ. כִּי אָכַל אֶת יַעֲקֹב וְאֶת

⋙§ שְׁפֹךְ חֲמָתְךָ — *Pour Your wrath upon the nations . . .*

203. Why are these verses inserted at this point in the Seder?

Abarbanel asserts that the second "half" of Hallel refers to the future redemption which will take place with the advent of the Messiah (see question 199), unlike the beginning of Hallel, which harks back to the events of the Exodus. Indeed, the verbs in this second part of Hallel are in the future tense or in the imperative mode, while the first two paragraphs (*Psalms*, Chaps. 113-114), which were recited before the meal, are in the past tense. The opening verse of this second half of

to His anointed, to David and to his descendants forever.[1] He Who makes peace in His heights, may He make peace upon us and upon all Israel. Now respond: Amen!

Fear HASHEM, You — His holy ones — for there is no deprivation for His reverent ones.[2] Young lions may want and hunger, but those who seek HASHEM will not lack any good. Give thanks to HASHEM for He is good; His kindness endures forever.[3] You open Your hand and satisfy the desire of every living thing.[4] Blessed is the man who trusts in HASHEM, then HASHEM will be his security.[5] I was a youth and also have aged, and I have not seen a righteous man forsaken, with his children begging for bread.[6] HASHEM will give might to His nation; HASHEM will bless His nation with peace.[7]

Upon completion of *Bircas HaMazon* the blessing over wine is recited and the third cup is drunk while reclining on the left side. It is preferable to drink the entire cup, but at the very least, most of the cup should be drained.

Blessed are You, HASHEM our God, King of the universe, Who creates the fruit of the vine.

The fourth cup is poured. According to most customs, the Cup of Elijah is poured at this point, after which the door is opened in accordance with the verse, "It is a guarded night." Then the following paragraph is recited.

Pour Your wrath upon the nations that do not recognize You and upon the kingdoms that do not invoke Your Name. For they have devoured Jacob and

(1) *Psalms* 18:51. (2) 34:10-11. (3) 136:1 et al. (4) 145:16.
(5) *Jeremiah* 17:7. (6) *Psalms* 37:25. (7) 29:11.

Hallel — *"Not for our sake, O Lord . . . but for Your Name's sake . . ."* — is an ambiguous way to open a new section of the Haggadah, as its frame of reference is not clear: Exactly what should God do for His Name's sake? To provide a background for these paragraphs and a reference point for the second half of Hallel, these verses are recited as an introduction. The message of these verses is thus: "God, we have seen how You have done wonders in avenging the persecution of the Jews of the generation of the Exodus from their Egyptian tormentors who did not recognize You (*Exodus* 5:2). Now pour out Your wrath against those nations who still do not recognize You, who persecute and

נָוֵהוּ הֵשַׁמּוּ.¹ שְׁפָךְ עֲלֵיהֶם זַעְמֶךָ וַחֲרוֹן אַפְּךָ יַשִּׂיגֵם.² תִּרְדֹּף בְּאַף וְתַשְׁמִידֵם מִתַּחַת שְׁמֵי יהוה.³

הלל

The door is closed and the recitation of the Haggadah is continued.

לֹא לָנוּ יהוה לֹא לָנוּ, כִּי לְשִׁמְךָ תֵּן כָּבוֹד, עַל חַסְדְּךָ עַל אֲמִתֶּךָ. לָמָּה יֹאמְרוּ הַגּוֹיִם, אַיֵּה נָא אֱלֹהֵיהֶם. וֵאלֹהֵינוּ בַשָּׁמָיִם, כֹּל אֲשֶׁר חָפֵץ עָשָׂה. עֲצַבֵּיהֶם כֶּסֶף וְזָהָב, מַעֲשֵׂה יְדֵי אָדָם. פֶּה לָהֶם וְלֹא יְדַבֵּרוּ, עֵינַיִם לָהֶם וְלֹא יִרְאוּ. אָזְנַיִם לָהֶם וְלֹא יִשְׁמָעוּ, אַף לָהֶם וְלֹא יְרִיחוּן. יְדֵיהֶם וְלֹא יְמִישׁוּן, רַגְלֵיהֶם וְלֹא יְהַלֵּכוּ, לֹא יֶהְגּוּ בִּגְרוֹנָם. כְּמוֹהֶם יִהְיוּ עֹשֵׂיהֶם, כֹּל אֲשֶׁר בֹּטֵחַ בָּהֶם. יִשְׂרָאֵל בְּטַח בַּיהוה, עֶזְרָם וּמָגִנָּם הוּא. בֵּית אַהֲרֹן בִּטְחוּ בַיהוה, עֶזְרָם וּמָגִנָּם הוּא. יִרְאֵי יהוה בִּטְחוּ בַיהוה, עֶזְרָם וּמָגִנָּם הוּא.

---

torment Jacob, and who have gone even further than the Egyptians, in that they destroyed the Temple. And even if we ourselves are not deserving of such miraculous salvation, do it not for us, but for Your Name . . ."

204. Why is it customary to open the door at this point in the Seder?

Bircas Avraham says that opening the door is demonstrating our firm belief in the coming of the Messiah. This being the night not only of the redemption from Egypt but of the future redemption as well, we take this opportunity to show our faith that our deliverance is near. We hope that in the merit of our faith we will indeed be privileged to quickly see our hopes realized.

Maharal explains that this custom, and the custom of filling a cup of wine for Elijah at this point, are instructional tools through which we

destroyed His dwelling.[1] Pour Your fury on them and let Your fiery wrath overtake them.[2] Pursue them with wrath and annihilate them from beneath the heavens of HASHEM.[3]

HALLEL

The door is closed and the recitation of the Haggadah is continued.

Not for our sake, HASHEM, not for our sake, but for Your Name's sake give glory, for Your kindness and for Your truth! Why should the nations say: 'Where is their God?" Our God is in the heavens; whatever He pleases, He does! Their idols are silver and gold, the handiwork of man. They have a mouth, but cannot speak; they have eyes, but cannot see; they have ears, but cannot hear; they have a nose, but cannot smell; their hands — they cannot feel; their feet — they cannot walk; they cannot utter a sound with their throat. Those who make them should become like them, whoever trusts in them. O Israel, trust in HASHEM; their help and their shield is He! House of Aaron, trust in HASHEM; their help and their shield is He. You who fear HASHEM trust in HASHEM, their help and their shield is He!

---

(1) *Psalms* 79:6-7. (2) 69:25. (3) *Lamentations* 3:66.

---

transmit to our children that before the Messiah comes to deliver us from our exile, he will be preceded by Elijah the Prophet (*Malachi* 3:23). This principle is significant in that it prevents us from straying after false Messiahs. These practices are done at this particular point in the Seder because we are about to begin the second part of Hallel. It is here that we praise God and beseech him to bring about the future redemption. The opening of the door and pouring of the cup symbolize the entrance of Elijah as a precursor to Hallel which alludes to the coming of the Messiah.

יהוה זְכָרָנוּ יְבָרֵךְ, יְבָרֵךְ אֶת בֵּית יִשְׂרָאֵל, יְבָרֵךְ אֶת בֵּית אַהֲרֹן. יְבָרֵךְ יִרְאֵי יהוה, הַקְּטַנִּים עִם הַגְּדֹלִים. יֹסֵף יהוה עֲלֵיכֶם, עֲלֵיכֶם וְעַל בְּנֵיכֶם. בְּרוּכִים אַתֶּם לַיהוה, עֹשֵׂה שָׁמַיִם וָאָרֶץ. הַשָּׁמַיִם שָׁמַיִם לַיהוה, וְהָאָרֶץ נָתַן לִבְנֵי אָדָם. לֹא הַמֵּתִים יְהַלְלוּ יָהּ, וְלֹא כָּל יֹרְדֵי דוּמָה. וַאֲנַחְנוּ נְבָרֵךְ יָהּ, מֵעַתָּה וְעַד עוֹלָם, הַלְלוּיָהּ.[1]

אָהַבְתִּי כִּי יִשְׁמַע יהוה, אֶת קוֹלִי תַּחֲנוּנָי. כִּי הִטָּה אָזְנוֹ לִי, וּבְיָמַי אֶקְרָא. אֲפָפוּנִי חֶבְלֵי מָוֶת, וּמְצָרֵי שְׁאוֹל מְצָאוּנִי, צָרָה וְיָגוֹן אֶמְצָא. וּבְשֵׁם יהוה אֶקְרָא, אָנָּה יהוה מַלְּטָה נַפְשִׁי. חַנּוּן יהוה וְצַדִּיק, וֵאלֹהֵינוּ מְרַחֵם. שֹׁמֵר פְּתָאִים יהוה, דַּלּוֹתִי וְלִי יְהוֹשִׁיעַ. שׁוּבִי נַפְשִׁי לִמְנוּחָיְכִי, כִּי יהוה גָּמַל עָלָיְכִי. כִּי חִלַּצְתָּ נַפְשִׁי מִמָּוֶת, אֶת עֵינִי מִן דִּמְעָה, אֶת רַגְלִי מִדֶּחִי. אֶתְהַלֵּךְ לִפְנֵי יהוה, בְּאַרְצוֹת הַחַיִּים. הֶאֱמַנְתִּי כִּי אֲדַבֵּר, אֲנִי עָנִיתִי מְאֹד. אֲנִי אָמַרְתִּי בְחָפְזִי, כָּל הָאָדָם כֹּזֵב.

מָה אָשִׁיב לַיהוה, כָּל תַּגְמוּלוֹהִי עָלָי. כּוֹס יְשׁוּעוֹת אֶשָּׂא, וּבְשֵׁם יהוה אֶקְרָא. נְדָרַי לַיהוה אֲשַׁלֵּם, נֶגְדָה נָּא לְכָל עַמּוֹ. יָקָר בְּעֵינֵי יהוה, הַמָּוְתָה לַחֲסִידָיו. אָנָּה יהוה כִּי אֲנִי עַבְדֶּךָ, אֲנִי עַבְדְּךָ, בֶּן אֲמָתֶךָ, פִּתַּחְתָּ לְמוֹסֵרָי. לְךָ אֶזְבַּח זֶבַח תּוֹדָה, וּבְשֵׁם יהוה אֶקְרָא. נְדָרַי לַיהוה אֲשַׁלֵּם, נֶגְדָה נָּא לְכָל עַמּוֹ. בְּחַצְרוֹת בֵּית יהוה, בְּתוֹכֵכִי יְרוּשָׁלָיִם הַלְלוּיָהּ.[1]

HASHEM Who has remembered us will bless — He will bless the House of Israel; He will bless the House of Aaron; He will bless those who fear HASHEM, the small as well as the great. May HASHEM increase upon you, upon you and your children! You are blessed of HASHEM, Maker of heaven and earth. As for the heavens — the heavens are HASHEM's, but the earth He has given to mankind. Neither the dead can praise God, nor any who descend into silence; but we will bless God from this time and forever. Halleluyah![1]

I love Him, for HASHEM hears my voice, my supplications. For He has inclined His ear to me, so in my days shall I call. The pains of death encircled me; the confines of the grave have found me; trouble and sorrow I would find. Then I would invoke the Name of HASHEM: "Please, HASHEM, save my soul," Gracious is HASHEM and righteous, our God is merciful. HASHEM protects the simple; I was brought low, but He saved me. Return my soul, to your rest; for HASHEM has been kind to you. For You have delivered my soul from death, my eyes from tears, my feet from stumbling. I shall walk before HASHEM in the lands of the living. I have kept faith although I say: "I suffer exceedingly." I said in my haste: "All mankind is deceitful."

How can I repay HASHEM for all His kindness to me? I will raise the cup of salvations, and the Name of HASHEM I will invoke. My vows to HASHEM I will pay, in the presence, now, of His entire people. Difficult in the eyes of HASHEM is the death for His devout ones. Please, HASHEM — for I am Your servant, I am Your servant, son of Your handmaid — You have released my bonds. To You I will sacrifice thanksgiving-offerings, and the Name of HASHEM I will invoke. My vows to HASHEM I will pay, in the presence, now, of His entire people. In the courtyards of the House of HASHEM, in your midst, O Jerusalem, Halleluyah.[2]

---

(1) *Psalms* 115. (2) 116.

הַלְלוּ אֶת יהוה, כָּל גּוֹיִם, שַׁבְּחוּהוּ כָּל הָאֻמִּים. כִּי גָבַר עָלֵינוּ חַסְדּוֹ, וֶאֱמֶת יהוה לְעוֹלָם, הַלְלוּיָהּ.[1]

הוֹדוּ לַיהוה כִּי טוֹב,   כִּי לְעוֹלָם חַסְדּוֹ.

יֹאמַר נָא יִשְׂרָאֵל,   כִּי לְעוֹלָם חַסְדּוֹ.

יֹאמְרוּ נָא בֵית אַהֲרֹן,   כִּי לְעוֹלָם חַסְדּוֹ.

יֹאמְרוּ נָא יִרְאֵי יהוה,   כִּי לְעוֹלָם חַסְדּוֹ.

מִן הַמֵּצַר קָרָאתִי יָּהּ, עָנָנִי בַמֶּרְחָב יָהּ. יהוה לִי לֹא אִירָא, מַה יַּעֲשֶׂה לִי אָדָם. יהוה לִי בְּעֹזְרָי, וַאֲנִי אֶרְאֶה בְשֹׂנְאָי. טוֹב לַחֲסוֹת בַּיהוה, מִבְּטֹחַ בָּאָדָם. טוֹב לַחֲסוֹת בַּיהוה, מִבְּטֹחַ בִּנְדִיבִים. כָּל גּוֹיִם סְבָבוּנִי, בְּשֵׁם יהוה כִּי אֲמִילַם. סַבּוּנִי גַם סְבָבוּנִי, בְּשֵׁם יהוה כִּי אֲמִילַם. סַבּוּנִי כִדְבֹרִים דֹּעֲכוּ כְּאֵשׁ קוֹצִים, בְּשֵׁם יהוה כִּי אֲמִילַם. דָּחֹה דְחִיתַנִי לִנְפֹּל, וַיהוה עֲזָרָנִי. עָזִּי וְזִמְרָת יָהּ, וַיְהִי לִי לִישׁוּעָה. קוֹל רִנָּה וִישׁוּעָה, בְּאָהֳלֵי צַדִּיקִים, יְמִין יהוה עֹשָׂה חָיִל. יְמִין יהוה רוֹמֵמָה, יְמִין יהוה עֹשָׂה חָיִל. לֹא אָמוּת כִּי אֶחְיֶה, וַאֲסַפֵּר מַעֲשֵׂי יָהּ. יַסֹּר יִסְּרַנִּי יָּהּ, וְלַמָּוֶת לֹא נְתָנָנִי. פִּתְחוּ לִי שַׁעֲרֵי צֶדֶק, אָבֹא בָם אוֹדֶה יָהּ. זֶה הַשַּׁעַר לַיהוה, צַדִּיקִים יָבֹאוּ בוֹ. אוֹדְךָ כִּי עֲנִיתָנִי, וַתְּהִי לִי לִישׁוּעָה. אוֹדְךָ כִּי עֲנִיתָנִי, וַתְּהִי לִי לִישׁוּעָה. אֶבֶן מָאֲסוּ הַבּוֹנִים, הָיְתָה לְרֹאשׁ פִּנָּה. אֶבֶן מָאֲסוּ הַבּוֹנִים, הָיְתָה לְרֹאשׁ פִּנָּה. מֵאֵת יהוה הָיְתָה זֹּאת, הִיא נִפְלָאת בְּעֵינֵינוּ. מֵאֵת יהוה הָיְתָה זֹּאת, הִיא נִפְלָאת בְּעֵינֵינוּ. זֶה הַיּוֹם עָשָׂה יהוה, נָגִילָה וְנִשְׂמְחָה

---

(1) *Psalms* 117.

Praise HASHEM, all nations; praise Him, all the states! For His kindness has overwhelmed us, and the truth of HASHEM is eternal. Halleluyah![1]

Give thanks to HASHEM for He is good;
His kindness endures forever!
Let Israel say now: His kindness endures forever!
Let the House of Aaron say now: His kindness endures forever!
Let those who fear HASHEM say now:
His kindness endures forever!

From the straits did I call to God; God answered me with expansiveness. HASHEM is with me, I have no fear; how can man affect me? HASHEM is with me through my helpers; therefore I can face my foes. It is better to take refuge in HASHEM than to rely on man. It is better to take refuge in HASHEM than to rely on nobles. All the nations surround me; in the Name of HASHEM I cut them down. They encircle me, they also surround me; in the Name of Hashem, I cut them down! They encircle me like bees, but they are extinguished as a fire does thorns; in the name of HASHEM I cut them down! You pushed me hard that I might fall, but HASHEM assisted me. God is my might and my praise, and He was a salvation for me. The sound of rejoicing and salvation is in the tents of the righteous. "HASHEM'S right hand does valiantly! HASHEM'S right hand is raised triumphantly! HASHEM'S right hand does valiantly!" I shall not die! But I shall live and relate the deeds of God. God has chastened me exceedingly, but He did not let me die. Open for me the gates of righteousness, I will enter them and thank God. This is the gate of HASHEM; the righteous shall enter through it. I thank You, for You have answered me and become my salvation! I thank You, for You have answered me and become my salvation! The stone the builders despised has become the cornerstone. The stone the builders despised has become the cornerstone. This emanated from HASHEM; it is wondrous in our eyes. This emanated from HASHEM; it is wondrous in our eyes. This is the day HASHEM has made; let us rejoice and be glad

בּוֹ. זֶה הַיּוֹם עָשָׂה יהוה, נָגִילָה וְנִשְׂמְחָה בוֹ.

אָנָּא יהוה הוֹשִׁיעָה נָּא.

אָנָּא יהוה הוֹשִׁיעָה נָּא.

אָנָּא יהוה הַצְלִיחָה נָא.

אָנָּא יהוה הַצְלִיחָה נָא.

בָּרוּךְ הַבָּא בְּשֵׁם יהוה, בֵּרַכְנוּכֶם מִבֵּית יהוה. בָּרוּךְ
הַבָּא בְּשֵׁם יהוה, בֵּרַכְנוּכֶם מִבֵּית יהוה. אֵל
יהוה וַיָּאֶר לָנוּ, אִסְרוּ חַג בַּעֲבֹתִים, עַד קַרְנוֹת הַמִּזְבֵּחַ.
אֵל יהוה וַיָּאֶר לָנוּ, אִסְרוּ חַג בַּעֲבֹתִים, עַד קַרְנוֹת
הַמִּזְבֵּחַ. אֵלִי אַתָּה וְאוֹדֶךָּ, אֱלֹהַי אֲרוֹמְמֶךָּ. אֵלִי אַתָּה
וְאוֹדֶךָּ, אֱלֹהַי אֲרוֹמְמֶךָּ. הוֹדוּ לַיהוה כִּי טוֹב, כִּי לְעוֹלָם
חַסְדּוֹ. הוֹדוּ לַיהוה כִּי טוֹב, כִּי לְעוֹלָם חַסְדּוֹ.[1]

יְהַלְלוּךָ יהוה אֱלֹהֵינוּ כָּל מַעֲשֶׂיךָ, וַחֲסִידֶיךָ צַדִּיקִים
עוֹשֵׂי רְצוֹנֶךָ, וְכָל עַמְּךָ בֵּית יִשְׂרָאֵל בְּרִנָּה
יוֹדוּ וִיבָרְכוּ וִישַׁבְּחוּ וִיפָאֲרוּ וִירוֹמְמוּ וְיַעֲרִיצוּ וְיַקְדִּישׁוּ
וְיַמְלִיכוּ אֶת שִׁמְךָ מַלְכֵּנוּ, כִּי לְךָ טוֹב לְהוֹדוֹת וּלְשִׁמְךָ
נָאֶה לְזַמֵּר, כִּי מֵעוֹלָם וְעַד עוֹלָם אַתָּה אֵל.

הוֹדוּ לַיהוה כִּי טוֹב	כִּי לְעוֹלָם חַסְדּוֹ.
הוֹדוּ לֵאלֹהֵי הָאֱלֹהִים	כִּי לְעוֹלָם חַסְדּוֹ.
הוֹדוּ לַאֲדֹנֵי הָאֲדֹנִים	כִּי לְעוֹלָם חַסְדּוֹ.
לְעֹשֵׂה נִפְלָאוֹת גְּדֹלוֹת לְבַדּוֹ	כִּי לְעוֹלָם חַסְדּוֹ.
לְעֹשֵׂה הַשָּׁמַיִם בִּתְבוּנָה	כִּי לְעוֹלָם חַסְדּוֹ.

---

(1) *Psalms* 118.

on it. This is the day HASHEM has made; let us rejoice and be glad
on it.

Please HASHEM, save now!
  Please HASHEM, save now!
Please HASHEM, bring success now!
  Please HASHEM, bring success now!

Blessed is he who comes in the Name of HASHEM; we bless
you from the House of HASHEM. Blessed is he who comes in
the Name of HASHEM; we bless you from the House of HASHEM.
HASHEM is God, He illuminated for us; bind the festival offering
with cords until the corners of the Altar. HASHEM is God, He
illuminated for us; bind the festival offering with cords until the
corners of the Altar.You are my God, and I will thank You; my
God, I will exalt You. You are my God, and I will thank You; my
God, I will exalt You. Give thanks to HASHEM, for He is good; His
kindness endures forever. Give thanks to HASHEM, for He is good;
His kindness endures forever.[1]

All Your works shall praise You, HASHEM our God. And Your
devout ones, the righteous, who do Your will, and Your entire
people, the House of Israel, with glad song will thank, bless,
praise, glorify, exalt, extol, sanctify, and proclaim the sovereignty of Your Name, our King. For to You it is fitting to give
thanks, and unto Your Name it is proper to sing praises, for from
This World to the World to Come You are God.

Give thanks to HASHEM for He is good,
                for His kindness endures forever.
Give thanks to the God of the heavenly powers,
                for His kindness endures forever.
Give thanks to the Lord of the lords,
                for His kindness endures forever.
To Him Who alone performs great wonders,
                for His kindness endures forever.
To Him Who made the heavens with understanding,
                for His kindness endures forever.

לְרֹקַע הָאָרֶץ עַל הַמָּיִם	כִּי לְעוֹלָם חַסְדּוֹ.
לְעֹשֵׂה אוֹרִים גְּדֹלִים	כִּי לְעוֹלָם חַסְדּוֹ.
אֶת הַשֶּׁמֶשׁ לְמֶמְשֶׁלֶת בַּיּוֹם	כִּי לְעוֹלָם חַסְדּוֹ.
אֶת הַיָּרֵחַ וְכוֹכָבִים לְמֶמְשְׁלוֹת בַּלָּיְלָה	
	כִּי לְעוֹלָם חַסְדּוֹ.
לְמַכֵּה מִצְרַיִם בִּבְכוֹרֵיהֶם	כִּי לְעוֹלָם חַסְדּוֹ.
וַיּוֹצֵא יִשְׂרָאֵל מִתּוֹכָם	כִּי לְעוֹלָם חַסְדּוֹ.
בְּיָד חֲזָקָה וּבִזְרוֹעַ נְטוּיָה	כִּי לְעוֹלָם חַסְדּוֹ.
לְגֹזֵר יַם סוּף לִגְזָרִים	כִּי לְעוֹלָם חַסְדּוֹ.
וְהֶעֱבִיר יִשְׂרָאֵל בְּתוֹכוֹ	כִּי לְעוֹלָם חַסְדּוֹ.
וְנִעֵר פַּרְעֹה וְחֵילוֹ בְיַם סוּף	כִּי לְעוֹלָם חַסְדּוֹ.
לְמוֹלִיךְ עַמּוֹ בַּמִּדְבָּר	כִּי לְעוֹלָם חַסְדּוֹ.
לְמַכֵּה מְלָכִים גְּדֹלִים	כִּי לְעוֹלָם חַסְדּוֹ.
וַיַּהֲרֹג מְלָכִים אַדִּירִים	כִּי לְעוֹלָם חַסְדּוֹ.
לְסִיחוֹן מֶלֶךְ הָאֱמֹרִי	כִּי לְעוֹלָם חַסְדּוֹ.
וּלְעוֹג מֶלֶךְ הַבָּשָׁן	כִּי לְעוֹלָם חַסְדּוֹ.
וְנָתַן אַרְצָם לְנַחֲלָה	כִּי לְעוֹלָם חַסְדּוֹ.
נַחֲלָה לְיִשְׂרָאֵל עַבְדּוֹ	כִּי לְעוֹלָם חַסְדּוֹ.
שֶׁבְּשִׁפְלֵנוּ זָכַר לָנוּ	כִּי לְעוֹלָם חַסְדּוֹ.
וַיִּפְרְקֵנוּ מִצָּרֵינוּ	כִּי לְעוֹלָם חַסְדּוֹ.
נֹתֵן לֶחֶם לְכָל בָּשָׂר	כִּי לְעוֹלָם חַסְדּוֹ.
הוֹדוּ לְאֵל הַשָּׁמָיִם	כִּי לְעוֹלָם חַסְדּוֹ.[1]

---

(1) *Psalms* 136.

To Him Who spread out the earth over the waters,
> for His kindness endures forever.

To Him Who makes great lights,
> for His kindness endures forever.

The sun for the reign of the day, for His kindness endures forever.

The moon and the stars for the reign of the night,
> for His kindness endures forever.

To Him Who smote Egypt through their firstborn,
> for His kindness endures forever.

And brought Israel forth from their midst,
> for His kindness endures forever.

With strong hand and outstretched arm,
> for His kindness endures forever.

To Him Who divided the Sea of Reeds into parts,
> for His kindness endures forever.

And caused Israel to pass through it,
> for His kindness endures forever.

And threw Pharaoh and his army into the Sea of Reeds,
> for His kindness endures forever.

To Him Who led His people through the Wilderness,
> for His kindness endures forever.

To Him Who smote great kings, for His kindness endures forever.

And slew mighty kings,   for His kindness endures forever.

Sichon, king of the Emorites, for His kindness endures forever.

And Og, king of Bashan,   for His kindness endures forever.

And presented their land as a heritage,
> for His kindness endures forever.

A heritage for Israel, His servant, for His kindness endures forever.

In our lowliness He remembered us,
> for His kindness endures forever.

And released us from our tormentors,
> for His kindness endures forever.

He gives nourishment to all flesh,
> for His kindness endures forever.

Give thanks to God of the heavens,
> for His kindness endures forever.[1]

נִשְׁמַת כָּל חַי תְּבָרֵךְ אֶת שִׁמְךָ יְהוָה אֱלֹהֵינוּ, וְרוּחַ כָּל בָּשָׂר תְּפָאֵר וּתְרוֹמֵם זִכְרְךָ מַלְכֵּנוּ תָּמִיד. מִן הָעוֹלָם וְעַד הָעוֹלָם אַתָּה אֵל, וּמִבַּלְעָדֶיךָ אֵין לָנוּ מֶלֶךְ גּוֹאֵל וּמוֹשִׁיעַ. פּוֹדֶה וּמַצִּיל וּמְפַרְנֵס וּמְרַחֵם בְּכָל עֵת צָרָה וְצוּקָה. אֵין לָנוּ מֶלֶךְ אֶלָּא אָתָּה. אֱלֹהֵי הָרִאשׁוֹנִים וְהָאַחֲרוֹנִים אֱלוֹהַּ כָּל בְּרִיּוֹת אֲדוֹן כָּל תּוֹלָדוֹת הַמְהֻלָּל בְּרֹב הַתִּשְׁבָּחוֹת הַמְנַהֵג עוֹלָמוֹ בְּחֶסֶד וּבְרִיּוֹתָיו בְּרַחֲמִים וַיהוָה לֹא יָנוּם וְלֹא יִישָׁן. הַמְעוֹרֵר יְשֵׁנִים וְהַמֵּקִיץ נִרְדָּמִים וְהַמֵּשִׂיחַ אִלְּמִים וְהַמַּתִּיר אֲסוּרִים וְהַסּוֹמֵךְ נוֹפְלִים וְהַזּוֹקֵף כְּפוּפִים לְךָ לְבַדְּךָ אֲנַחְנוּ מוֹדִים. אִלּוּ פִינוּ מָלֵא שִׁירָה כַּיָּם וּלְשׁוֹנֵנוּ רִנָּה כַּהֲמוֹן גַּלָּיו וְשִׂפְתוֹתֵינוּ שֶׁבַח כְּמֶרְחֲבֵי רָקִיעַ וְעֵינֵינוּ מְאִירוֹת כַּשֶּׁמֶשׁ וְכַיָּרֵחַ וְיָדֵינוּ פְרוּשׂוֹת כְּנִשְׁרֵי שָׁמַיִם וְרַגְלֵינוּ קַלּוֹת כָּאַיָּלוֹת, אֵין אֲנַחְנוּ מַסְפִּיקִים לְהוֹדוֹת לְךָ יְהוָה אֱלֹהֵינוּ וֵאלֹהֵי אֲבוֹתֵינוּ וּלְבָרֵךְ אֶת שִׁמְךָ עַל אַחַת מֵאֶלֶף אֶלֶף אַלְפֵי אֲלָפִים וְרִבֵּי רְבָבוֹת פְּעָמִים הַטּוֹבוֹת שֶׁעָשִׂיתָ עִם אֲבוֹתֵינוּ וְעִמָּנוּ. מִמִּצְרַיִם גְּאַלְתָּנוּ יְהוָה אֱלֹהֵינוּ וּמִבֵּית עֲבָדִים פְּדִיתָנוּ בְּרָעָב זַנְתָּנוּ וּבְשָׂבָע כִּלְכַּלְתָּנוּ מֵחֶרֶב הִצַּלְתָּנוּ וּמִדֶּבֶר מִלַּטְתָּנוּ וּמֵחֳלָיִם רָעִים וְנֶאֱמָנִים דִּלִּיתָנוּ. עַד הֵנָּה עֲזָרוּנוּ רַחֲמֶיךָ וְלֹא עֲזָבוּנוּ חֲסָדֶיךָ וְאַל תִּטְּשֵׁנוּ יְהוָה אֱלֹהֵינוּ לָנֶצַח. עַל כֵּן אֵבָרִים שֶׁפִּלַּגְתָּ בָּנוּ וְרוּחַ וּנְשָׁמָה שֶׁנָּפַחְתָּ בְּאַפֵּינוּ וְלָשׁוֹן אֲשֶׁר שַׂמְתָּ בְּפִינוּ הֵן הֵם יוֹדוּ וִיבָרְכוּ וִישַׁבְּחוּ וִיפָאֲרוּ וִירוֹמְמוּ וְיַעֲרִיצוּ וְיַקְדִּישׁוּ וְיַמְלִיכוּ אֶת שִׁמְךָ מַלְכֵּנוּ. כִּי כָל פֶּה לְךָ יוֹדֶה וְכָל לָשׁוֹן לְךָ תִשָּׁבַע

The soul of every living being shall bless Your Name, HASHEM, our God; and the spirit of all flesh shall always glorify and exalt Your remembrance, our King. From This World to the World to Come, You are God and other than You we have no king, redeemer or savior. Liberator, Rescuer, Sustainer and Merciful One in every time of distress and anguish, we have no King but You! — God of the first and of the last, God of all creatures, Master of all generations, Who is extolled through a multitude of praises, Who guides His world with kindness and His creatures with mercy. HASHEM neither slumbers nor sleeps. He Who rouses the sleepers and awakens the slumberers, Who makes the mute speak and releases the bound; Who supports the fallen and straightens the bent. To You alone we give thanks. Were our mouth as full of song as the sea, and our tongue as full of joyous song as its multitude of waves, and our lips as full of praise as the breadth of the heavens, and our eyes as brilliant as the sun and the moon, and our hands as outspread as eagles of the sky and our feet as swift as hinds — we still could not thank You sufficiently HASHEM, our God and God of our forefather fathers and to bless Your name for even one of the thousand thousand; thousands of thousands and myriad myriads of favors that You performed for our ancestors and for us. You redeemed us from Egypt, HASHEM, our God, and liberated us from the house of bondage. In famine You nourished us and in plenty You sustained us. From sword You saved us; from plague you let us escape; and from severe and enduring diseases You spared us. Until now Your mercy has helped us and Your kindness has not forsaken us. Do not abandon us HASHEM, our God, forever. Therefore the organs that You set within us, and the spirit and soul that You breathed into our nostrils, and the tongue that You placed in our mouth — all of them shall thank and bless, praise and glorify, exalt and revere, sanctify and declare the sovereignty of Your Name, our King. For every mouth shall offer thanks to You; every tongue shall vow allegiance to You;

וְכָל בֶּרֶךְ לְךָ תִכְרַע וְכָל קוֹמָה לְפָנֶיךָ תִשְׁתַּחֲוֶה וְכָל לְבָבוֹת יִירָאוּךָ וְכָל קֶרֶב וּכְלָיוֹת יְזַמְּרוּ לִשְׁמֶךָ. כַּדָּבָר שֶׁכָּתוּב כָּל עַצְמֹתַי תֹּאמַרְנָה יהוה מִי כָמוֹךָ מַצִּיל עָנִי מֵחָזָק מִמֶּנּוּ וְעָנִי וְאֶבְיוֹן מִגֹּזְלוֹ.[1] מִי יִדְמֶה לָּךְ וּמִי יִשְׁוֶה לָּךְ וּמִי יַעֲרָךְ לָךְ הָאֵל הַגָּדוֹל הַגִּבּוֹר וְהַנּוֹרָא אֵל עֶלְיוֹן קֹנֵה שָׁמַיִם וָאָרֶץ. נְהַלֶּלְךָ וּנְשַׁבֵּחֲךָ וּנְפָאֶרְךָ וּנְבָרֵךְ אֶת שֵׁם קָדְשֶׁךָ כָּאָמוּר לְדָוִד בָּרְכִי נַפְשִׁי אֶת יהוה וְכָל קְרָבַי אֶת שֵׁם קָדְשׁוֹ.[2]

הָאֵל בְּתַעֲצֻמוֹת עֻזֶּךָ הַגָּדוֹל בִּכְבוֹד שְׁמֶךָ הַגִּבּוֹר לָנֶצַח וְהַנּוֹרָא בְּנוֹרְאוֹתֶיךָ הַמֶּלֶךְ הַיּוֹשֵׁב עַל כִּסֵּא רָם וְנִשָּׂא.

שׁוֹכֵן עַד מָרוֹם וְקָדוֹשׁ שְׁמוֹ. וְכָתוּב רַנְּנוּ צַדִּיקִים בַּיהוה לַיְשָׁרִים נָאוָה תְהִלָּה.[3] בְּפִי יְשָׁרִים תִּתְהַלָּל וּבְדִבְרֵי צַדִּיקִים תִּתְבָּרַךְ וּבִלְשׁוֹן חֲסִידִים תִּתְרוֹמָם וּבְקֶרֶב קְדוֹשִׁים תִּתְקַדָּשׁ:

וּבְמַקְהֲלוֹת רִבְבוֹת עַמְּךָ בֵּית יִשְׂרָאֵל בְּרִנָּה יִתְפָּאַר שִׁמְךָ מַלְכֵּנוּ בְּכָל דּוֹר וָדוֹר שֶׁכֵּן חוֹבַת כָּל הַיְצוּרִים לְפָנֶיךָ יהוה אֱלֹהֵינוּ וֵאלֹהֵי אֲבוֹתֵינוּ לְהוֹדוֹת לְהַלֵּל לְשַׁבֵּחַ לְפָאֵר לְרוֹמֵם לְהַדֵּר לְבָרֵךְ לְעַלֵּה וּלְקַלֵּס עַל כָּל דִּבְרֵי שִׁירוֹת וְתִשְׁבְּחוֹת דָּוִד בֶּן יִשַׁי עַבְדְּךָ מְשִׁיחֶךָ.

יִשְׁתַּבַּח שִׁמְךָ לָעַד מַלְכֵּנוּ הָאֵל הַמֶּלֶךְ הַגָּדוֹל וְהַקָּדוֹשׁ בַּשָּׁמַיִם וּבָאָרֶץ כִּי לְךָ נָאֶה יהוה אֱלֹהֵינוּ וֵאלֹהֵי אֲבוֹתֵינוּ שִׁיר וּשְׁבָחָה הַלֵּל וְזִמְרָה עֹז

every knee shall bend to You; every erect spine shall prostrate itself before You; all hearts shall fear You, and all innermost feelings and thoughts shall sing praises to Your Name, as it is written: "All my bones shall say, HASHEM, who is like You? You save the poor man from one stronger than he, the poor and destitute from one who would rob him."[1] Who is like unto You? Who is equal to You? Who can be compared to You? O great, mighty, and awesome God, the supreme God, Creator of heaven and earth. We shall laud, praise and glorify You and bless Your holy Name, as it says: "Of David: Bless HASHEM o my soul, and let all my innermost being bless His holy Name."[2]

O God, in the omnipotence of Your strength, great in the glory of Your name, mighty forever and awesome through Your awesome deeds. O King enthroned upon a high and lofty throne!

He Who abides forever, exalted and holy is His Name. As it is written: "Sing joyfully, O righteous, before HASHEM; for the upright, praise is fitting."[3] By the mouth of the upright shall You be lauded; by the words of the righteous shall You be blessed; by the tongue of the devout shall You be exalted; and amid the holy shall You be sanctified.

And in the assemblies of the myriads of Your people, the House of Israel, with joyous song shall Your Name be glorified, our King, throughout every generation. For such is the duty of all creatures — before you, HASHEM, our God, God of our forefathers, to thank, laud, praise, glorify, exalt, adorn, bless, raise high, and sing praises — even beyond all expressions of the songs and praises of David the son of Jesse, Your servant, Your anointed.

May Your Name be praised forever — our King, the God, the great and holy King — in heaven and on earth. Because for You is fitting — O HASHEM, our God, and the God of our forefathers — song and praise, lauding

---

(1) *Psalms* 35:10.(2) 103:1. (3) 33:1.

וּמֶמְשָׁלָה נֶצַח גְּדֻלָּה וּגְבוּרָה תְּהִלָּה וְתִפְאֶרֶת קְדֻשָּׁה וּמַלְכוּת בְּרָכוֹת וְהוֹדָאוֹת מֵעַתָּה וְעַד עוֹלָם: בָּרוּךְ אַתָּה יהוה אֵל מֶלֶךְ גָּדוֹל בַּתִּשְׁבָּחוֹת אֵל הַהוֹדָאוֹת אֲדוֹן הַנִּפְלָאוֹת הַבּוֹחֵר בְּשִׁירֵי זִמְרָה מֶלֶךְ אֵל חֵי הָעוֹלָמִים.

The blessing over wine is recited and the fourth cup is drunk while reclining to the left side. It is preferable that the entire cup be drunk.

בָּרוּךְ אַתָּה יהוה אֱלֹהֵינוּ מֶלֶךְ הָעוֹלָם, בּוֹרֵא פְּרִי הַגָּפֶן.

After drinking the fourth cup, the concluding blessing is recited. On the Sabbath include the passage in parentheses.

בָּרוּךְ אַתָּה יהוה אֱלֹהֵינוּ מֶלֶךְ הָעוֹלָם, עַל הַגֶּפֶן וְעַל פְּרִי הַגֶּפֶן וְעַל תְּנוּבַת הַשָּׂדֶה וְעַל אֶרֶץ חֶמְדָּה טוֹבָה וּרְחָבָה שֶׁרָצִיתָ וְהִנְחַלְתָּ לַאֲבוֹתֵינוּ לֶאֱכוֹל מִפִּרְיָהּ וְלִשְׂבּוֹעַ מִטּוּבָהּ. רַחֵם נָא יהוה אֱלֹהֵינוּ עַל יִשְׂרָאֵל עַמֶּךְ וְעַל יְרוּשָׁלַיִם עִירֶךְ וְעַל צִיּוֹן מִשְׁכַּן כְּבוֹדֶךְ וְעַל מִזְבְּחֶךְ וְעַל הֵיכָלֶךְ. וּבְנֵה יְרוּשָׁלַיִם עִיר הַקֹּדֶשׁ בִּמְהֵרָה בְיָמֵינוּ וְהַעֲלֵנוּ לְתוֹכָהּ וְשַׂמְּחֵנוּ בְּבִנְיָנָהּ וְנֹאכַל מִפִּרְיָהּ וְנִשְׂבַּע מִטּוּבָהּ וּנְבָרֶכְךָ עָלֶיהָ בִּקְדֻשָּׁה וּבְטָהֳרָה. [וּרְצֵה וְהַחֲלִיצֵנוּ בְּיוֹם הַשַּׁבָּת הַזֶּה] וְשַׂמְּחֵנוּ בְּיוֹם חַג הַמַּצּוֹת הַזֶּה. כִּי אַתָּה יהוה טוֹב וּמֵטִיב לַכֹּל וְנוֹדֶה לְּךָ עַל הָאָרֶץ וְעַל פְּרִי הַגָּפֶן. בָּרוּךְ אַתָּה יהוה עַל הָאָרֶץ וְעַל פְּרִי הַגָּפֶן.

נרצה

חֲסַל סִדּוּר פֶּסַח כְּהִלְכָתוֹ. כְּכָל מִשְׁפָּטוֹ וְחֻקָּתוֹ. כַּאֲשֶׁר זָכִינוּ לְסַדֵּר אוֹתוֹ. כֵּן נִזְכֶּה לַעֲשׂוֹתוֹ.

and hymns, power and dominion, triumph, greatness and strength, praise and splendor; holiness and sovereignty, blessings and thanksgivings, from this time and forever. Blessed are You, HASHEM, God, King exalted through praises, God of thanksgiving, Master of wonders, Who chooses musical songs of praise — King, God, Life-giver of the world.

The blessing over wine is recited and the fourth cup is drunk while reclining to the left side.
It is preferable that the entire cup be drunk.

Blessed are You, HASHEM, our God, King of the universe, Who creates the fruit of the vine.

After drinking the fourth cup, the concluding blessing is recited.
On the Sabbath include the passage in parentheses.

Blessed are You, HASHEM, our God, King of the universe, for the vine and the fruit of the vine, and the produce of the field, and for the precious, good and spacious land that You willed to give as an inheritance to our ancestors, to eat of its fruit and to be sated by its goodness. Have mercy, please, HASHEM, our God, on Israel, Your people, and on Jerusalem, Your city, and on Zion, the abode of Your glory, and on Your Altar and on Your Temple. Rebuild Jerusalem, the city of sanctity, speedily in our lifetimes. Bring us up into it and let us rejoice in its reconstruction. Let us eat of its fruits and be sated by its goodness. May we bless You over it in holiness and purity (and may it be Your will to fortify us on this Sabbath day), and may You bring us joy on this day of the Festival of Matzos. For You, HASHEM, are good and do good to all, and we thank You for the land and the fruit of the vine. Blessed are You, HASHEM, for the land and the fruit of the vine.

NIRTZAH

The Seder is now concluded in accordance with its laws, with all its ordinances and statutes. Just as we were privileged to arrange it, so may we merit to perform it.

זָךְ שׁוֹכֵן מְעוֹנָה. קוֹמֵם קְהַל עֲדַת מִי מָנָה. בְּקָרוֹב נַהֵל נִטְעֵי כַנָּה. פְּדוּיִם לְצִיּוֹן בְּרִנָּה.

לְשָׁנָה הַבָּאָה בִּירוּשָׁלָיִם.

On the first night recite the following.
On the second night continue on page 232.

וּבְכֵן וַיְהִי בַּחֲצִי הַלַּיְלָה.

אָז רוֹב נִסִּים הִפְלֵאתָ   בַּלַּיְלָה.

בְּרֹאשׁ אַשְׁמוֹרֶת זֶה   הַלַּיְלָה.

גֵּר צֶדֶק נִצַּחְתּוֹ כְּנֶחֱלַק לוֹ   לַיְלָה.

וַיְהִי בַּחֲצִי הַלַּיְלָה.

דַּנְתָּ מֶלֶךְ גְּרָר בַּחֲלוֹם   הַלַּיְלָה.

הִפְחַדְתָּ אֲרַמִּי בְּאֶמֶשׁ   לַיְלָה.

וַיָּשַׂר יִשְׂרָאֵל לְמַלְאָךְ וַיּוּכַל לוֹ   לַיְלָה.

וַיְהִי בַּחֲצִי הַלַּיְלָה.

זֶרַע בְּכוֹרֵי פַתְרוֹס מָחַצְתָּ בַּחֲצִי   הַלַּיְלָה.

חֵילָם לֹא מָצְאוּ בְּקוּמָם   בַּלַּיְלָה.

טִיסַת נְגִיד חֲרוֹשֶׁת סִלִּיתָ בְּכוֹכְבֵי   לַיְלָה.

וַיְהִי בַּחֲצִי הַלַּיְלָה.

◆§ וַיְהִי בַּחֲצִי הַלַּיְלָה — *It happened at midnight.*

This poem is taken from the additional prayers for *Shabbos Hagadol*, the Sabbath which precedes Passover. It is based on the *midrashic* statement (*Bamidbar Rabbah* 20:12, *Tanchuma*, *Balak* 11) that when the Torah says, "It is a night of watching for Hashem . . . a watching for all the Children of Israel for their generations," it means that when enemies stood up against the Jewish nation, the enemies were miraculously destroyed at night. The *midrash* seems to imply that the night on which

228 / הגדה של פסח — כי ישאלך בנך

O Pure One, Who dwells on high, raise up the countless congregation, soon — guide the offshoots of Your plants, redeemed, to Zion, with glad song.

Next year in Jerusalem!

On the first night recite the following.
On the second night continue on page 232.

It happened at midnight.

Then You performed wondrous miracles at   night.
  At the first watch of this   night.
You brought victory to the righteous convert
  [Abraham] by dividing for him the   night.
      It happened at midnight.

You judged the king of Gerar [Abimelech]
  in a dream of the   night.
You terrified the Aramean [Laban] in the dark of   night.
And Israel [Jacob] fought with an angel
  and overcame him at   night.
      It happened at midnight.

You bruised the firstborn seed
  of Pasros [Egypt] at   midnight.
They did not find their legions
  when they arose at   night.
The swift armies of the prince of Charoshes [Sisera]
  You crushed with the stars of   night.
      It happened at midnight.

---

all these miracles happened was, in fact, the "night of watching for all generations" — the night of the fifteenth of Nissan. Among the example mentioned in the *midrashim* are: God's nocturnal appearances to Abimelech (*Genesis* 20:3) and Laban (ibid. 31:24), the moving of Israel's protective cloud to the skies over the attacking Egyptian army (*Exodus* 14:20).

Aruch HaShulchan believes that the poem suggests a question-and-

יָעֵץ מְחָרֵף לְנוֹפֵף אִוּי הוֹבַשְׁתָּ פְגָרָיו בַּלַּיְלָה.
בָּרַע בֵּל וּמַצָּבוֹ בְּאִישׁוֹן לַיְלָה.
לְאִישׁ חֲמוּדוֹת נִגְלָה רָז חֲזוֹת לַיְלָה.
וַיְהִי בַּחֲצִי הַלַּיְלָה.

מִשְׁתַּכֵּר בִּכְלֵי קֹדֶשׁ נֶהֱרַג בּוֹ בַּלַּיְלָה.
נוֹשַׁע מִבּוֹר אֲרָיוֹת פּוֹתֵר בִּעֲתוּתֵי לַיְלָה.
שִׂנְאָה נָטַר אֲגָגִי וְכָתַב סְפָרִים בַּלַּיְלָה.
וַיְהִי בַּחֲצִי הַלַּיְלָה.

עוֹרַרְתָּ נִצְחֲךָ עָלָיו בְּנֶדֶד שְׁנַת לַיְלָה.
פּוּרָה תִדְרוֹךְ לְשֹׁמֵר מַה מִלַּיְלָה.
צָרַח כַּשּׁוֹמֵר וְשָׂח אָתָא בֹקֶר וְגַם לַיְלָה.
וַיְהִי בַּחֲצִי הַלַּיְלָה.

קָרֵב יוֹם אֲשֶׁר הוּא לֹא יוֹם וְלֹא לַיְלָה.
רָם הוֹדַע כִּי לְךָ הַיּוֹם אַף לְךָ הַלַּיְלָה.
שׁוֹמְרִים הַפְקֵד לְעִירְךָ כָּל הַיּוֹם וְכָל הַלַּיְלָה.
תָּאִיר כְּאוֹר יוֹם חֶשְׁכַּת לַיְלָה.
וַיְהִי בַּחֲצִי הַלַּיְלָה.

---

answer format. It is well known that "night" is used as a metaphor for periods of distress or exile, and "morning" or "daytime" is used to represent deliverance. Why, then, do we find that throughout history, salvation seems to happen at night? The answer is, *"It happened at midnight."* Nighttime is indeed a time that symbolizes the darkness and gloom of unfortunate times, but only the *beginning* of the night. Midnight, as the Kabbalah tells us (see commentaries to *Shulchan Aruch, Orach Chaim* 1), is a time of mercy and receptiveness in Heaven.

The blasphemer [Sennacherib] schemed to raise
   his hand menacingly [over the precious city].
      You made his corpses rot at   night.
Bel [the Babylonian pagan deity] and his
   pedestal fell in the black of   night.
To the beloved man [Daniel] was revealed
   the secret of the visions of   night.
              It happened at midnight.

He who guzzled out of the sacred vessels
   [Belshazzar, king of Babylonia] was killed on that night.
The one who was saved from the lions' den
   interpreted the terrors of the   night.
The Aggagite [Haman] nurtured hatred
   and wrote decrees at   night.
              It happened at midnight.

You initiated Your triumph against him
   by disturbing the sleep [of Ahasuerus] at   night.
You will tread a winepress [in peace after victory]
   for him who cries out [Israel]: Our Guardian!
   What will be of this   night?
Like a guardian You will call out in response:
   The morning has come, as well as the   night.
              It happened at midnight.

The day is approaching which is neither day nor   night.
Most High! Make it known that Yours are
   both the day and the   night.
Appoint watchmen over Your city all day and all   night.
Illuminate like the light of day the darkness of   night.
              It will happen at midnight.

Thus it is indeed appropriate that all these miracles occurred at night,
for *it happened at midnight.*

On the first night continue on page 234.
On the second night recite the following.

וּבְכֵן וַאֲמַרְתֶּם זֶבַח פֶּסַח:

בְּפֶסַח.   אִמֶץ גְּבוּרוֹתֶיךָ הִפְלֵאתָ

פֶּסַח.   בְּרֹאשׁ כָּל מוֹעֲדוֹת נִשֵּׂאתָ

פֶּסַח.   גִּלִּיתָ לְאֶזְרָחִי חֲצוֹת לֵיל

וַאֲמַרְתֶּם זֶבַח פֶּסַח.

בְּפֶסַח.   דְּלָתָיו דָּפַקְתָּ כְּחֹם הַיּוֹם

בְּפֶסַח.   הִסְעִיד נוֹצְצִים עֻגוֹת מַצּוֹת

פֶּסַח.   וְאֶל הַבָּקָר רָץ זֵכֶר לְשׁוֹר עֵרֶךְ

וַאֲמַרְתֶּם זֶבַח פֶּסַח.

בְּפֶסַח.   זוֹעֲמוּ סְדוֹמִים וְלוֹהֲטוּ בָּאֵשׁ

פֶּסַח.   חֻלַּץ לוֹט מֵהֶם וּמַצּוֹת אָפָה בְּקֵץ

בְּפֶסַח.   טֵאטֵאתָ אַדְמַת מוֹף וְנוֹף בְּעָבְרְךָ

וַאֲמַרְתֶּם זֶבַח פֶּסַח.

---

§⊷ וּבְכֵן וַאֲמַרְתֶּם זֶבַח פֶּסַח — *And you will say:*
"A feast of Passover."

---

205. What is the meaning of the refrain of this poem? Who is supposed to say, "A feast of Passover" and for what purpose?

Aruch HaShulchan notes that throughout the Torah the seven-day holiday we call Pesach is referred to as "The festival of matzos," while "Pesach" is used to describe the day *before* the holiday, the day on which the Pesach sacrifice was slaughtered. In Talmudic times the Biblical name fell into disuse and the present practice of calling the holiday "Pesach" began. Why was this new name for the holiday adopted? *Aruch HaShulchan* suggests that this was done because the name "Pesach" (meaning "passing over") recalls the miracles of the Exodus, when God smote the firstborn of Egypt but "skipped over" the

On the first night continue on page 234.
On the second night recite the following.

And you will say: A feast of Passover.

The power of Your mighty deeds
  You showed wondrously on   Passover.
Foremost of all festivals You exalted   Passover.
You revealed to Abraham
  the events of the night of   Passover.
      And you will say: A feast of Passover.

You knocked on his doors
  during the heat of the day on   Passover.
He gave bright angels a meal of cakes of
  matzah on   Passover.
He ran to fetch an ox in commemoration of
  the ox sacrificed [as the *Korban Chagigah* —
  the festival offering] on   Passover.
      And you will say: A feast of Passover.

The Sodomites provoked Hashem
  and were set ablaze on   Passover.
Lot escaped from them and baked matzos
  at the end of   Passover.
You swept clean the land of Mof and Nof
  [Egyptian cities] on   Passover.
      And you will say: A feast of Passover.

Jewish households, while "the festival of matzos" does not have so direct an association.

The intent of the poem may thus be explained as follows: Since *"the power of Your mighty deeds you showed wondrously"* at the time of the original Pesach sacrifice, and hence *"foremost of all festivals You exalted"* that night of Pesach, and, because the importance of this date was known to You centuries before these events, when *"You revealed to Abraham the events of the night of Passover,"* therefore we say that this is *"A feast of Passover."* The other stanzas may be interpreted accordingly.

יָהּ רֹאשׁ כָּל אוֹן מָחַצְתָּ בְּלֵיל שִׁמּוּר פֶּסַח.

כַּבִּיר עַל בֵּן בְּכוֹר פָּסַחְתָּ בְּדַם פֶּסַח.

לְבִלְתִּי תֵּת מַשְׁחִית לָבֹא בִּפְתָחַי בַּפֶּסַח.

וַאֲמַרְתֶּם זֶבַח פֶּסַח.

מְסֻגֶּרֶת סֻגָּרָה בְּעִתּוֹתֵי פֶּסַח.

נִשְׁמְדָה מִדְיָן בִּצְלִיל שְׂעוֹרֵי עֹמֶר פֶּסַח.

שׂוֹרְפוּ מִשְׁמַנֵּי פּוּל וְלוּד בִּיקַד יְקוֹד פֶּסַח.

וַאֲמַרְתֶּם זֶבַח פֶּסַח.

עוֹד הַיּוֹם בְּנֹב לַעֲמוֹד עַד גָּעָה עוֹנַת פֶּסַח.

פַּס יַד כָּתְבָה לְקַעֲקֵעַ צוּל בַּפֶּסַח.

צָפֹה הַצָּפִית עָרוֹךְ הַשֻּׁלְחָן בַּפֶּסַח.

וַאֲמַרְתֶּם זֶבַח פֶּסַח.

קָהָל כִּנְּסָה הֲדַסָּה צוֹם לְשַׁלֵּשׁ בַּפֶּסַח.

רֹאשׁ מִבֵּית רָשָׁע מָחַצְתָּ בְּעֵץ חֲמִשִּׁים בַּפֶּסַח.

שְׁתֵּי אֵלֶּה רֶגַע תָּבִיא לְעוּצִית בַּפֶּסַח.

תָּעֹז יָדְךָ וְתָרוּם יְמִינְךָ כְּלֵיל הִתְקַדֶּשׁ חַג פֶּסַח.

וַאֲמַרְתֶּם זֶבַח פֶּסַח.

On both nights continue here:

כִּי לוֹ נָאֶה, כִּי לוֹ יָאֶה:

⋖ כִּי לוֹ נָאֶה, כִּי לוֹ יָאֶה — *To Him it is fitting.*
To Him it is due.

---

206. How does this tribute to God's majesty fit into the Haggadah?

Abarbanel explains the connection between the theme of extolling God's kingship over the world and Pesach. He notes that it was on this day that the nations of the world recognized that it was not Pharaoh who

HASHEM, the first issue of strength You bruised
   on the watchful night of   Passover.
Mighty One, You skipped over the firstborn son
   because of the blood of   Passover,
Not to allow the destroyer to enter my doors on Passover.
         And you will say: A feast of Passover.

The closed city [Jericho] was handed over
   [to the Jews] at the time of   Passover.
Midian was destroyed [by the Jews
   under the leadership of Gidon]
   through the merit of a cake of the *omer* on   Passover.
The mighty nobles of Pul and Lud [the Assyrians
   in the days of King Hezekiah]
   were burnt in a conflagration on   Passover.
         And you will say: A feast of Passover.

He [Sennacherib] would have stood at Nob,
   but the time of Passover arrived.
A hand wrote the decree of annihilation against Zul
   [Babylonia] on   Passover.
Their scout went to look for the enemy while their table
   was festively set on   Passover.
         And you will say: A feast of Passover.

Hadassah [Esther] gathered an assembly for
   a three-day fast on   Passover.
The head of the evil house [Haman] You killed
   on a fifty-cubit pole on   Passover.
Bring bereavement and widowhood to Utzis
   [Edom] in an instant on   Passover.
Strengthen Your hand, raise Your right hand as on
   the night that the festival of Passover was sanctified.
         And you will say: A feast of Passover.

On both nights continue here:

To Him it is fitting. To Him it is due.

אַדִּיר בִּמְלוּכָה, בָּחוּר כַּהֲלָכָה, גְּדוּדָיו יֹאמְרוּ לוֹ, לְךָ
וּלְךָ, לְךָ כִּי לְךָ, לְךָ אַף לְךָ, לְךָ יהוה הַמַּמְלָכָה, כִּי לוֹ
נָאֶה, כִּי לוֹ יָאֶה.

דָּגוּל בִּמְלוּכָה, הָדוּר כַּהֲלָכָה, וָתִיקָיו יֹאמְרוּ לוֹ, לְךָ
וּלְךָ, לְךָ כִּי לְךָ, לְךָ אַף לְךָ, לְךָ יהוה הַמַּמְלָכָה, כִּי לוֹ
נָאֶה, כִּי לוֹ יָאֶה.

זַכַּאי בִּמְלוּכָה, חָסִין כַּהֲלָכָה, טַפְסְרָיו יֹאמְרוּ לוֹ, לְךָ
וּלְךָ, לְךָ כִּי לְךָ, לְךָ אַף לְךָ, לְךָ יהוה הַמַּמְלָכָה, כִּי לוֹ
נָאֶה, כִּי לוֹ יָאֶה.

יָחִיד בִּמְלוּכָה, כַּבִּיר כַּהֲלָכָה, לִמּוּדָיו יֹאמְרוּ לוֹ, לְךָ
וּלְךָ, לְךָ כִּי לְךָ, לְךָ אַף לְךָ, לְךָ יהוה הַמַּמְלָכָה, כִּי לוֹ
נָאֶה, כִּי לוֹ יָאֶה.

מוֹשֵׁל בִּמְלוּכָה, נוֹרָא כַּהֲלָכָה, סְבִיבָיו יֹאמְרוּ לוֹ, לְךָ
וּלְךָ, לְךָ כִּי לְךָ, לְךָ אַף לְךָ, לְךָ יהוה הַמַּמְלָכָה, כִּי לוֹ
נָאֶה, כִּי לוֹ יָאֶה.

עָנָיו בִּמְלוּכָה, פּוֹדֶה כַּהֲלָכָה, צַדִּיקָיו יֹאמְרוּ לוֹ, לְךָ
וּלְךָ, לְךָ כִּי לְךָ, לְךָ אַף לְךָ, לְךָ יהוה הַמַּמְלָכָה, כִּי לוֹ
נָאֶה, כִּי לוֹ יָאֶה.

קָדוֹשׁ בִּמְלוּכָה, רַחוּם כַּהֲלָכָה, שִׁנְאַנָּיו יֹאמְרוּ לוֹ, לְךָ
וּלְךָ, לְךָ כִּי לְךָ, לְךָ אַף לְךָ, לְךָ יהוה הַמַּמְלָכָה, כִּי לוֹ
נָאֶה, כִּי לוֹ יָאֶה.

---

was the mightiest ruler in the world, but God. It was through the Exodus
that "the chieftains of Edom were confounded, trembling gripped the
powers of Moab. . ." (*Exodus* 15:15), and all kingdoms realized how puny
and insignificant they were in His presence.

Abarbanel also gives another interpretation of the word *na'eh* —
generally translated as *"fitting"* or "proper." He believes it is related to the

Mighty in royalty, chosen by right, His legions say to Him: Yours and only Yours; Yours, yes Yours, Yours, surely Yours; Yours, HASHEM, is the sovereignty of the world. To Him it is fitting. To Him it is due.

Distinguished in royalty, glorious of right. His faithful say to Him: Yours and only Yours; Yours, yes Yours; Yours, surely Yours; Yours, HASHEM, is the sovereignty of the world. To Him it is fitting. To Him it is due.

Pure in royalty, firm of right. His courtiers say to Him: Yours and only Yours; Yours, yes Yours; Yours, surely Yours; Yours, HASHEM, is the sovereignty of the world. To Him it is fitting. To Him it is due.

Unique in royalty, mighty of right. His disciples say to Him: Yours and only Yours; Yours, yes Yours; Yours, surely Yours; Yours, HASHEM, is the sovereignty of the world. To Him it is fitting. To Him it is due.

Ruling in royalty, feared of right. Those who surround Him say to Him: Yours and only Yours; Yours, yes Yours; Yours, surely Yours; Yours, HASHEM, is the sovereignty of the world. To Him it is fitting. To Him it is due.

Humble in royalty, redeeming by right. His righteous ones say to Him: Yours and only Yours; Yours, yes Yours; Yours, surely Yours; Yours, HASHEM, is the sovereignty of the world. To Him it is fitting. To Him it is due.

Holy in royalty, merciful of right. His angels say to Him: Yours and only Yours; Yours, yes Yours; Yours, surely Yours; Yours, HASHEM, is the sovereignty of the world. To Him it is fitting. To Him it is due.

Aramaic word meaning "soft." This indicates that God is easy to appease when one seeks His forgiveness through repentance and good deeds.

תַּקִּיף בִּמְלוּכָה, **תּוֹמֵךְ** כַּהֲלָכָה, תְּמִימָיו יֹאמְרוּ לוֹ, לְךָ וּלְךָ, לְךָ כִּי לְךָ, לְךָ אַף לְךָ, לְךָ יהוה הַמַּמְלָכָה, כִּי לוֹ נָאֶה, כִּי לוֹ יָאֶה.

אַדִּיר הוּא יִבְנֶה בֵיתוֹ בְּקָרוֹב, בִּמְהֵרָה, בִּמְהֵרָה, בְּיָמֵינוּ בְּקָרוֹב. אֵל בְּנֵה, אֵל בְּנֵה, בְּנֵה בֵיתְךָ בְּקָרוֹב.

בָּחוּר הוּא. **גָּדוֹל** הוּא. **דָּגוּל** הוּא. יִבְנֶה בֵיתוֹ בְּקָרוֹב, בִּמְהֵרָה, בִּמְהֵרָה, בְּיָמֵינוּ בְּקָרוֹב. אֵל בְּנֵה, אֵל בְּנֵה, בְּנֵה בֵיתְךָ בְּקָרוֹב.

הָדוּר הוּא. **וָתִיק** הוּא. **זַכַּאי** הוּא. **חָסִיד** הוּא. יִבְנֶה בֵיתוֹ בְּקָרוֹב, בִּמְהֵרָה, בִּמְהֵרָה, בְּיָמֵינוּ בְּקָרוֹב. אֵל בְּנֵה, אֵל בְּנֵה, בְּנֵה בֵיתְךָ בְּקָרוֹב.

טָהוֹר הוּא. **יָחִיד** הוּא. **כַּבִּיר** הוּא. **לָמוּד** הוּא. **מֶלֶךְ** הוּא. **נוֹרָא** הוּא. **סַגִּיב** הוּא. **עִזּוּז** הוּא. **פּוֹדֶה** הוּא. **צַדִּיק** הוּא. יִבְנֶה בֵיתוֹ בְּקָרוֹב, בִּמְהֵרָה, בְּיָמֵינוּ בְּקָרוֹב. אֵל בְּנֵה, אֵל בְּנֵה, בְּנֵה בֵיתְךָ בְּקָרוֹב.

קָדוֹשׁ הוּא. **רַחוּם** הוּא. **שַׁדַּי** הוּא. **תַּקִּיף** הוּא. יִבְנֶה בֵיתוֹ בְּקָרוֹב, בִּמְהֵרָה, בִּמְהֵרָה, בְּיָמֵינוּ בְּקָרוֹב. אֵל בְּנֵה, אֵל בְּנֵה, בְּנֵה בֵיתְךָ בְּקָרוֹב.

אֶחָד מִי יוֹדֵעַ? אֶחָד אֲנִי יוֹדֵעַ. אֶחָד אֱלֹהֵינוּ שֶׁבַּשָּׁמַיִם וּבָאָרֶץ.

אַדִּיר הוּא — *Mighty is He*

Yalkut Shimoni explains that we recite this prayer for the rebuilding of the Temple on this night because our future deliverance through the Messiah is supposed to come during Nissan (*Rosh Hashanah* 11a). We express our

Powerful in royalty, sustaining of right. His perfect ones say to Him: Yours and only Yours; Yours, yes Yours; Yours, surely Yours; Yours, HASHEM, is the sovereignty of the world. To Him it is fitting. To Him it is due.

Mighty is He. May He build His house soon; quickly, quickly, in our lifetimes, soon. God, build; God, build; build Your house soon.

Exalted is He, great is He, distinguished is He. May He build His house soon; quickly, quickly, in our lifetimes, soon. God, build; God, build; build Your house soon.

Glorious is He, faithful is He, guiltless is He, righteous is He. May He build His house soon; quickly, quickly, in our lifetimes, soon. God, build; God, build; build Your house soon.

Pure is He, unique is He, powerful is He, all-wise is He, the King is He, awesome is He, sublime is He, all-powerful is He, the Redeemer is He, all-righteous is He. May He build His house soon; quickly, quickly, in our lifetimes, soon. God, build; God, build; build Your house soon.

Holy is He, compassionate is He, Almighty is He, Omnipotent is He. May He build His house soon; quickly, quickly, in our lifetimes, soon. God, rebuild; God, build; build Your house soon.

Who knows one? I know one.
One is our God in the heavens and the earth.

---

hope that this might happen "quickly, quickly" — that is, immediately, on this very night.

Although the rule is that the building of the Temple may not be carried out on Yom Tov (Shevuos 15b), Rashi tells us in several places that the Third Temple will not be built by human hands, but by supernatural means, by God's own hand, as it were. Thus the poem continues, "God, build; God, build" — that is, since it is You, God, Who will build the Temple it is possible that we can pray now for this to happen immediately.

⇜ אֶחָד מִי יוֹדֵעַ ⇝ — *Who knows one?*

---

207. What does this song have to do with Pesach?

239 / THE HAGGADAH WITH ANSWERS

שְׁנַיִם מִי יוֹדֵעַ? שְׁנַיִם אֲנִי יוֹדֵעַ. שְׁנֵי לֻחוֹת הַבְּרִית, אֶחָד אֱלֹהֵינוּ שֶׁבַּשָּׁמַיִם וּבָאָרֶץ.

שְׁלֹשָׁה מִי יוֹדֵעַ? שְׁלֹשָׁה אֲנִי יוֹדֵעַ. שְׁלֹשָׁה אָבוֹת, שְׁנֵי לֻחוֹת הַבְּרִית, אֶחָד אֱלֹהֵינוּ שֶׁבַּשָּׁמַיִם וּבָאָרֶץ.

אַרְבַּע מִי יוֹדֵעַ? אַרְבַּע אֲנִי יוֹדֵעַ. אַרְבַּע אִמָּהוֹת, שְׁלֹשָׁה אָבוֹת, שְׁנֵי לֻחוֹת הַבְּרִית, אֶחָד אֱלֹהֵינוּ שֶׁבַּשָּׁמַיִם וּבָאָרֶץ.

חֲמִשָּׁה מִי יוֹדֵעַ? חֲמִשָּׁה אֲנִי יוֹדֵעַ. חֲמִשָּׁה חֻמְשֵׁי תוֹרָה, אַרְבַּע אִמָּהוֹת, שְׁלֹשָׁה אָבוֹת, שְׁנֵי לֻחוֹת הַבְּרִית, אֶחָד אֱלֹהֵינוּ שֶׁבַּשָּׁמַיִם וּבָאָרֶץ.

שִׁשָּׁה מִי יוֹדֵעַ? שִׁשָּׁה אֲנִי יוֹדֵעַ. שִׁשָּׁה סִדְרֵי מִשְׁנָה, חֲמִשָּׁה חֻמְשֵׁי תוֹרָה, אַרְבַּע אִמָּהוֹת, שְׁלֹשָׁה אָבוֹת, שְׁנֵי לֻחוֹת הַבְּרִית, אֶחָד אֱלֹהֵינוּ שֶׁבַּשָּׁמַיִם וּבָאָרֶץ.

שִׁבְעָה מִי יוֹדֵעַ? שִׁבְעָה אֲנִי יוֹדֵעַ. שִׁבְעָה יְמֵי שַׁבַּתָּא, שִׁשָּׁה סִדְרֵי מִשְׁנָה, חֲמִשָּׁה חֻמְשֵׁי תוֹרָה, אַרְבַּע אִמָּהוֹת, שְׁלֹשָׁה אָבוֹת, שְׁנֵי לֻחוֹת הַבְּרִית, אֶחָד אֱלֹהֵינוּ שֶׁבַּשָּׁמַיִם וּבָאָרֶץ.

The following explanation is found in *Simchas HaRegel*, quoting the *Chasam Sofer*. The belief of the ancient heretics was that it is impossible for one being to be the source of both the good and the bad that exist in the world. It is for this reason that they postulated the existence of two separate gods, one who was the source of all good in the world, and the other who was the root of all evil. The truth is, of course, that the one God does indeed have control over all that takes place. And while it is true that bad things cannot emanate from a being that is totally and unremittingly good, bad things *do* come from God through His, to some extent, removing His providence from a given person or nation, and their destruction follows as a result of the lack of God's

Who knows two? I know two. Two are the Tablets of the Covenant. One is our God in the heavens and the earth.

Who knows three? I know three. Three are the Patriarchs. Two are the Tablets of the Covenant. One is our God in the heavens and the earth.

Who knows four? I know four. Four are the Matriarchs. Three are the Patriarchs. Two are the Tablets of the Covenant. One is our God in the heavens and the earth.

Who knows five? I know five. Five are the Books of the Torah. Four are the Matriarchs. Three are the Patriarchs. Two are the Tablets of the Covenant. One is our God in the heavens and the earth.

Who knows six? I know six. Six are the Orders of the *Mishnah.* Five are the Books of the Torah. Four are the Matriarchs. Three are the Patriarchs. Two are the Tablets of the Covenant. One is our God in the heavens and the earth.

Who knows seven? I know seven. Seven are the days of the week. Six are the Orders of the *Mishnah.* Five are the Books of the Torah. Four are the Matriarchs. Three are the Patriarchs. Two are the Tablets of the Covenant. One is our God in the heavens and the earth.

---

protection (see *Ramban, Genesis* 18:19). God "personally" administered the plague of the firstborn and brought out the Jews from Egypt, without the use of angels or other heavenly agents, as the Haggadah established earlier. God, in His ultimate and unparalleled purity and sanctity descended, as it were, to Egypt, the most impure and spiritually contaminated place in the world. By doing so He showed that, despite the apparent disparity between God's sanctity and Egypt's profanity, He was in fact in complete control of both realms. This display of Unity is thus quite relevant to the events of Pesach, and it is this theme that this song addresses.

Iyun Tefillah is of the opinion that this poem is simply a riddle designed to arouse the children's curiosity and to be an incentive for them to stay awake even after the meal is finished.

שְׁמוֹנָה מִי יוֹדֵעַ? שְׁמוֹנָה אֲנִי יוֹדֵעַ. שְׁמוֹנָה יְמֵי מִילָה, שִׁבְעָה יְמֵי שַׁבַּתָּא, שִׁשָּׁה סִדְרֵי מִשְׁנָה, חֲמִשָּׁה חֻמְשֵׁי תוֹרָה, אַרְבַּע אִמָּהוֹת, שְׁלֹשָׁה אָבוֹת, שְׁנֵי לֻחוֹת הַבְּרִית, אֶחָד אֱלֹהֵינוּ שֶׁבַּשָּׁמַיִם וּבָאָרֶץ.

תִּשְׁעָה מִי יוֹדֵעַ? תִּשְׁעָה אֲנִי יוֹדֵעַ. תִּשְׁעָה יַרְחֵי לֵדָה, שְׁמוֹנָה יְמֵי מִילָה, שִׁבְעָה יְמֵי שַׁבַּתָּא, שִׁשָּׁה סִדְרֵי מִשְׁנָה, חֲמִשָּׁה חֻמְשֵׁי תוֹרָה, אַרְבַּע אִמָּהוֹת, שְׁלֹשָׁה אָבוֹת, שְׁנֵי לֻחוֹת הַבְּרִית, אֶחָד אֱלֹהֵינוּ שֶׁבַּשָּׁמַיִם וּבָאָרֶץ.

עֲשָׂרָה מִי יוֹדֵעַ? עֲשָׂרָה אֲנִי יוֹדֵעַ. עֲשָׂרָה דִבְּרַיָּא, תִּשְׁעָה יַרְחֵי לֵדָה, שְׁמוֹנָה יְמֵי מִילָה, שִׁבְעָה יְמֵי שַׁבַּתָּא, שִׁשָּׁה סִדְרֵי מִשְׁנָה, חֲמִשָּׁה חֻמְשֵׁי תוֹרָה, אַרְבַּע אִמָּהוֹת, שְׁלֹשָׁה אָבוֹת, שְׁנֵי לֻחוֹת הַבְּרִית, אֶחָד אֱלֹהֵינוּ שֶׁבַּשָּׁמַיִם וּבָאָרֶץ.

אַחַד עָשָׂר מִי יוֹדֵעַ? אַחַד עָשָׂר אֲנִי יוֹדֵעַ. אַחַד עָשָׂר כּוֹכְבַיָּא, עֲשָׂרָה דִבְּרַיָּא, תִּשְׁעָה יַרְחֵי לֵדָה, שְׁמוֹנָה יְמֵי מִילָה, שִׁבְעָה יְמֵי שַׁבַּתָּא, שִׁשָּׁה סִדְרֵי מִשְׁנָה, חֲמִשָּׁה חֻמְשֵׁי תוֹרָה, אַרְבַּע אִמָּהוֹת, שְׁלֹשָׁה אָבוֹת, שְׁנֵי לֻחוֹת הַבְּרִית, אֶחָד אֱלֹהֵינוּ שֶׁבַּשָּׁמַיִם וּבָאָרֶץ.

שְׁנֵים עָשָׂר מִי יוֹדֵעַ? שְׁנֵים עָשָׂר אֲנִי יוֹדֵעַ. שְׁנֵים עָשָׂר שִׁבְטַיָּא, אַחַד עָשָׂר כּוֹכְבַיָּא, עֲשָׂרָה דִבְּרַיָּא, תִּשְׁעָה יַרְחֵי לֵדָה, שְׁמוֹנָה יְמֵי מִילָה, שִׁבְעָה יְמֵי שַׁבַּתָּא, שִׁשָּׁה סִדְרֵי מִשְׁנָה, חֲמִשָּׁה חֻמְשֵׁי תוֹרָה, אַרְבַּע אִמָּהוֹת, שְׁלֹשָׁה אָבוֹת, שְׁנֵי לֻחוֹת הַבְּרִית, אֶחָד אֱלֹהֵינוּ שֶׁבַּשָּׁמַיִם וּבָאָרֶץ.

שְׁלֹשָׁה עָשָׂר מִי יוֹדֵעַ? שְׁלֹשָׁה עָשָׂר אֲנִי יוֹדֵעַ. שְׁלֹשָׁה עָשָׂר מִדַּיָּא, שְׁנֵים עָשָׂר שִׁבְטַיָּא, אַחַד עָשָׂר כּוֹכְבַיָּא,

Who knows eight? I know eight. Eight are the days of circumcision. Seven are the days of the week. Six are the Orders of the *Mishnah.* Five are the Books of the Torah. Four are the Matriarchs. Three are the Patriarchs. Two are the Tablets of the Covenant. One is our God in the heavens and the earth.

Who knows nine? I know nine. Nine are the months of pregnancy. Eight are the days of circumcision. Seven are the days of the week. Six are the Orders of the *Mishnah.* Five are the Books of the Torah. Four are the Matriarchs. Three are the Patriarchs. Two are the Tablets of the Covenant. One is our God in the heavens and the earth.

Who knows ten? I know ten. Ten are the Commandments. Nine are the months of pregnancy. Eight are the days of circumcision. Seven are the days of the week. Six are the Orders of the *Mishnah.* Five are the Books of the Torah. Four are the Matriarchs. Three are the Patriarchs. Two are the Tablets of the Covenant. One is our God in the heavens and the earth.

Who knows eleven? I know eleven. Eleven are the stars [of Yosef's dream]. Ten are the Commandments. Nine are the months of pregnancy. Eight are the days of circumcision. Seven are the days of the week. Six are the Orders of the *Mishnah.* Five are the Books of the Torah. Four are the Matriarchs. Three are the Patriarchs. Two are the Tablets of the Covenant. One is our God in the heavens and the earth.

Who knows twelve? I know twelve. Twelve are the tribes. Eleven are the stars. Ten are the Commandments. Nine are the months of pregnancy. Eight are the days of circumcision. Seven are the days of the week. Six are the Orders of the *Mishnah.* Five are the Books of the Torah. Four are the Matriarchs. Three are the Patriarchs. Two are the Tablets of the Covenant. One is our God in the heavens and the earth.

Who knows thirteen? I know thirteen. Thirteen are the Attributes of God. Twelve are the tribes. Eleven are the stars.

עֲשָׂרָה דִבְּרַיָּא, תִּשְׁעָה יַרְחֵי לֵדָה, שְׁמוֹנָה יְמֵי מִילָה, שִׁבְעָה יְמֵי שַׁבַּתָּא, שִׁשָּׁה סִדְרֵי מִשְׁנָה, חֲמִשָּׁה חֻמְשֵׁי תוֹרָה, אַרְבַּע אִמָּהוֹת, שְׁלֹשָׁה אָבוֹת, שְׁנֵי לֻחוֹת הַבְּרִית, אֶחָד אֱלֹהֵינוּ שֶׁבַּשָּׁמַיִם וּבָאָרֶץ.

חַד גַּדְיָא, חַד גַּדְיָא, דְּזַבִּין אַבָּא בִּתְרֵי זוּזֵי, חַד גַּדְיָא חַד גַּדְיָא.

וְאָתָא **שׁוּנְרָא** וְאָכְלָה לְגַדְיָא, דְּזַבִּין אַבָּא בִּתְרֵי זוּזֵי, חַד גַּדְיָא חַד גַּדְיָא.

וְאָתָא **כַלְבָּא** וְנָשַׁךְ לְשׁוּנְרָא, דְּאָכְלָה לְגַדְיָא, דְּזַבִּין אַבָּא בִּתְרֵי זוּזֵי, חַד גַּדְיָא חַד גַּדְיָא.

---

§ חַד גַּדְיָא — *One kid, one kid*

The commentators ascribe deep significance to this poem, explaining that it is far more than merely an entertaining children's song.

The Haggadah *Simchas HaRegel,* quoting *Chasam Sofer,* comments that the paragraph "*Ha Lachma Anya,*" at the beginning of the Haggadah, is a lament over the fact that we are no longer able to bring our Pesach sacrifices to the Temple in Jerusalem. It is written in Aramaic because Aramaic was the predominant language at the time that it was composed. The same, he continues, may be said of "*Chad Gadya*": It too bemoans the suspension of the Pesach sacrifice now that the Temple has been destroyed. The double expression "*one kid, one kid*" refers to two sacrifices the Jews offered for Pesach — the Pesach offering and the *Chagigah* sacrifice which generally accompanied the Pesach. The halachah requires (*Chagigah* 6a) that the *Chagigah* offering be worth at least two pieces of silver; hence, the reference to "*father*" buying it for two *zuzim* is to our ancestors having spent two silver pieces on purchasing the *Chagigah* offering, and we now long for those days. The repetition of the phrase "*one kid, one kid*" at the end of each stich is a lament designed to convey our feelings of longing for this past period of glory.

Aruch HaShulchan sees the kid as being a reference to the goat that was slaughtered by Joseph's brothers after they sold him into slavery.

Ten are the Commandments. Nine are the months of pregnancy. Eight are the days of circumcision. Seven are the days of the week. Six are the Orders of the *Mishnah*. Five are the Books of the Torah. Four are the Matriarchs. Three are the Patriarchs. Two are the Tablets of the Covenant. One is our God in the heavens and the earth.

One kid, one kid that father bought for two *zuzim*. One kid, one kid.

And the cat came and ate the kid that father bought for two *zuzim*. One kid, one kid.

And the dog came and bit the cat that ate the kid that father bought for two *zuzim*. One kid, one kid.

Joseph was sold for 20 pieces of silver, so each of his ten brothers would have received a share of two silver pieces, which is alluded to by the words *"two zuzim."* The *"father"* refers to Joseph, for the Aramaic word *"Abba"* is often used as a title of importance, and is used by Targum to refer to Joseph himself (*Genesis* 41:43). According to this interpretation, the refrain should be translated thus: "One goat, one goat, [that was used] when they sold the great man for two *zuzim.*" The brother's sale of Joseph set off the chain of events which ultimately led to our enslavement in Egypt, and subsequently to the Exodus, the conquest of *Eretz Yisrael*, and the entire odyssey of Jewish history which followed. The various stages of the kid's experiences reflect the stages in the Jewish people's experience.

Maase Nissim, citing a variety of Talmudic and midrashic sources to support his analogies, offers a running commentary on the entire song: The *"kid"* represents the Temple. The *midrash* tells us that when David purchased the Temple Mount from the Jebusite farmer Araunah he collected two golden pieces from each of the tribes of Israel. Thus, the *"kid"* was bought for two *"zuzim."* The *"cat"* is Nebuchadnezzar, who destroyed the *"kid."* He was eventually neutralized by the favorable decrees of the Persian king Cyrus, who is compared to a *"dog."* The *"stick"* that beat the dog represents Greece, who conquered the Persians. The Hashmoneans, the *Kohanim* who overthrew the Greek rulers of *Eretz Yisrael*, are referred to as *"fire,"* for *Kohanim* are called *"fire."* The Romans, who destroyed the Second Temple, are compared to

וְאָתָא **חוּטְרָא** וְהִכָּה לְכַלְבָּא, דְּנָשַׁךְ לְשׁוּנְרָא, דְּאָכְלָה לְגַדְיָא, דְּזַבִּין אַבָּא בִּתְרֵי זוּזֵי, חַד גַּדְיָא חַד גַּדְיָא.

וְאָתָא **נוּרָא** וְשָׂרַף לְחוּטְרָא, דְּהִכָּה לְכַלְבָּא, דְּנָשַׁךְ לְשׁוּנְרָא, דְּאָכְלָה לְגַדְיָא, דְּזַבִּין אַבָּא בִּתְרֵי זוּזֵי, חַד גַּדְיָא חַד גַּדְיָא.

וְאָתָא **מַיָּא** וְכָבָה לְנוּרָא, דְּשָׂרַף לְחוּטְרָא, דְּהִכָּה לְכַלְבָּא, דְּנָשַׁךְ לְשׁוּנְרָא, דְּאָכְלָה לְגַדְיָא, דְּזַבִּין אַבָּא בִּתְרֵי זוּזֵי, חַד גַּדְיָא חַד גַּדְיָא.

וְאָתָא **תוֹרָא** וְשָׁתָה לְמַיָּא, דְּכָבָה לְנוּרָא, דְּשָׂרַף לְחוּטְרָא, דְּהִכָּה לְכַלְבָּא, דְּנָשַׁךְ לְשׁוּנְרָא, דְּאָכְלָה לְגַדְיָא, דְּזַבִּין אַבָּא בִּתְרֵי זוּזֵי, חַד גַּדְיָא חַד גַּדְיָא.

וְאָתָא **הַשּׁוֹחֵט** וְשָׁחַט לְתוֹרָא, דְּשָׁתָא לְמַיָּא, דְּכָבָה לְנוּרָא, דְּשָׂרַף לְחוּטְרָא, דְּהִכָּה לְכַלְבָּא, דְּנָשַׁךְ לְשׁוּנְרָא, דְּאָכְלָה לְגַדְיָא, דְּזַבִּין אַבָּא בִּתְרֵי זוּזֵי, חַד גַּדְיָא חַד גַּדְיָא.

וְאָתָא **מַלְאַךְ הַמָּוֶת** וְשָׁחַט לְשׁוֹחֵט, דְּשָׁחַט לְתוֹרָא, דְּשָׁתָה לְמַיָּא, דְּכָבָה לְנוּרָא, דְּשָׂרַף לְחוּטְרָא, דְּהִכָּה לְכַלְבָּא, דְּנָשַׁךְ לְשׁוּנְרָא, דְּאָכְלָה לְגַדְיָא, דְּזַבִּין אַבָּא בִּתְרֵי זוּזֵי, חַד גַּדְיָא חַד גַּדְיָא.

וְאָתָא **הַקָּדוֹשׁ בָּרוּךְ הוּא** וְשָׁחַט לְמַלְאַךְ הַמָּוֶת, דְּשָׁחַט לְשׁוֹחֵט, דְּשָׁחַט לְתוֹרָא, דְּשָׁתָה לְמַיָּא, דְּכָבָה לְנוּרָא, דְּשָׂרַף לְחוּטְרָא, דְּהִכָּה לְכַלְבָּא, דְּנָשַׁךְ לְשׁוּנְרָא, דְּאָכְלָה לְגַדְיָא, דְּזַבִּין אַבָּא בִּתְרֵי זוּזֵי, חַד גַּדְיָא חַד גַּדְיָא.

Although the Haggadah formally ends at this point, one should continue to occupy himself with the story of the Exodus, and the laws of Passover, until sleep overtakes him. Many recite Song of Songs after the Haggadah.

And the stick came and beat the dog that bit the cat that ate the kid that father bought for two *zuzim*. One kid, one kid.

And the fire came and burned the stick that beat the dog that bit the cat that ate the kid that father bought for two *zuzim*. One kid, one kid.

And the water came and doused the fire that burned the stick that beat the dog that bit the cat that ate the kid that father bought for two *zuzim*. One kid, one kid.

And the ox came and drank the water that doused the fire that burned the stick that beat the dog that bit the cat that ate the kid that father bought for two *zuzim*. One kid, one kid.

And the slaughterer came and slaughtered the ox that drank the water that doused the fire that burned the stick that beat the dog that bit the cat that ate the kid that father bought for two *zuzim*. One kid, one kid.

And the angel of death came and slaughtered the slaughterer who slaughtered the ox that drank the water that doused the fire that burned the stick that beat the dog that bit the cat that ate the kid that father bought for two *zuzim*. One kid, one kid.

The Holy One, Blessed is He, then came and slaughtered the angel of death who slaughtered the slaughterer who slaughtered the ox that drank the water that doused the fire that burned the stick that beat the dog that bit the cat that ate the kid that father bought for two *zuzim*. One kid, one kid.

Although the Haggadah formally ends at this point, one should continue to occupy himself with the story of the Exodus, and the laws of Passover, until sleep overtakes him. Many recite Song of Songs after the Haggadah.

"water." The Arabs (Ishmael) took the Land of Israel from the Romans, and they are represented by an *"ox."* The *"slaughterer"* of the *"ox"* is Mashiach ben Joseph, who is destined to reclaim *Eretz Yisrael* from the Arabs. We are told that Mashiach ben Joseph will be killed by the angel of death. Ultimately, the Holy One, Blessed is He, will come and redeem the Land of Israel in the End of Days.

This volume is part of
THE ARTSCROLL SERIES®
an ongoing project of
translations, commentaries and expositions
on Scripture, Mishnah, Talmud, Halachah,
liturgy, history and the classic Rabbinic writings;
and biographies, and thought.

For a brochure of current publications
visit your local Hebrew bookseller
or contact the publisher:

Mesorah Publications, ltd

4401 Second Avenue
Brooklyn, New York 11232
(718) 921-9000